ALSO BY HERBERT GOLD

Novels

Short Stories

Essays

THE MAGIC WILL

STORIES AN

THE
MAGIC
WILL

HERBERT
GOLD

ESSAYS OF A DECADE

RANDOM HOUSE • NEW YORK

ISBN: 0-394-46018-9

Library of Congress Catalog Card Number: 73-143993

Some of these essays first appeared in *The Atlantic Monthly, Harper's Magazine, Rolling Stone, The Hudson Review, Holiday, The Reporter, Encounter, Esquire, Look, Tri-Quarterly,* and "Biafra Goodbye," published by Two Windows Press.

Manufactured in the United States of America by H. Wolff Book Manufacturing Co., N.Y.

Designed by Antonina Krass

98765432

First Edition

FOR BUNNY AND DICK

PREFACE

IF IT IS true that all novels of any persistent value are about love and death, it's perhaps also true that the shorter forms, stories and essays, are about catastrophe and desire. An essay reforms the world in the imagination, organizes some meanings, and ventilates reality as well as illuminates it. A story does the same things—with the addition of magic. It wants to make strange, make pious and impious, make uncanny, make real. But a worthwhile essay—analysis, history or argument—also makes the world magical. So the line between the two forms is not even a dotted one. There is a constant skirmish and fading over and across.

Some of the chapters in this book are stories and the others are essays. The cross-fertilization of fiction and fact, true lies and partial perspectives is a motley one. I try to remember when I was really there and when I only thought I was, though sometimes the thought of being there is more powerful than the actual history of travel and trouble in my own shoes. What begins as a notion or an anecdote ends, if nerve is awakened, as an image of fate. At least this is the writer's hope: to fix the real within the unreal within the real.

To put on the shoes of others—of the New York writer, say, or the Midwestern divorced office worker, or the boyish Vietnam-time love casualty, or the Bohemian painter—means to try on a strange life in order to make sense of one's own.

There is a risk of gains and failures. I used to say, in answer to the question *Why do you write?*: "To master my own experience and make the real world vivid." Now it seems more complex: to make the real world unreal and magical, and make the unreal and magical world real and practical. And all to make the expense of human life in the twentieth century seem worthwhile, at least for a span, at least for someone. The work of the writer is a way out and a way in, and both at the same time, and that's why this book faces two ways.

H. G.

CONTENTS

· CONTENTS ·

THE MAGIC WILL

PROGRAMMING
THE PECULIAR THINGS
1

"Peculiar things happen to you."

He had a peculiar look on his face.

My friend was right, I decided. But then I defended myself against the undemocratic inference. Peculiar things happen to all of us, especially if we are paying attention. The first is being born, the last is dying. And in between, the magic will works to give us eyes and a heart, a register and a judging apparatus constructed over the millions of years by fishy juices and sponges, a history and a soul. Of course, it's helped by genes and habits, but these we can take as natural, like the smog we breathe.

To construct a proper privacy, making it a privilege rather than a burden, we first need to construct a community—love, family, politics, art. If the two-legged bird without feathers is to be more than a plucked chicken, we must connect ourselves with the privacy and fantasy of others, and run the risks of the general madness. My own peculiar things belong to everyone, or by right ought to. This is the writer's intention as he puts together the discrete facts of his experience, all the experiences he has had, mind and body, history and dream, trying to make sense of them—*meaning*. God, Spinoza said, is the principle of organization. (I think he meant a "principle of rationality," but not all organizing and structure are rational.)

In my stories and essays I have tried to understand some of the peculiar things, which means to make them stand still in memory and take shape in relation to each other. To tell what I know, as Dylan Thomas said, and also what I don't know. To grasp the mystery, which is like grasping a cloud. There is a crucial difference between those who grasp at the cloud of mortality and those who cannot abide the risk—no, the inevitability of failure. Feet, do your work; words, move. Charlatanism, vain rhetorical insistence or a calloused and dull-witted passivity await failure at either end. Hysteria and despair measure the boundaries for those who strive too much or strive not enough.

If the writer were a holy man or a merely moral one, he could take his chances on trying to live a decent life. He could pick a right path and follow it. As it is, he must resort to fun and art and the expense of feeling, using what brains he has; he may mutilate himself, carving his own path, some of it over his own body; but no other way for the likes of him, and no other way to test his humanity, either. *To live* is a verb in transit to something else.

2

IN THE tradition, men have usually assumed that understanding and will, the two primary qualities of the human mind, cannot be reduced to formulae or mechanical models. The complexity is not merely one of degree, but of quality. Recent attempts to define the mind as a peculiarly advanced computer have generated great enthusiasm and given limited results. The Frankenstein computer, laughing, weeping and dominating, is something of which the human mind can conceive, but the computer is not born yet which can make love.

I had a brief experience working as a tutor to a Direct English Access computer, trying to teach the machine to be funny and poetic. The job didn't last long, not because the machine

wasn't ready for me (it wasn't), but because of personnel dis-
agreements and also because I was discouraged by abrupt revelation of the military financing of the research. Nevertheless, I
can assure anyone who doubts it that thinking machines still
think very primitively. The basic integrating factors in the human mind cannot be programmed. Imitations of understanding and will can be routed on the discs; the process can be
broken down into a series of off-on steps; but the desire and
need soaked in our blood and history cannot be programmed.
A histrionic, hysterical, overadaptable girl is not a woman,
even though she says what a woman says, is overprinted with
modern guilt and therapy; we all learn to recognize this after
some experience.

Perhaps a clearer analogy to the computer from real life is
the cold and unfeeling writer, of whom there are more than a
few, who is clever enough to put "heart" and "soul" and
"love" and stylish echoes of sensibility into his work because
he knows they are supposed to be there. Do we feel the lack in
such a writer? We do; eventually we do, despite all cleverness;
the music is hollow. We are also deceived by the clever paranoid or the effective and energetic psychopath, but the failures
of contact and sensibility eventually make us react with weariness or outrage. Our belief does not endure past the high moment of chic when everybody is talking about this writer and
the hope of feeling is invested in his work. After a season the
audience turns to another flicker.

When we meet a computer programmed for warmth and
depth, we still know that the machine will burn out, leaving a
husk; the creature emits signals when there is an operator for
it, but despite its noisy clacking present, there is indifference
and a void in its future. Mourning an obsolete thermostat
seems unlikely, even if the thermostat gives birth to ancestor-
worshiping Mark IIs. Somehow we know it is still either hard-
ware or software or a combination of the two, while our bodies
contain (symbolize?) something more.

Scientific development, in other words, has given us models that are useful but advertise themselves with an authority which does not satisfy our deepest needs. And needs not just for faith or hope, but also for intellectual completeness, elegance and rigor.

The infinite variety of possibility in the use of language, in innovation, in construction of new patterns, in violations of old patterns, is—as Noam Chomsky points out—clear signal that the old analogies of human will to mechanical will and desire and growth to stimulus-response mechanisms are inadequate. It is not my purpose to argue the linguistic case for the meaning of "will" (it's not in my capacity, anyway); what the stories and essays of our time would intend to illustrate, if they had intentions, is the power and pervasive working of will and its corruptions in some specific cases within the American experience. Of course stories don't have clear intentions, and neither do storytellers. But they use mind, experience, and self to point to reality or to engulf it, not really knowing how smart they can be, sometimes still fearing the charlatan's hysteria or the cynic's boredom.

During my brief experience as tutor to the bright young computer, I encountered some difficulties with its parents and staff. We had meetings on such problems as that of programming wit and humor. The assembled linguists, mathematicians, engineers, and computer scientists loved their creature and tended to limit the universe to its possibilities, exactly as a nurse might limit her outings to the nearby parks and the possibilities of the bratlet in her charge. At one meeting I suggested that while simulations of ardor, pity, and horniness, for example, might be programmed into a machine, they would necessarily have a certain thinness in the aura. The process of history and growth, extending back into the womb and beyond, the weight of body and time, intimations of mortality, intentions about defying mortality, all are bound up in the simplest as well as the most complex attitudes. These were

6

matters inaccessible to the tapes and storage discs of our machines, I said. Authenticity would be a difficult job; that's where soul comes in.

A brilliant lady mathematician, Ph.D., MIT, ballpoint pen behind her ear and little blue dots in her left palm, had been brooding about my presentation of doctrine and illustration. She said, "Mr. Gold, if you can tell me what horniness is, I can program it."

"Well, it's a complex interpenetration of circumstances and energies, plus memories, hopes and, um, desire—"

"I said if you can tell me what it is, I can program it."

"It's a willingness to move in certain ways, impelled by a history of stillness and movement . . ."

She had a triumphant frown on her face. I'm sure I had a fussy look of imprecision on my face; I knew I wasn't getting through. "Well, some girls make me feel it and some don't . . ."

She grinned. She had won. "That's what I mean," she said. "If you knew what it was, I could program it."

Well, programming sincerity, faith, sacrifice, soul, is at least a possible art if we accept the notion that human beings can duplicate (*replicate*) themselves, in combinations and variations. Just repeat the unique being and you have another unique being, only with the difference that—well, there's another just like it. But then give it different circumstances and you're home free. Dr. Michael Scriven, philosopher of science at the University of California, believes that the question of whether or not to give computers the vote must normally come up in a few years; and after their enfranchisement, once we admit they can choose as intelligently as other electors, it will be natural for a computer to want to run for President. It's a hectic thought, but why not?

Our imaginations are still so tuned to accident, magic, and will that we can do little more than chuckle tolerantly or shiver with fear at the notion of an IBM chief executive, perhaps with Mr. Nixon stepping down to serve as Vice President. Why not? Why not? Why not? Because we still want magic and accident, no matter how deadly they may come to be in a world of apocalyptic options. We still want magic and will? *Okay, then, Mr. Gold, if you can define magic and will, we can program them.*

3

IF THE poet—or philosopher or novelist or preacher or politician—has found the truth, why is this pen wobbling between his fingers, why this tongue murking in his mouth? Why add a trivial noise to his midnight or morning discovery? Answer: Because the truth is not found until sung or acted, heard and reacted against, carved with cuneiform doggedness into clay and examined by the community. In action, and in the action of joining the community of hearers and speakers, the writer *really* finds the truth he claims for his moments of vision.

The act of writing is not, as some assume, a passive and languid yielding to feeling, with the pen somehow worked by abstracted and twitching muscles. Rather, it is a physical act of considerable rigor, like sculpting. The pencil is an awl, the typewriter a riveting machine, the pen a knife, and the eraser a buffer. Whiplash injuries can occur, I know by personal experience, from a sprung, seated attack on an unfinished novel. The doctor said that automobile accidents and love-making are the most frequent causes of whiplash; book writing was new to his practice. I don't suppose that reading a novel ever puts anyone in traction, but still the reader's act of imagination is similar to that of the writer. Below the reverie line, there's lots of motion. But one of the great differences between the creative act of reading and the creative act of writing is that the reader, despite his turmoil of suspense, holds the entire book in his hands; he knows it's there and the tale will unwind somehow; his fingers clutch it and his dollars bought it. The writer doesn't know anything yet, and writes about things he doesn't know, with a language not yet or ever in his final possession. If he knows, if he has a clear outline and a finished diction, then it isn't worth doing. What justifies the aching back is the chance to carve what has never yet been carved out of the void. To do, in fact, what cannot be done.

The painter Jean Varda, now nearly eighty years old, claims that he was a charlatan until about thirty years ago. "Then I became an artist." Perhaps he is protecting his recent work; the fear of charlatanism must always come along with the hope of style. A style that doesn't work is mere manner. A point of view which strains for genius most likely reaches only as far as absurdity. There may be an element of con in great art, more than in a lesser work, since the supreme artist is striving to express what he doesn't know and to name the un-namable. One of his mysterious secrets is sincerity; that is, fooling himself that this time, this time, oh this time he will find the truth. He reaches his dirty hands into the void and says, seizing air, *Now I've got it!* (Or perhaps he seizes only his other hand.) An art is rhetorical, vapid, and pretentious when the artist is interested in an effect of knowing rather than in knowledge, when he drowns out the doubts by shout-ing, when he insists with poor grounds for insisting.

Of course, he always stands in quicksand, but it must be *firm* quicksand. When his ambiguous dreams and passionate hopes are not quite fulfilled and he presses forward anyway— well, that is the blessed charlatanism which leads to the deep-est knowledge: power over what is unwilled, knowledge of the unknowable, a finger and gaze toward the stars, which can never be reached. There is a chronic moral vertigo in this in-tention: *Do I mean it? Do I really know what I say I know?*

The American fantasy of absolutely free will on earth is beautifully exaggerated by the Reverend Jefferson F. Poland, founder of the Sexual Freedom League, who has argued in an impassioned editorial that much remains to be accomplished

9

before freedom is really planted in place. We have all the sexual freedoms now, he said, except for one—the freedom to rape. Why does some girl have the right to say no to us just because she wants to or doesn't want to or never has before? Outrage in the reverend's willful heart. What have we here? What kind of broad? Who does she think she is—someone different from anyone else? We must not relax, comrades, we must press on. As Thomas Jefferson (of Montecello, Virginia) said, the tree of liberty must be watered with the blood of patriots. The Rev. J. F. Poland (of San Francisco, California) turns on a fury of lemme. Lemme, I wanna, lemme; he is an American and a Californian, he sees no reason for limits in a democracy, he wants to water the tree of liberty with the blood of virgins.

The American experience is terrifying and full of charms. However I try to grasp it, with poems, stories, novels, essays, I find myself with a handful of words falling through my fingers. The linear arrangement of words is only one of the elements which trouble those who seek understanding; we want to get our heads on straight, and heads are not really made to fit straight onto our necks, bodies, hearts, souls, legs. The kidnapping beat of rock music and the thermal avalanche of the movies are attempts to enter the world fully by a total exit from the self. I love these forms, too, but finally they do not succeed in straightening our heads and we are left again with words, words, words. We try to make the words echo, ricochet, reverberate. ("You're thinking again," the teenie says reproachfully to her old man.) We try to keep our fingers together and make a cup for the words. *This sieve*—says the poet—*this time*—he insists—*will hold water.*

When the words are all wadded up together like a snowball, maybe they will stick. They may melt, but they can still do damage or build glorious snow monsters. They can both amuse and threaten, and straighten heads by jarring the soul. Sentences and paragraphs make judgments and cross-refer to themselves as they move along in a way more sly and delicate than pictures, rhythms, or the mass drenching of electronic media. They leave a great deal of freedom to the reader. He makes choices in the process, and therefore, like the writer's, his perspective can be individual and magical at the same time.

My own essays are stories—imaginary histories of voyaging in the world; my stories are essays—"attempts to perform and accomplish something," as the dictionary says. There are no secrets from the reader but the most terrible ones, the ones he and I already know and hide from ourselves with speed and rock, movies and drugs and television and war. We hide ourselves in our daily routines, marriages, children, jobs. And they must be revealed! Made general and particular!

I have circled about the matter of literature with the habit of a teller of stories, on the theory that you cannot see a blinding truth by merely looking at it. We must prepare. Exactly as we cannot look directly at the car onrushing down the highway toward us at night, we cannot look directly at love and death; the headlights blind; we gasp, we gaze to the side and place the glare in the perspective of ditch and thicket; we prepare our nerves with peripheral vision.

A writer cannot give away his secrets even if he wants to, since the process of traveling along these roads is what gives the conclusions whatever weight they possess. To fix and name forever the sense of the magic will of America is a task for a great philosopher-poet if we ever produce one. In the meantime, doubting the possibility of fixing and naming forever, but believing that this remains the great task, the writer takes what consolation he can from his personal approximations.

I dedicated this story to a girl who wept and wept, saying, "I don't feel twenty-five, I feel thirty-five!" It was the greatest age she could imagine, it was the disaster of senility for a star of the year of Swinging London, the Summer of Love in San Francisco, flower children on the march through LSD and the Beatles.

I was forty-two and what was I doing in this world? It made me need to face my own early twenties—the end of a war, the shaky return to the cold war, and what the weeping girl was imagining in her own way: the inevitability of death and that something must be done about it. As Americans, we think we can take these matters in our own hands. We're wrong.

A curious epilogue to the story in its publishing history. Playboy wanted to buy it, but wanted to cut all except the part about the war. That is, what dealt with aging and mortality had to go, and what would remain would be an anecdote about young men dying in their bloom. The story was instead published in Harper's.

A Playboy editor later told me, "We can't tell our readers you're forty!"

"But it's obvious, if I'm writing about the war—"

"Yes, but we can't rub their noses in it, Herb."

A SELFISH STORY

A STORY

Not long ago one of my daughters asked me, "Daddy, were you in World War One or Two?" At about the same time, a girl whom I consider as grown-up as myself told me that she remembers my war because she remembers the boots her father wore while washing the car. She was an infant on an Army post. And yet, for those of us who enlisted near our eighteenth birthdays in the early forties, the war is still immediate, our youth is not disappeared, and yet time and history have rolled over us, despite our will to give sense to the present and future in the light of the past. Now I must subjugate the past in order to tell about it. It turns out that I am still its willing groom, moving and mated to it.

In 1942 I embraced New York City. I had spent a year wandering on the road, living out a fantasy of rebellion from Cleveland, part of it in the flophouses of the Bowery and Bleecker Street, but now I had washed and scrubbed myself, turned seventeen and a half, and entered Columbia College. Morningside Heights was as far from my scrounging boy bum days as any place could be; Irwin Edman and Mark Van Doren replaced the gamblers and shills on Key Largo, the enraged, oversteamed chefs in restaurant kitchens all up and down the eastern seaboard, the hobos, wildballs, and predators of the risky America I had pursued. Having so much eccentric fun made me morose and serious. I was an adjusted misfit.

The return to college structure was brief. We freshmen, turning eighteen, believed we might finish our first year before going to war. Autumn, black winter, reluctant spring. We read Homer, Thucydides, Herodotus, Humanities and Contemporary Civilization, and felt up the Barnard girls near the spiked metal fence on Broadway, and thought about our silver wings, our marksmen's medals, our future citations and press dispatches. We had no imagination for death, for our own inevitable future deaths, the death of everyone, and for the plain fact that a certain proportion of these readers of bloody Homer would be dead early, very soon now, before the end of the war.

However, there are fits in the process of growing up and imagining one's own mortality. Living is a flux and flow, but knowledge comes at moments. A serious illness is one start, the death of a parent is another. And sometimes even the incident of education can educate. By pure good fortune, one of these occasions occurred on a lazy late-winter afternoon in

Hamilton Hall; the steam heat was boiling, there was a smell of chalk in the air, a seminar on "Lucretius and Time" was occupying a group of solemn freshmen and our professor, O. J. Campbell, a distinguished scholar of Shakespeare. Up until this afternoon, I must note, I had not formed any real friend-ships at school, although I admired the mad Cuban of Hartley Hall, who ran naked up and down the corridors, working out, and a boy with a Maine accent who wanted to be either a missionary or a dean, and an irritable young man from White Plains who felt misused because he was adopted into a rich family rather than born to it. Jack Kerouac was on the football team, a popular kid; I had spent a year on the road and felt cut off from him and the other middle-class youngsters making their way on squads and in clubs. I didn't even write for the *Jester*, the college review, or the *Spectator*, though I was a se-cret poet and journal keeper.

On that sleepy, still afternoon in Hamilton Hall, a crucial discovery was opened to me, and with it, I also made my first close college friend. Professor Campbell, looking out over the dozen of us slouched around a table, talking about time and time's end, life and mortality, suddenly remarked to this serious crew of freshmen, "I was dead once, and I came back. I was dead and I remember it." He had had a heart attack; he had gone under; then he had returned. "I was dead. I still re-member it." The words were ordinary, but in the act of utter-ing them, he suddenly forgot to speak. He put his head down and remembered. Thick gray eyebrows, a heavy, handsome old head. A look of withdrawal, a look of the deepest seriousness possessed him. There was an uneasy silence in the room.

Ahead of my first risk in the war, ahead of my first danger-ous illness, ahead of the first death of someone close to me, I suddenly had a premonition of what death might mean, be-yond the drama of grief and mourning. My own heart stopped. There was the excitement of discovery and a terrible loneli-ness.

At that moment, and perhaps just as Professor Campbell began to speak once more of Lucretius, I noticed a fellow student, whom I shall now call Marvin Shapiro. Purplish hickies stood out in the pallor of his face. He was stunned by this reminiscence of death, as I had been, and he too felt that premonitory grief and loneliness. And then he flushed as the blood returned.

After class I approached Shapiro and we talked. We cut the rest of our classes that day, strolled the campus, ate ice cream, circled the track, told our stories, listened to our stories, and finally got around to the subject of girls. This led naturally to a number of pitchers of beer at the West End Tavern on Broadway. By closing time we decided we were lifelong friends, and so we were. Marvin was a skinny boy with bad skin, a deep voice and a surcharged Adam's apple, and a family in Brooklyn. He wanted to be a radio announcer, a physicist, and a lover of beautiful women. I shared the latter ambition, but aimed at poetry and philosophy as the means to this dreamed-of end. I also told him (me from Lakewood, Ohio) that he was my first Jewish friend. Marvin looked at me as if I must be crazy. He knew nothing about Lakewood, Ohio.

Expanding our horizons, we organized expeditions to eat eggplant parmigiana on First Avenue and fish at Joe's on South Street near the market. We were voyeurs who stopped at every doorway. And after we had peeked, we discussed what it all meant. The sting of prying was a philosophical lust, we thought; but also we were perpetually horny. Strolling through the fish market, we saw a child idly piddling his hands in a barrel of shrimp. It was a boy of eight or nine in a corduroy jumper-jacket; he had a bored, sallow, pretty, Italian face, and he was dipping his hands into the crisp pink shells and letting them spill through his fingers like doubloons in a pirate movie; he was watching the stand for his father. One withered leg was encased in a shiny paraphernalia of metal braces. Marvin's eyes filled with tears.

Disasters and horrors are familiar in the city. Only a few days before we had seen a dead man propped against a wall near St. Mark's on the Bowery. Marvin was shaking his head and tears were rolling down his cheeks. "What's the matter?" I asked him.

"That kid'll never get laid," he said.

Like most young men in those days, circa 1943, we had a sure means of solving all our problems with college, girls, boredom, and anxiety: we could be heroes in the war. When Marvin and I began to talk about it, however, it seemed different to us. Professor Campbell's eyes looking downward, looking inward, had changed our feeling about the days to come. We were infected by the beginning of the imagination of death, and it lay beneath our friendship as a shared battle. We too had been born twice.

In all friendships between adolescent boys there are curious contradictions, rivalries and family difficulties. I was surely jealous of Marvin's great fortune with girls, whom he met and conquered in subway crowds, on campus walks, wherever he deigned to point his ardent, demanding eyes, his shiny beak, and his disturbed, acne-bothered face. He would take a girl for a walk and an ice cream, and not get back to Hartley Hall until his first morning class. Unless he lurked outside, imagining my envy all through the grimy New York night, I had to assume that he figured out someplace to go with the lady after the walk, the hamburgers and the balcony of the Forty-second Street movie.

On the other hand, he envied me too—my lack of "nervousness." In those days I seemed calm. To Marvin I was a rock, though I knew myself to be volcanic lava, in inexorable motion. Also he envied me my year underground, hitchhiking, working at odd jobs on the Florida Keys, escaping the Ivy League, as he called it, somehow including Brooklyn. No wonder I was calm, he told me: life had not passed me by. All *he* had to his credit was satisfied lust.

Poor Marvin. I would have given up the life that had not
passed me by for one, two, or three—as many as the genie
might allow me—of the girls with whom Marvin strolled. Satisfied lust! But I would offer them deep feeling, each and every
one. He shrugged. They couldn't resist him, he said, but that
was not life. Every time he traveled in a crowded subway he
made a new conquest, and that was not life either. That was
just rubbing. Each and every one would have been appalled by
my morose deep feeling. They liked Marvin—cheerful rubbing.

I discovered, I think, why Marvin charmed women. It only
seemed to be mere cheerful rubbing. He needed them, he
really needed and wanted girls, this one and that one, each one
in particular. He was born for women. We walked around Van
Am Quad, a little space of brick and grass, endlessly turning in
the damp midnight, while he explained, "Some people are
ambitious. You wake up and write poems at dawn—"

"I kill myself, I'm so horny—"

"Shush. I wake all cold and gray and I know I'll die if I can't
curve into her body."

"Whose, Marvin?"

"So the next day I take a subway ride at rush hour. I find
someone. I sniff it out and wiggle in, sometimes we never even
look at each other's face—sometimes we walk out together
and go to her place . . ."

"What do you talk about?"

He grinned in the darkness. "I tell her how much I need
her. I love her. I desire her. I treasure her. I adore her. I'll do
anything for her, and more to her. Aitch-bert, when I talk like
that, I'll tell you, they always listen closely."

The bust of Van Am glistened in the diffuse gray of a globe
lamp. There were blackout curtains on the dormitory windows
nearby, and lights where the V-12 program Navy boys were
doing calculus and navigation problems. We walked round
and round. Marvin contained a famine which he offered up in

tribute to womankind. He did not hide his need. He surrounded them with joyous hunger. He gave it freely, and thus they could forgive everything. He may not have been sincere, but he was desperate. Girls had the key; friends had the key; excitement and variety and new adventures had the key. Everyone was grateful to be able to do so much for Marvin. He responded with the tenderness of a gratified child. He could barely remember their names.

He also met a Barnard girl named Ellen who wore black woolen dresses, had long black hair, a long maternal figure; she wept when he took her into the cold bushes, wept when he brought her out, and wept all the way to her parents' apartment when they had left it empty for the weekend. Marvin reported, somewhat worried, that she was still weeping when they emerged on a fine sunny winter afternoon. He had enjoyed the love of a good woman, and he found it wet.

For my own reasons, partly connected with the war, partly with the sag of midyear at college, partly with my lack of the love of a good or a bad woman, I began to figure on not waiting until the end of the school year to go into the Army. Casually one day I mentioned this to Marvin. He must have spent an unusually damp evening with Ellen because his answer was short and to the point: "Yeah!" The jukebox at the West End was playing, I recall, a song with this line: "Get outta here and get me some money, too . . ."

It solved the problem of cuts in classes, the itch for adventure, the discomfort of school, the failures of successes with girls. We would go in together, and be heroes together. We enlisted together.

Before telling his parents that he was about to go into the Air Corps, he asked me to spend a night with him in Brooklyn. I expected to be bored—*parents*—but instead I was amazed. No plump, dull Brooklyn lawyer, Mr. Shapiro was a jaunty man who wore a yachting cap indoors and liked to drink, eat exotic foods, and go out fishing. He had his own boat. He

talked about mizzens and fore and aft; I was learning Latin
and French but had no grasp of yachting. His face was weath-
ered by Long Island Sound. I had never met a sailing Jew before. Mrs. Shapiro was a soft sweet woman with a small,
pretty, girlish face; she read good books and listened to Beethoven and smiled at her husband's jokes. He did calisthenics
on a bar above the bed in their room. It was a jazzy household,
unlike anything I had expected in that large, old-fashioned,
furniture-filled house on a leafy Brooklyn street. There was
also another son, younger than Marvin, to whom little attention was paid. Marvin was clearly the hope of the family, and
Mr. Shapiro was delighted by his son's wildness. He twisted
and dodged through life in a way which would have hurt him
at thirty, but at eighteen he was a charmer. He had fun when I
sought Meaning. He had style. From afar I admired a sense of
luxuriousness. Even now, when rubbing up against strange
girls in the subway does not seem very stylish, I carry the
memory of a lively boy, with a swollen Adam's apple, a deep
laugh in a skinny body, doted on by his parents and allowing
himself all pleasures.

Marvin told them we were both going to war soon. This
followed a discussion about orientals in which we all agreed
that there was something puzzling about the newspapers' de-
scriptions of how to tell the face of a Japanese—sneaky, yellow, totalitarian—from that of a Chinese. The Chinese face in
those days was open, smiling, friendly, and democratic. Marvin's father had a wild, high, energetic laugh at this. He said
that the objective testimony of witnesses was sometimes inaccurate. He liked the way his son thought ahead.

"Aitch-bert and I are going to enlist," Marvin said suddenly.
"It's time. Otherwise all the good jobs'll be taken."

His mother dropped a spoon; it made a little chime against
her foot. Silent tears. His father clapped him on the back and
said, "I knew it, why not? You'll tear 'em apart. They'll give
up as soon as they get the news." His eyes glittered with envy.

Marvin's kid brother looked adoring and pleased. No one fretted about his mother's tears until Marvin kissed her on the neck and she sobbed wildly.

The night before Marvin and I went to Camp Upton, we bought tickets for *The Skin of Our Teeth*, with Tallulah Bankhead. She wiggled and chanted the Joycean lines. If only she had known we were about to go off to die for our country, we both thought, she would have been absolutely indifferent to us anyway. The next day we shipped out, were stripped naked, and began to put on our new lives.

As with girls, so with the war. Marvin seemed to have all the luck. His reflexes and his eyes were sharp. He became what both of us had wanted to be, a fighter pilot. I went to the infantry, and then to a school to learn Russian, toward a vague Army hope that I might help to provide liaison with our gallant Soviet allies. In the periods between drill, study, and fret, we deep Russian scholars continued real life by drinking, writing letters, and chasing girls at the USO. Most of us were successful at the first two projects, less at the third. I corresponded with Marvin, with Ellen, and with Marvin's mother. He was in England, flying missions over the Continent. I was in wet white Maryland that next winter, doing maneuvers through an American landscape—barns, churches, apple orchards—all traced and spelled in Russian on our maps. O'er the steppes of Maryland I wandered, dressed like a wolf, carrying a compass, a full pack and a new vocabulary.

Marvin's mother wrote that she missed our coming out to Brooklyn to eat fish on Saturdays. Her husband spent his weekends in his small sailboat, digging salt fish out of the salt sea. He was also doing civilian patrol work. She was worried about her son and wanted me to reassure her.

Ellen wrote that she was crazy in love with Marvin and he

didn't write often enough. So she wanted to receive letters from me, since I was his best friend.

Marvin wrote that the English girls were peculiar but co-operative. He was now a first lieutenant, and what with his silver bars and all, he didn't like to do it standing up in the alleys of Piccadilly. So he had found girls who were willing to take him home. They liked chocolate and they liked to rock with him as the bombs fell and the sirens shrieked.

I remember this particularly now because it takes me back to the time when prowess, position, and opportunity were the great issues in love. It was technical and it was to be shared among men. Marvin was collecting his reward for being a fighter pilot and a man. He could dream of a girl in a flowing skirt, flowers and sunlight in a field, and also admire the technique of the wife of a Pakistani colonel (or perhaps he was an English colonel stationed in India).

Poor Marvin's mother, whose innocent boy was practicing the rites of killing and lust.

Poor Ellen, who imagined him pining for her, needing her.

Poor me, crawling around in Russian in the snowbanks and slushy mud of Maryland in winter. Our officers were combat dropouts—men so ineffective at war that they were sent back to train future intelligence officers.

The only one not to be pitied seemed to be Marvin himself, handsome, his acne drying under doses of adrenalin, collecting missions and medals and the wives of our allies. He made captain. The boy quick into the bushes of Riverside Drive was also quick in the sky against the stubby German fighters. Ellen, his mother, and I all formed his audience against the backdrop of horror and destruction, explosions and fire, brandy and good jokes. Seen from our distance, the garish light lit his face and made it angelic, made it devilishly smile.

One winter night my group returned to Camp Ritchie, the intelligence training post in Maryland, after nearly a week of simulated war in marshes and orchards. We had been frozen and misled; we had been fired upon and tested; we had conducted a strange war among Maryland mountain people to whom we were not allowed to speak English. We needed shaves; we were jittery with stimulants; we smelled bad. Our mission had been a failure because our officer, who had been responsible for a minor disaster at Anzio, still believed that his own sense of direction was superior to that of a compass. He knew the way; could a compass think? Consequently we had been lost for three days in a prickly, cutover pine desert. I felt as if ice had been packed into my ears. We had the usual gripes against officers. They became the real enemy. We stood in our long khaki overcoats against a camp stove, smelling the chicken-feather singe as we tried to get warm, slurping coffee from our mess kits and reading the accumulated mail. Our officer went to sulk because north was not where north used to be in the Alabama National Guard. I tore open my little stack of mail.

A letter from Marvin described a weekend in London. What fun, what sparkle amid the blackout. A duke's daughter, he claimed; mentally I made him out a liar but read on, envying. She loved him, she really did. He cared for her a lot, of course, but not that much. Ellen was writing him weepy letters and he supposed he would have to close now in order to drop her a line.

Ellen wrote to ask if I had heard from Marvin. She was worried. He must be ill or something.

The last letter was from his mother. It was the most recent. Marvin had been shot down over Germany; others in the squadron had seen his parachute open, but it was being fired on. There seemed to have been a hit in the air. He was presumed dead.

I crawled outside into the snow as if I were seasick. I heaved and gagged and groaned because I had forgotten how to weep. I was too old to cry, and not yet old enough; later I would

learn again. But now there was only this churning physical turmoil like seasickness, like jealousy, like lust and dread. The
desire to run away or to deny was changed into an eating of
the lining of my belly. I was simply sick, a trivial response to
death, I then thought and still believe. I remembered Professor Campbell, his head down, contemplating the Fact. I remembered the awe Marvin and I had shared, which had been
the foundation of our friendship before the matter of girls and
career and the war came to give us the details of intimacy. I
was appalled that I dared to feel my own body, even in sick-
ness, when Marvin was simply without feeling, without soul,
dead. I recalled with disgust Dostoevsky's denunciation of
Turgenev: When he watches a shipwreck, children drowning,
he feels only the tears running down his own face. And yet I
now had only myself. In the midst of this unreal war which I
was fighting and for which I was merely preparing, I had lost
my emblem of vitality and true life, my friend. I was bereft.
I was gagging in the deep, silent Maryland winter, with nearby
slush piles and garbage cans and the debris of soldiering and,
just beyond, a horizon of scrub and poor soil itching through
the snow and a whiteness of hills and winter sky. The earth
was an ache. This was the third death I had known in my life,
and perhaps the beginning of the sense of my own death. I
saw Marvin's face—grinning, acne-pocked, delighted by life—
under his parachute swinging down and then exploded in midair as he hung between heaven and hell. I have seen him there
for twenty years, and so he will be always.

Like Dostoevsky's Turgenev, I am telling a selfish story.
After grief, how does the vain young poet survive? He writes a
vain young poem, of course. It was a long elegy to the memory
of Captain Marvin Shapiro (1924–1945) and I typed it in the
company orderly room at Camp Ritchie, Maryland, and sent
it to the *Atlantic Monthly*, 8 Arlington Street, Boston, Massachusetts. Presently it was returned with a long letter signed by
a lady who had apparently been moved by this death in my

life. I haven't seen the poem since the end of the war, but I am reasonably certain it was not a good one. I remember little about it other than its shape on the page and the rhyme scheme. I believe the editor wrote to me because I was a soldier mourning a dead friend and there was a war on. Shortly afterward I was shipped out and lost track of the poem. I carried the letter from Marvin's mother with me.

His body was never found. He had written to me that it was odd to have the initial on the dog tags that identified him as a Jew when he might have to parachute into Germany; but he kept the initial. Anyway, he was destroyed in the sky.

The class of '46, my class, mostly returned to begin college again as twenty-one-year-old sophomores. We counted our losses and secretly watched out of the corners of our eyes those with missing limbs or raw, still-healing, burned scars. Some of us were in line for plastic surgery, some were outpatients, many were on partial disability pensions. Our hairlines had changed. Moony faces were lean and looney. There was confusion, the GI Bill, and a host of babies who claimed to be college students, too. I could not take up school as I had before, in a dormitory, with a roommate. I rented a room off Broadway and thought to enter adult life after the three years of murderous limbo. Our bodies twitched with unfulfilled destruction. How dare we live, how dare we not live. A friend and I jumped a thuggish heckler at a street-corner Henry Wallace rally. A group of us formed a klepto-bibliomaniacal society, stealing books, food, anything small and large. We called it the Book Find Club. Our motto was: Steal four books and get a fruit cake free from the A & P. We initiated girls into the sport. In their confusion they thought the war heroes must know what they were doing. They thought we were heroes and nervous. We were, in fact, nervous.

Around my thoughts of Marvin, on whose behalf I was taking certain revenges against the world, whom I was sometimes imitating in the subway, I came gradually to think of his mother, his father, and Ellen. Probably I did not know how to meet the grief of others. I was busy installing myself in the Bohemian student life of those days, all of us in khaki, sullen, arrogant. But gradually, as the months went by, I decided to visit Marvin's survivors. At last I telephoned Mrs. Shapiro in Brooklyn and she reminded me of how to get to Avenue K by subway. I used to know the way. My ears felt different in the roar of the tunnel.

At the subway entrance I began to think of the smoked eel I had eaten for the first time at their house. Marvin had said, bragging, "We have eels all the time—crabs, lobsters, oysters, shrimp. Snails. Clams."

"Do you eat pork?" I asked.

"*Feh*, unclean," he said. "You know that joke?"

I remembered pausing at the newsstand to pick up a copy of *PM*. They were selling the New York *Post* with the same old headlines, and I thought it was the same man with the papers, fret on his face, hair in his ears, waiting out his time. Still alive.

I expected the house to be shaded, dark with mourning. Instead, it was light and sunny, with the curtains pulled back and the surprising winter sunlight filling the rooms. But it seemed empty. Even some of the furniture was gone. It was emptied of its men. After his death Marvin's father had enlisted, not as a lawyer but as an expert sailor, and had commanded a landing craft, and had fought as an overage captain through southern France. After the end of the war he had simply not returned. Mrs. Shapiro, smiling, told me that he had found a girl in Marseilles. I couldn't imagine what a Brooklyn lawyer would do in Marseilles—Jean Gabin yes, Mr. Shapiro no—and I saw him in a corduroy cap, on the waterfront, a handsome, stocky, make-out, middle-aged settler in France, with a young high-breasted chick with wooden soles on her shoes. Mrs. Shapiro said simply, "It broke up our family. We

25

were a good family, I think, but we needed Marvin." Her other son was now at Yale, going very white shoe.

She made tea. We talked about Marvin. Tea, raisin toast, orange marmalade, chocolate cookies. I thought of Marvin's hickies—"zits," the freshmen now called them. She told me a little about her marriage and, I knew, would later want to tell me more. My need for a community of mourning gave way to embarrassment. I could not be husband and son to her, and when I slipped out into the deep early night, I tried to feel sadness and sympathy; I felt sympathy and sadness, and I felt relief to escape. Marvin was my friend in the past. What community I sought could not be built of nostalgia.

Still, I wanted to find Ellen. When I finally met her again, she was also in mourning, wearing an ugly shapeless woolen dress, flat shoes, her hair untended, smelling of anxiety and poor caring. She was a graduate student and had a reputation for persistent moping. Never a very pretty girl, she had been a sweetly attractive one. Now at age twenty-three, she looked ravaged, as if she had been left out in funky weather. I had a bit more patience with her than with Marvin's mother. We took coffee and meals together near campus. She wanted to drink at the West End because Marvin and I had gone there with her so often. Three times, I think. She imagined for herself a deep love affair, she imported it backward into history, she imagined widowhood. At first I shared the play, stunned by her conception of him, which seemed so much deeper than my own. They had been truly in love, they had been deep true lovers; it was not wrestling in the grass, it was not couch work in her parents' apartment on Central Park West, it was an immortal passion; her hero had been blásted out of the skies by fate and she would treasure his memory forever. Marvin and Ellen stood in the great tradition of doomed lovers. She was a graduate student in literature.

After a few immersions in her fantasy of the past, I began to feel discomfort and then resentment. Marvin had been my best friend and his memory made me ache. But he slipped away in the tumult of Ellen's ardent dream. I found new resources of coldness in myself. I would watch impatiently for her to finish her beer and then deliver her to her room on West 113th Street. Once, when she managed to order another beer, I felt myself ready to groan with boredom. And when she wanted me to come to her room, tiptoing past the other rooms, past the common kitchen, I felt as if I were being led into a trap. Her wet beery kisses were not for me. I twisted away and cried out, "You're lying to yourself! Never cared about you! He had girls everywhere, in England, Brooklyn, everywhere!"

She started to run down the darkened hall. I caught her at the door, held her in my arms as she struggled, and pointed out that it was not my room from which she was running, but her own. *She* should stay and *I* should go. Be rational. Be logical. Make sense. I'm sorry, but it's the truth.

I believed myself to be proudly surgical, but also I was smelling the stench of a woman's hysteria for the first time in my life. Little popping explosions of rage and hatred were going off in my arms. "You think you can play God! You think you're God and my judge!" she shrieked at me.

The practice of playing God and Judge sometimes exhausts itself with time. I have the disease worse than most (*Ellen, wherever you are*).

I dragged her back to her room. Invisible ears were pressed to the shut bedroom doors. Community kitchen, community crises. Shush, shush, I said. The stringent, leaping sobs subsided; she was simply weeping; I put her in bed with her clothes on, covered her and sat stroking her hand. Toward dawn she fell asleep. Cold-eyed I felt. I tiptoed out.

Back on the street, I saw a metal case of milk at the door of a short-order restaurant. For the first time in my life—not the last—I had spent a night trying to calm a woman made mad by something I had said. And for the last time in my life I felt that, well, it wasn't really my fault at all, I was right, I had done the right thing, I was right. So I told myself. So I told myself again. Still insisting, I believed that I had committed an obscenity. I stood at the doorway of the diner: CLOSED. GO AWAY.

They had no right to be rude. I was hungry and thirsty. I was a veteran. They were turning a veteran from their door.

The metal case of milk glittered in the early light. I looked at the bottles. My hand felt a premonitory sensual coolness, like touching a loved woman. It would be sweet to drink long cool swallows from the bottle and then heave it into the street. I was thirsty and hungry and cold and feverish and I decided not to steal a bottle of milk.

I stood there, squinting at the metal case. I would leave it in a moment. I would leave without a bottle for myself. This was a new reaction for me. The night had brought me much that was new.

When next I saw Ellen, she had changed her hair, cut it stylishly, and her clothes looked recently dry-cleaned. Now she was a handsome, perhaps too-mature twenty-three-year-old woman. She was going with someone. She had a *friend* (stare, blush, angry stare). We met as acquaintances, not as friends. She made it clear that I had sacrificed our past friendship. But she bore me no ill will; she smiled and inquired about my doings. I had little to say to her. Our life together was all in the past. I had projects for the future. She was married within the year, gave up graduate work, got pregnant, left New York. Though I insisted to myself that I had done the right thing, she made me uncomfortable. It was much easier for me not to see her on campus.

Now the years have passed and I think of my friend who died when he and I were mere children. The event still seems real when I remember it, but like a reality glimpsed through a thick glass, without the physical heft of life.

Recently, however, an immediate grief seemed to break the glass of memory and Marvin came tumbling free and alive again. The distancing of history is fatal, and yet it can be reversed. I am accustomed to his death. And yet, when I needed an occasion to express my grief at something else, at something happening to me, in my own life, I found Marvin waiting like a boy, ready to play. I told the story about him to a friend who was a baby when he flew over Germany. "He was dead before he had time to lose his adolescent acne." I had no tears for Marvin's mother or Ellen, but now, telling it, I fought for control of myself. A peculiar humping under my palate.

My friend reminded me coolly, "Ellen has a child ready for college. Marvin's father, if he is still alive and eating eels, must be nearly seventy—more. Do you think he's still in Marseilles? His mother is an old woman. His kid brother is a middle-aged professor."

"At Williams College, I heard."

"So," she said. "So it was a long time ago."

Yes, child, that was mere history. Yet there are new wars for which we must prepare ourselves, and I am still ready. I am also ready to join the company of O. J. Campbell, remembering my own deaths.

THE MAGIC WILL
1

CATASTROPHE and desire are linked in our lives as the moon is linked to that reflected light from the sun which enables the eye to see it. Dreadful fears and dreaming hope are conjoined in the same spirit. The mildest among us holds ferocious contradictions in his heart. Surviving, we aim to judge these fantastic extremes as everyday, whether we keep busy avoiding sharp, dung-smeared sticks in Vietnam or the pitfalls of permissive child rearing in Cleveland. The risks and boredoms of life in the world have a hidden undersurface: the continual dreaming of violence, the perpetual nostalgia for an imagined sweetness. Murder and love are the specific aims of the dark inward life, plus flight, revenge, pleasure.

Everyday our actions seem; catastrophic they appear to us in dreams; we travel on through gratified desire toward further desire and fear more than anything else the loss of desire, the melancholia of Senior City.

Now permit me to testify for myself by telling about the Haitian poet, about the girl I loved at age thirteen, about the man whose growth stocks went down—he wanted to kill. And about the cruising beasts, saw-toothed eels and lizards run amuck through the caprices of evolution. And how the Cuban missile crisis pleased so many who secretly seek suicide. And how the murder of a President is employed as a means to create a community of terror, but a community all the same.

"Freak out!" as the hard-rock song says. My connections may cross yours in infinite space, where parallel lines do meet.

30

2

THE Haitian poet was a lively, light-skinned, handsome man who deployed his hands with elegance and wore sunglasses day and night. In sunglasses he looked like a suave actor. Without sunglasses it became evident that one of his eyes shot off out of control—a disconnected muscle. His laugh was nervous, his English good, his culture international. About him it was told, "Ce youn masters-of," which was the Creole way of saying he had received a master's degree, from Columbia University. His poetry had been published in French, English, and Creole. He drank more rum-soda than was good for him, but less than most Haitian poets drank. He had a pretty wife, who liked to wear a single long earring. He had two children. He scavenged for a living, sometimes for the government, sometimes for UNESCO, sometimes as a journalist. I'll call him Gerard Lorraine.

Like all visitors to Haiti, I was curious about voodoo. It made him laugh. He explained it; he had written a monograph about it; finally it bored him, and he indulged the visiting anthropologists, professional and amateur, just because he was agreeable. Personally, he did not believe there was much to it. "Hysteria, obsession. Oh yes, and it's a pedigreed religion, too, y'know—a way of explaining the world." But that was all. It was mainly a joke to him. "Stillborn science," he said, "the peasants trying to learn something without knowing anything. Silly business."

One evening I was sitting at home in Bourdon, on the main road leading from Port-au-Prince to the hillside suburb of Pétionville, when there came a pounding at the door. I opened. Gerard fell in, covered with dirt and brambles, flecks of foam at the mouth, in a state of exhaustion and whimpering misery. He fell to the floor. His eye was a blank rolling map of burst capillaries, a disaster area.

He asked to be alone. I gave him clothes to wear. He took a shower.

Half an hour later he was sipping a rum-soda with me on the terrace. He was laughing. We could hear the drums calling Papa Legba, guardian of the crossroads, from the ravine of Canapé-Vert; we could hear the Adventists chanting their opposing ceremony from the mission nearby. He had on his sunglasses and the bad eye was hidden. Finally I asked again, "What happened?"

He laughed. "I had a bad dream," he said.

I shook my head.

"What's the matter?" he demanded. "Don't you ever have bad dreams?"

"You acted as if someone was chasing you."

"In my bad dream someone was chasing me."

"But it was only a dream."

He looked handsome, young, sleek. "I agree. It was only a dream. But a very bad dream and it frightened me." He giggled nervously. "You don't have bad dreams?"

"Yes, but not like that."

"Lucky chap. Sometimes my dreams take over—like a fit, you know? But I remembered where you live, *mon ami*, and you would take care of me."

"I'm glad you came here," I said.

It would be foolish to speak with him of the irrationality of nature which lies beneath professions and civilizations; he understood all about that. It was unnecessary to speak of nightmares as a form of revelation, of the intentions we put into the form of fears, of the language of excess. Voodoo and the hysteria of elections, power and powerlessness, race prejudice and the exercise of sex for reasons other than lust and love—these had been our subjects during many long evenings. "Le Cénacle des Philosophes," Gerard had named a little group of Haitians who met on a coffee merchant's terrace to be homesick for the *Partisan Review* or Saint-Germain-des-Prés among the weights and scales and sacks of green coffee beans. He had too much style to take clucking sympathy from me for his mysterious access. His humor was so firm that he didn't even need to be ashamed of being caught in weakness. He was tough. He didn't suffer from the usual Haitian aches and pains—color, money, pride, envy. He took his victimization by his own mind as just another peculiar trick which life on earth plays on men who have not yet made their way to paradise. His view of the universe could be defined as *We're Up On It, and if we're not, we're not.*

And so we only stared at each other for a while. Finally Gerard sighed and stretched and rubbed his knuckles in his wet hair as if he were sleepy. "*Ouais*," he said in the Creole way, "*mes-z-amis*. I can't explain it. Allhallows Eve—you say that?"

"Halloween."

"Oh yes, trick or treat. Ah, the garbage cans tipped all over Ninety-second Street! Well. That explains even less. My bad dreams."

"I have them too," I said.

"They tell me something, but I don't know what it is. Sometimes people murder or become great heroes," he remarked softly, "for no better reason. Me, I get very frightened and run. It's not death that pursues me, or my fate. I wouldn't be so frightened of that, of those—just such things—would I, friend? It must be something serious."

"Or just a fit, the *fear*—I got the fear, they used to call it."

"Having no power corrupts. Having absolutely no power corrupts absolutely." He began to laugh his peculiar chopping chuckle. "Maybe it's just Papa Legba and he has a claim on me. I never put the cakes and rum on my mother's grave, y'know? There are so many things I've meant to do, not done. Papa Legba is kind of sore at me, probably has his reasons. Or Ogoun Ferraille. Or who knows, Erzulie herself: you have no idea, friend, how I've insulted love at times."

"Regrets, everybody has them."

He gazed at me with his hilarious grin and asked, "Then why should I suffer so, please?"

3

Now to come closer to home. I am addicted to falling in love, to nostalgia, to dreaming of perfect ladies; we can cut that short, it's a common disease and a familiar story. I walk more than most men, sleep sometimes uneasily, wake often at dawn, find perfect beauty passing in an automobile, her lips compressed with a fret I'll never share: this is more and more familiar, isn't it? I don't even take down the license number of the car, hire a private detective, track her down, and woo her with unshakable persistence and cunning.

But one curious subsidiary plight in the history of vain hope comes from the occasional unearned victory of vain and foolish hopes. At age thirteen I discovered that I could defeat the monsters of sleeplessness (they are plural) by walking the nighttime streets of Lakewood, Ohio, which found their mystery when the suburb was bedded down. Cops, milk trucks, the dawn newsboys with the *Plain Dealer* were my demons, comrades, moving spectors in the dim glow of the city. Ghosts walked, crunching acorns. The wind rustled down the driveways of two-family houses. Then lights flashed on in kitchens and bathrooms! Signal of life, making toast, and the silhouettes were helpless and tender as they never seemed to be during the inoculated day.

And night after night, dawn after dawn, I sent out my rays of mystic power to Donna Smith. Make her come walking to Lakewood Park, there to discover me! Put sand in her rest, and force her onto the rocky shoreline of Lake Erie at sunrise, where she would stumble on the world's greatest thirteen-year-old poet. I even dramatized our conversation: "Hello!" "Hello . . ." "What are you doing here?" "What are *you* doing here?" Filled with irony, understatement, and crazy lust.

And then it got even more poetic. I violated her dreams with clairvoyant itching and telepathic madness. And it ended with love, true love, Donna Smith sheltered by my strong arms in a light which hid my hickies.

Night after night, dawn after dawn, I explored the city with no reward but fantasy, my mighty will churning in the void, its propellers catching no sweet air or water. I saw faces in trees and rocks, heard caressing voices in the wind, ran anthropomorphically amuck. Only later did I learn to take the keen gifts of a city for themselves and to expect nothing more. Streets, squares, and urban spaces are not girls, nor were they meant to be, though they are meant to rouse the spirit.

First, however, I had to suffer fulfillment. One afternoon I left high school amid the mob flooding from the doors, boiling, released. I found Donna Smith waiting, bouncing a little red ball. In a calm eddy behind a door. A bride of quietness, still unravished. With one red ball and bouncing it. "Carry my books home, care to?" she asked through her chewing gum.

I must have said something. I was carrying her books home. My heart was seeking a way out through my lumber jacket, but thump and batter as it might, the corduroy of those days was too tough. My mighty corduroy jacket kept my heart imprisoned in my body. Only my heart, and not my Bailey's jacket, had built-in obsolescence. It was a difficult time for the world, but a friendly epoch in the history of corduroy.

Donna, with fetching elegance, put her gum in a piece of paper and let it trail onto a lawn. She put her rubber ball into her purse. She put little chirping words into the air between us.

Across all these years, how to recall those words? About French class; we both took French, and where do you put the tongue when you say "u," as in "pure"? About the school paper: I was an editor and kept a green eyeshade in my desk. About the football team: does junior high football really count? I thought not. I considered, and decided that French and journalism are deeper talents. It was autumn, Indian summer, and Midwestern oak leaves crackled underfoot; so did maple and birch leaves . . . "That Lewis Snyder, he's a nert."

Which is the one sentence I definitely remember. It is imprinted. Tender, satisfying and tantalizing, it has a shapely perfection—a certain *je sais quoi*. It told me that my rival, Lewis Snyder, had his own problems with Donna, though I believed they were going steady and surely he had poured many a malted along with many a movie down her avid consumer's gullet. "Nert" seemed to me an exceptionally thoughtful way to say "nut" (nit? nought?). Donna was doing everything she could to make me comfortable.

We took the entire afternoon to wander down the gentle slope from Lakewood High School toward Edgewater Drive, near Lake Erie, where Donna lived. I carried her books. She carried the rubber ball in her purse and my heart in her hand. It didn't break the corduroy. It had slipped past my lumber jacket, out the opening of the zipper; it had left me definitively; and yet, miraculously, another heart beat in its place. But I knew that Donna had taken possession.

The flow of late-afternoon kids, heading home, thinned out. We saw delivery trucks, streetcars, a train. We commented on clouds (how beautiful) and weather (how nice). We just slid through the remainder of the afternoon, coasting downhill. It was as dreamy as my lonely midnights and dawns, when my parents slept without knowing how oddly I wandered.

At the door of the apartment house where she lived, clever Donna, an only child, paused, thinking. I did not press the issue. "Come on up!" she said.

Into the dark, damp, and silent hallway.

"Ride the elevator with me! Hop in!"

What a treat. Everyone else lived in the little suburban houses. Sophisticated Donna lived in an apartment house with an elevator.

Into the metallic, suspended box. Controlled by buttons. And a switch for the light.

Donna pressed a button. We rose toward the stratosphere, slowly creaking. Oh space and gravity and Otis!

I think she was five flights up. I was five flights high. As the elevator drifted upward, she grinned crazily, she let her purse slide to the floor, we were in this cell together, we were alone, she pressed the switch and it was night.

All my walks, my dreams, my insomnias, my mighty will had attempted to force her from her bed onto the beach, under the stars, under the street lamps, under the oaks and maples. But here we were in a dark capsule, rising. Her cashmere on me. Her lips on me. Her mouth opening. Sweet saliva and hot breath.

It was my first kiss. Then the platform trembled, the door opened and dim hall light dribbled in. Well, this was her stop. We were there. She paused a moment. She pressed the Close button. Again darkness shrouded our eyes; cashmere, lips and tongue. And then the door opened once more and we stepped out. Laughing, she led me down the hall, hanging on my arm as if she were coiled there. I had never known cashmere before. She put her key in the lock. Her parents both had jobs. "Psst! Wait!" She peeked in. Her mother was not home yet. "Wait!"

I was ready for anything. I was ready to be taught anything. I was stunned by desire and fulfillment all compounded together—bliss. She poked her head in. She was ready to ask me to tarry awhile if no one was home. No one was home. Donna was calculating with the speed of flying cashmere—fast.

"Ooops, can't," she said. "Beds not made."

And flop, good-bye, the door was shut, good-bye, maybe see you tomorrow, huh? Good-bye. I was standing in a cold hallway of 1937, no longer what I had been.

What a penalty I paid for that moment. Though it was not at midnight or at dawn, on the beach or in the vistas of boulevard through which I marched in all seasons, my dream had been magically fulfilled, my magic will was done. Had I been rewarded for the poet's longing? It seemed so, but a charge was put against my account in heaven, and the interest payments were destined to keep me stripped to boyishness past my natural time.

A poet begins life as a child with a man's desires, and later he continues as a man with a child's desires. And a crazy intention to fulfill them. He is addicted to his dreams come true, whether they come true or not. No matter that Donna never kissed me again, she snickered when she saw me, no matter; we had risen in the dark of that elevator together, her lower lip inverted, her tongue fluttering.

And no matter that she is now forty-six years old.

My magic will still insists on its desire.

4

IT IS now necessary to tell how I was hit from behind by a disappointed investor in growth stocks (white) while crossing Montgomery Street, which is the financial center of San Francisco, on my way to meet Leopold Sedar Senghor, President of the African republic of Senegal, a few days after San Francisco's race riot of Indian summer, 1966.

The war in Vietnam had been escalating and the stock market had also been heading the wrong way. It was down about twenty-five percent.

Because unemployment and prejudice and disappointment and ignorance . . . Well, for the usual reasons, including the usual killing by a cop of a fleeing suspected thief, a sixteen-year-old boy, there had been a night of riot in the Fillmore and Hunter's Point neighborhoods. The streets were shot up by the National Guard, the police, and the citizenry; the mayor made a firm statement; committees were formed to find jobs for the unemployed; spokesmen appeared on the TV—the standard thing for a great American city during a hot spell.

Under complex auspices, including the State Department, President Senghor, the great poet of *négritude,* was welcomed to San Francisco with a dinner at the World Trade Club. Poets, writers, black businessmen, and society people received invitations to break bread with him.

I was wearing a dark suit, a dark tie, shined shoes. I was walking down from Russian Hill toward the Embarcadero, crossing Montgomery Street, when a tall, heavy man, in clothes that looked neglected, with eyes that looked neglected, put his hand on my arm. "Say," he said, "my broker recommended growth stocks. I bought Aye Tee and Tee, I bought Gee Ee, I bought things like that. Eye Bee Emm. No dogs and cats, but if they're supposed to be growth stocks, why don't they grow?"

"I can't tell you," I said. "I really don't know much about it."

"Look, I asked you a civil question. We're supposed to have a four–five-percent national product in this country, he told me over the phone, my broker. What with careful growth stocks, maybe you can beat the inflation and make one heck of a lot of money, but instead the bastard sold me—"

"Gosh," I said, "it seems like a sound portfolio. I appreciate your interest in my opinion, but—"

I noticed that he had a roving eye, the pink and distracted eye of peculiar strangers. It had roved over my clothes. I represented the Market to him, the men who had deluded him, the broker, the enemy. I decided to be heading on.

"You'll have to excuse me," I said.

"They shouldn't call 'em 'growth' if you don't mean they'll grow."

I pulled my arm away. "Gee, that's too bad," I said. I started walking. Down Montgomery Street, past the chill and abandoned installation of Merrill, Lynch at eventide, past Sutro and Company when the cows are in the barn, past Francis I. du Pont in the gloaming, past Goodbody, Bache and Company, Dempsey-Tegeler, Hayden Stone Incorporated, E. F. Hutton & Company, past Eastman Dillon Union Securities as the mists swept in and only an occasional . . . Darkness shrouded my eyes, as Homer says. A thudding silence in my head. It was an odd sensation to drop from my own view. I was there, I was myself, I was present on earth, and then suddenly—nothing, nobody.

As I began to straighten up, I saw the objects which comprise a world dimly hurrying about in concentric circles to find their normal places. A street lamp stopped, as if to say: *Here.* A building paused and stood its ground. Automobiles deflated. I was in the middle of the street. Can I say I thought? I think I thought. I felt something. Like a candle: snuffed out. I began to consider among the possibilities: heart attack, an automobile, a stone from a cornice. I saw an automobile grill in front of me with its dollar grin. Honk, honk. I began to move out of the way. Oh, there were my glasses. I picked them up.

All this in only a few seconds. The world disappeared and then re-formed itself. The angry dollar grin told me to get a move-on.

A man ran up to me—a frayed, yellow-haired man—and cried excitedly, "There he is! There he is who done it!"

My friend the growth-stock expert was crouching in a doorway, peering out at me, wondering what I would think of next. He looked vaguely apelike, his arms hanging, panting with his effort to continue our analysis of his unsatisfactory effort to own a piece of American business. He had apparently run up behind me, and brought his fist down on my back. Now I was slightly discomfited, a little dizzy, but not hurt. However, my glands began to send up various commands, such as: You are angry. (I was.) I tasted blood. The snuffed, wickless sense—that state of being an object to myself—disappeared; I began to burn. The dizziness boiled away in a few seconds.

Adrenalin, thyroid, cerebral cortex, pituitary—what a wondrous creature is a man in a dark-blue suit who has just been hit hard from behind! Complaint, vanity, disgrace, righteous indignation, plus complex calculations about success in an endeavor of gaining quick revenge. I started toward the growth-stock expert. He crouched in the doorway, grinning at me, surprisingly light on his feet for a man of his weight in both flesh and disappointment. It was crazy to be so lithe. It was nuts of him to rock with such happy energy. It was paranoid of him to be so happy.

And I had an appointment with Leopold Sedar Senghor, President of the Republic of Senegal, whom important telephoners wanted me to meet. As a delegate to the French Assemblée Nationale, I was told, Senghor had been appointed to write the constitution of the Fourth Republic. How interesting. And now the great poet and statesman had his own new country, in which black and white dwelled together in peace and amity.

I advanced upon the growth-stock expert. He grinned.

I retreated, considering my options.

He took my thought to be fear. Perhaps it was—also prudence. He stepped toward me.

I moved into the doorway of a drugstore. Inside, a man was mopping. The door was locked. I was cornered. I called out, "Let me in! Call the police!"

The man mopping answered something in Spanish. I don't know Spanish. He didn't know what I was saying. His job is mostly to mop and not to discuss things with loud-mouthed Anglos. He leaned on his mop and asked me to explain. I turned toward the two-hundred-and-fifty-pound growth-stock expert who was stalking me. As he approached he seemed to gain weight. Three hundred pounds. All that cholesterol isn't good for a fellow's heart. Three hundred and fifty. Like a hippopotamus. Saliva dripping. Getting fat fast—up to four hundred now—and all the fat was muscle.

"Police! *Gendarmes! Polizei! Po-leez-ia!*" I yelled.

The sanitary engineer inside raised a finger in deft comprehension. He came toward me to unlock the *polizia*, which he apparently took to be the word for "door."

The five-hundred-pound scholar in investment situations advanced with a puzzled look on his face, which was a war-torn area, pitted with external ruin and internal chaos. I had an inspiration. I crouched and beckoned to him like a rival beast. "Come here! Come here!" I crooned.

This was unexpected.

"Come here, please."

And he took off.

He must not have wanted to do anything that would please me. My asking him to approach drove him to contrary impulses; he left; he absconded down Montgomery Street and around the corner, past a cigar stand and away, as fleet as the writer of a market letter explaining a change in the Dow-Jones charts. Perverse adversary. He was not a rational opponent. He wanted too much to please his fantasy, which involved displeasing me. Perhaps he also disliked the police.

The yellow-haired observer came up to me with a pouting, dismayed frown on his face. He showed me his lip. "Look!" he said. I saw what looked like a cold sore. "Last Saturday night. A friend, I thought he was a friend, he's a rating on this lovely submarine, he told me, and then we had a nice conversation and he hit me."

"On your lip like that?" I asked, this time careful to be interested. You never know when you might hurt a feeling.

"Just like that, he split the skin and it's still very tender."

"Well," I said, "I think maybe I'll see if I can find *my* friend, okay? But you be sure to put some cream on it."

The police were slow to arrive. I walked around the block, searching for the hefty author of oral market letters. His fantasy of an approachable enemy had interfered with my fantasy of freedom. I wanted to deliver a reply to his comment on the bear market. I disliked my employment in his dream. I was not Papa Legba or a tout for Sperry Rand. I wanted to remove him from the chance to draft strangers into his repertory of devils. He had disappeared into the city. I sought him for twenty minutes. Then I gave up and went to discuss the problems of primitive nations with Leopold Sedar Senghor.

5

WE ARE animals and children who are guided by our own limitations, by the law and by our ability to predict the future, including the prospects of retribution; and also by our hopes and our will to overcome the law and limitation. We have imagination. Sometimes we have conscience. We dream of symbolic disasters, like the Haitian poet. We dream of revenge and destruction, even as we dream of sweet wanderings with a loved creature on a beach.

What if my growth-stock fantast had found a brick in his hand or taken a pistol to our discussion? What if he had been standing at a window with a rifle? It was lucky that I was walking away from him, a little faster than was comfortable for a large and heavy older man, but what if he had had a good weapon in his fist instead of a rolled-up clutch of fingers?

He too, I am sure, has rolled many times in his sleep into the warm body of an imaginary woman who loved him. Who took his arm as if she loved him. Who breathed sweetly into his breath as if she loved him. But perhaps she was too often imaginary to give him the good comfort he needed.

I too have wanted to kill, and all who know their own desires can remember a few of the many times when they have suffered or exalted in the will to murder. Highways, classrooms, jobs, marriage, military service, habits, routines, duties —all stretch the demands on the lonely person. Civilization asks much. So does the primitive life. In return, we command our anarchic daydreams to give us ease. We promise to be adult, mature, and to put away childish things. But unless there is some gratifying answer of echo, the burden is too great. Any soul can leak. Echo says answer, but the answer comes: "No, no, you'll not get what you dream of." We carry the sac of fantasy encapsulated in history. It fills. It stretches. There are personal limits to the pressure that can be borne. Fantasy needs to flow. When it ruptures and spills out into reality, there is a poisoning, a corruption of intention, a murderous peritonitis. In a web and stink of need, conscience dissolves, expectations are grandiose, the mind cracks.

6

CAN WE live until we die, and without murdering others? Without at least dreaming of the murder of others? There is very little precedent for this either in history or in our fantasy about history. I made these notes during the Cuban missile crisis:

Today again the radio, television, and newspapers are screaming nuclear war, negotiation, fireball, shelter, breakdown, threat and counterthreat. It doesn't matter which crisis, in what corner of the crowded world, announces the imminence of annihilation this time. There was another a few months ago; there will be another to follow. The threat of the apocalypse is no longer something we shrug about when we meet it in a few street-corner fanatics, blowing their cold notes and vending their tracts. It is something the best of men are most aware of.

If we survive intact, many will not survive.

If we live, many will not live.

If disaster does not strike, disaster has already blighted our lives.

The primary axiom of which we need to be reminded is: All men are mortal. No matter what happens, we will each of us perish one day. *Man* may "prevail," as the Nobel laureate said, but *men* certainly will not, as the novelist Faulkner well knew. Even Americans die. The worst that the bomb and fallout can do is to speed up an inevitable process for all of us.

It can also end civilization, of course, but that is not what occupies most of our hopes. We are thinking of ourselves, our friends, those we love, our children.

Now children are weeping themselves to sleep, saying, "I don't want to die, please God, I don't want to die." Their parents are solemnly leading them to the television to watch speeches and news broadcasts. Their teachers are leading them through air-raid drills, teaching them to hide under desks with their hands on their heads. In San Francisco, parents are receiving mimeographed notes signed by the principals of the schools: *What shall we do with your child in case of a nuclear attack? Keep him in our shelter? Send him home? Wait for you to come and call for him? Check one.*

Children are being taught that life is an unlikely option for the future. Under a desk with hands on head disappoints even a six-year-old as an answer to nuclear attack. With all their usual fears and indecisions, the children are learning that their parents are also convinced that Nothingness lies ahead. With their childish selfishness and clarity, they see that the wrong things are being done and the grownups are being kept very busy doing them.

This makes for a specific death, not an abstract one.

These are real and specific deaths.

The continuing disaster is the destruction of human value *now*.

In offices and factories work is degraded. It has always been degraded partly by the fact that most men do work they cannot respect, work that does not engage them—work has been a means to things, then a means to leisure—and thus, exampled by work, the leisure and the things gained are also degraded. Certainly this is part of the reason why civilization has been bent the wrong way. We do not command our work. We are commanded. Paltry fantasies of work mean paltry play. An unused or failed imagination does not become healthy for the weekend. Sick fantasies are as contagious as the common cold, and bring fever, and bring a dull stuffiness, and the eyes turn rheumy and the ears go bad.

Now the transistors are out in force, shouting as if everyone were deaf. A deaf man bellows not because others cannot hear, but because *he* cannot hear, and many writers, artists, performers, politicians shout because *they* are deaf. They make us want to turn them off, like the transistors, like the music in elevators, like the news of the world.

The coffee breaks are extended by emergency, in order to cope with emergency. Another, grander World Series is in course. The papers publish extras as part of their circulation war. We lead lives of noisy desperation. An eager suspense and gossip fills the air: Is there a holocaust coming? Will we be here to collect our social security? Shouldn't we be off and getting drunk right now, or at least studying war-strategy maps and talking?

A silly, sad, hysterical man stopped me on Columbus yesterday, asking with a delighted grin on his face, "What you gonna do? I got my plan."

"What's your idea?"

"Oh man. I got the car all gassed up. I'm going to run up to Mendocino with some people I know and just have a picnic till it's all over. Man oh man, we'll have a ball."

I argued the futility of running away. He argued that there is no point in dying if you don't have to; Mendocino is out of the nuclear-target areas, and the prevailing winds are such that according to his hopeful calculations, he might even survive the fallout for a time. I uttered that usual protests about family, friends, and habits. He pointed out that many died in Europe because they were unable to respond to the disaster and stayed in their homes, surrounded by their families and friends, and then they all went into the furnace together. *Ha!* said his delighted face, feeling alive and justified.

And he pranced away, having won the debate. What he was really saying is that it's all over.

His wasted life is redeemed, he believes. Work and hope and love and children are all part of the short con. He has been smart all along. Ten minutes later I heard him stop another acquaintance, in a coffeehouse: "What you gonna do, pal? Listen, I got my plan."

The will to death is an element in all our lives. Our bodies perish steadily, providing a model for the wish of oblivion. The universe, running down as some scientists say it does, gives a merely abstract idea of fate. The threat of war is specific. The kind of nihilism it encourages is murder. We will live with it for an undetermined time now. Our children must live with it. We must learn to survive with the knowledge that the Mistake can take place at any time, and that it very possibly will.

Those who survive as human beings now, right now retaining their hope and sense of value, are the heroes of the time.

The rest wait and, waiting, die.

This is the present evidence of disaster: the photographs of the children cowering under desks in schoolrooms, their hands on their heads for protection against the nuclear fireball, weeping.

This is the disaster: grown men saying, There is no point in doing anything. I'm just keeping the car gassed up. That's my plan.

We must somehow learn to go about our business if we are to survive. Certainly we may all die suddenly or lingeringly; we may reach the moon with spaceships and wipe out our children by radiation; we may destroy ourselves as a species.

But the shrieking radios and headlines help us not at all. Shrieking fantasies are equally vulgar. The violent are victims, too.

They are killing us before the bomb lands. Sun, music, love, air, friendship, work—the joy of life is under attack *right now*. We must push our leaders where we can to make them guard us against catastrophe. We do not permit disaster: that's our plan. We can do little at the conference tables, at the rocket pads, in the centers of overkill; but we can say, *No, you must not*. And where we still really can, in our own daily lives, we must keep the universe alive.

Tolstoy said: If we are really dying, let us hear the rattle in our throats. If we are alive, let us go about our business.

The plan: to live until we die. And not to seek vividness by the murder of others.

7

WHEN the President was killed, I was traveling in Haiti, a primitive and anarchic tyranny where almost everyone dreams of murdering the dictator, and the dictator, in turn, dreams of a cataclysm, a mountain of corpses, which could make him as famous as Hitler. Contemplating the irony of Duvalier's celebration of the destruction of his enemy (there was a party at the Palais National that night), I returned home by stages—

Miami, New York, Cleveland, Detroit, San Francisco. Everywhere I was a curious exile in my own country. I am forever alien to the community of fear and grief created during the first days after the assassination. A friend who happened to be in Egypt on that day understands me. We remain on the outside of an event which briefly made America one nation indivisible. The dream was turned inside out; there was liberty and justice for no one; and for a few days, everyone wept in the same cause. The man in Egypt and the man in Haiti could not catch up.

Now there are people who regret that vivid time, as they might a snowstorm which briefly stills the cacaphony of cities and makes everyone friends; or a strike; or Christmas. The loneliness of private dreaming is profoundly disturbed in these times. I know a writer who suffered a nervous breakdown; he had been thinking so much of shooting the President that he now had nothing to live for. The doctors told him he felt guilt; he told them no, he was jealous of the killer.

Who can say what America thinks? It moves and it acts, but it is not an organism on the human model and it does not make logical shapes for itself and test them in imagination. If the medium of the American career is history, the medium is the message; but the content of history—the magic wills which lie embedded in public acts—remain a mystery to a confused race, self-created and headed into its nonmanifest destiny.

We don't know what we want. We are getting something else. The old rewards, both nostalgia for Arcadia and the dream of Progress, seem to be mere black comedy now to the swinging and the swung. Conscience is drenched in confusion.

8

FANTASY and murder, dream and possibility.
Now let us consider two beasts.

The lamprey is an undeveloped, ravenous, eel-like fish with inefficient eyes, trivial nerves, and a simplistic digestive system. It also possesses at the eating end a powerful circular sucking mouth with horny teeth for boring into the flesh of other fishes. It attaches itself. It sucks. It grinds, hanging in unconscious bliss. It feeds on the blood of its hosts until they die. Lamprey moved in up the St. Lawrence waterway, which provides a link for shipping between Cleveland and the ocean; lamprey took over the streams and the fresh water of Lake Erie, and destroyed the lovely trout, halibut, sweet game fish. They came from elsewhere; they multiplied; they destroyed. Now, after much labor, thanks to money, science, and the federal government, poison and electric fences have brought the lamprey under control. But the lake is dying anyway, thanks to sewerage; the sticky green algae feed on wastes, clot the water, strangle the few surviving fish. The lake is starved of oxygen; the cycle of destruction is tricky. The saw-toothed lamprey seems to be held at bay, but it awaits another chance. The lake on whose beaches I strolled, dreaming of Donna Smith, is a dead sea.

The axolotl is a primitive salamander, like a giant tadpole. It breeds in its larval state. It stops short. Somewhere in millennia past it hesitated. It never goes further—never naturally an adult, whatever that would be. But the mysteries of evolution! Put thyroid in the water and its gill slits grow marvelous lips, it develops lunglike structure, it swells up like a tomato fed on hormones, it lumbers out onto the land, immense, evolved, attaining a condition it never before knew, as if reminded of a forward or backward step in evolution which it once tried and rejected. It becomes another monster from the one it was. It lives a new life. It is very ugly. Mere thyroid does this.

When such creatures really exist, when they can be created by chemicals, what need have we of nightmares? Answer: To make it clear and certain that the lamprey and the axolotl really threaten us. Smoky bad dreams, visions of love, and drunken growth stocks are very personal. They are the dreamer's property alone. They belong to him, and he alone can act to answer them. Society and the public life are as they may be, and moving in; but the private will remains.

It is easy to see why Plato feared the poets. They bring monsters into the city. They delude. The morbid poet in every man is a monster which must be exorcised and can never be exterminated until its host dies. And so men cry in their sleep, *Kill kill kill*, or awake, *Burn baby burn*. Still, Plato made a great error in wanting to close the walls of the city to the risks and wastes of imagination. The invasion should not be turned off by walls. He looked for a utopia which is that of death. He was then an old man, dying peacefully to himself. He was melancholic, which means that the hope of love has been given up; even nostalgia is a better fate than the reconciliation of melancholia.

The magic will which makes us see the other side of our natures—dream and disaster, catastrophe and fulfillment—is the great permanent challenge of humanity. It tells us what we can do, want to do, must do, and even, if we listen very attentively, what price we will pay. Wars and lampreys, murder, riot, growth stocks, death. And Donna Smith's hot wet lips upon mine in the elevator.

Catastrophe and desire are the human fate everywhere. A civilized jungle like Manhattan covers them with quirks of manipulation, speedy recoveries, battening on others, shrewd appetites shrewdly dissatisfied. New York is a dream of power, abstract, a head-city, despite the smells of raunch, the luxuries of women, food, drink, and art, the screams of the elements grating against one another.

Now, what if a writer let himself slip into mere making out in Manhattan? What if he met one of those chiefs of Manhattan make-out, make-do? What if real life found them there in this easy slide and the real magic were not gone, and love exists as surely as death, death came as surely as love . . . ?

A DEATH
ON THE EAST SIDE

A STORY

"WHAT we like, my friend, is give away a lot of money so we can catch a little of the overflow for tax savings in line with—oh, well, the federal and state provisions." A boyish forty-nine-year-old man was winking at me. He was also engaged in instruction. "We find that money tends to stick in the nets, a little for everyone, nice like that. Not that you should bother your insides about it. You, sir, are beyond such distractions. You are an artist, head in the clouds, aren't you?"

I would have appreciated his ceasing the flirty winking, and at last, when I looked up from the oysters he was buying me at the Algonquin, he did. He was momentarily busy with his own

51

littlenecks—lemon, sauce, salt and wine—or perhaps he was just checking out his next move.

". . . the strength of oysters and the delicacy of clams," he was saying. "For spiritual sorts. The Baroness Blixen lived to nearly eighty on oysters and champagne." He rolled the last clam to its reward. "Isak Dinesen," he said. "We wanted to give her a year to write her final memoirs, but she said she couldn't spare the time. She said she was dying, and she was. Pity."

Philip Grove had served as vice president of various networks, he had been poetically handsome in his youth, he was a delight in middle age (luxuriant gray hair, ironic smiles); he had enjoyed twenty-five years of faithful drinking and seventeen years of psychoanalysis, both of them continuing nicely when we met. Two wives and three marriages confused matters; he had married one of the girls twice, numbers one and three—the oil lady from Tulsa had leapfrogged the chanteuse from Copenhagen and Cleveland. He was now redivorced from this first/third wife and paying her double indemnity, suicide, revenge, menopause, got-the-midnight-horrors alimony. Her wells had run dry. She was a three A.M. telephoner and even incited their daughter, Carol, to make trouble. "That hurts a bit," he said. "A lot."

A frequent refuge for Philip in times of stress was to enter public service. Now he was director of one of America's greatest second-rate foundations. They couldn't compete with Ford, Rockefeller, or Guggenheim, and that's how I came in: to help set up a program for catching the artistic fish and eels that the bigger endowments let slip through their valves.

Lunches at the Century Club, dinner at the Four Seasons. He wanted to get a positive result in whatever he did—even instructing me in how to live. I was flattered. We were both recently divorced, both trying out as gray-flecked Manhattan boys again. He had read my novels and thoughtfully quoted from me in conversation with me. That man knew how to make joy at small expense. (The person writing this story is no longer the person telling it.) I loved breathing the happy air. "Well, sir," he said with the courtly manner of a slightly older man who is signing all the checks, "I was probably paid more for reading your books than you were for writing them."

Somehow this made me feel important, though there was surely an edge to the compliment.

And advice on how to give money to artists? Now, there was a dreamy, restful deal. So I just let my mind expand, a few folds at a time. I suggested a program of special vacations for novelists, story writers, and poets. The idea was to waste and live well for a few weeks, to refresh the spirit with excess. A large sum of money would be handed out with the provision that it be squandered in less than a month. I invoked some traditional models—Dionysius, Bacchus, and C. Wright Mills (Philip expected nothing less from me). How would we check against the possibility of practical distortions—prudent mid-century poets laying on station wagons, laundry equipment, convertible preferreds for the children's education? Well, we could always go for receipts from Bahamian hotels and chorus girls freaked out on diet pills. Naturally, I preferred the honor system. I preferred to go that way.

Philip said he loved the idea, just loved it. As this meant he seemed to like it pretty well, I was sure the foundation would accept it, since he made all the important decisions. It was a brilliant day in the history of philanthropy. I was responsible for a great leap forward from the single flower of Puritanism into the thousand flowers of affluence and ecstasy. "Hmm," said Philip, "a keen article there for Gratefully Yours, the *Journal of Applied Philanthropy*. 'Affluence & Ecstasy: Expanding the Frontiers of Exemption . . .'" I was a mandarin ideologue in my first J. Press suit. Gongs, zithers, wine, silks and dancing girls for the contributors to the *Hudson Review*.

At the next regular meeting of the governing board my idea was rejected.

53

Ah, so. Another miscalculation. Another case of too much enthusiasm and trust on life's way. Again a deep brainstormer had misplaced his faith in the ability of others to understand innovations in quantum money dispersal. Well, no matter.

Our friendship survived this reverse. I expected a small check labeled "honorarium" for drafting the idea, typing it, too; but evidently the high-level decision was to pay me in lunches, dinners, oral quotation from my work, continuing instruction, and the companionship of Philip Grove. Well, some things are worth more than money, though perhaps a plate of oysters at the Algonquin is not one of them. I put away my mandarin dreams.

Nevertheless, taking a consistent pro-oyster position, one evening I accepted another session of charge-a-plate seafood. Philip wanted to explain. He was tender in his own heart, too. "I know what you think, I'm smart enough," he said, "but the fact is I really want to do something good every time I get into these—oh, complexities. The problem is making it happen. I don't mean gimmicks, I mean the clout, the thrust, the—" He smiled winningly. "The gimmick. I really hate it that you have reason not to respect me, pal. I *know* about respect and self-respect. Those are two of my fields."

It occurred to me, and I should have thought of it sooner, that he really wanted to commit fine acts, read beautiful words, think powerful thoughts, go to bed with sweet ladies.

"Ah-ah." He wagged a warning finger. "I have insights. I stay in touch."

"Sorry," I said. "I really like you, Philip."

"Not really," he said, "but you'll learn. However, I've called this little group together for another purpose." He hinted that he was looking about and planning to leave public service once more. It was not quite—well, take my delicious project, for example. A terrible loss, a personal embarrassment. How the bureaucracy of endowment misunderstands the creative temperament, both administrative and laboring in those lonely rooms which Sherwood Anderson of Elyria, Ohio, described so eloquently in his collected letters.

His large, dark, intense eyes bored into mine to see if I had caught his thought on the wing even before he had filed it along with the request for accrued vacation time.

Yes.

In my turn I hinted that I was nearing the end of the first draft of a new novel. Ah. New phases for both of us. We both sighed. We would digest all this news and return to it in the fullness of time.

We then settled down comfortably to discussing our mistreatment at the hands of women. We did not exactly wallow in our miseries, but we inoculated ourselves against cholesterol and useless fret by not keeping the secret. Although I had entered real life again, chasing limber ladies through the canyons and rushing gorges of Manhattan, I still took pleasure in these restful evenings of commentary and philosophy. Philip, ten years older, claimed to admire my energy, but liked to go at things a little more slowly. Bring them to him by taxi, for example, or by limou when one was available. The permanent truths—friendship, accomplishment, good taste—were what interested him. His daughter, Carol (a "teenie," as he described her), had let him down. "Patience and cunning," he said, "that's what a man needs. But no exile, it's impossible, the whole world is Manhattan now."

"I suppose."

"What good are victories?" he asked me. "What good is the hunt?"

"Are you asking me a question? I feel you're making a statement."

"Well, take Carol for openers. She is bad news for some old man, pal. If not for her dad, for some other chap."

In quest of permanent truth, he left the foundation and went to work for a buccaneer millionaire who had reached the stage in his development where he needed to finance art movies. On the day he told me about his new job I confessed to him that he looked a bit like a leading man. He was tall, slender, handsome, with suave weariness worn like a halo. That's a neat style. In his youth he had played polo. In his youth, he confessed in turn, he had wanted to be an actor, but: "I had too much—oh, premature afterthought you can call it. The lines they gave actors in those days—couldn't say 'em." His eyes were dark, soft and tender as he explained why he chose not to be a star of stage and screen. Producer—well, that's all the difference in the world. Because I had begun to weary of his dramatic cynicism, I redoubled my efforts to express friendship. After all, he had been good to me. But I began to suspect he was wearing eye liner to accentuate that dark, soft, and tender gaze.

Oh, it couldn't be.

I denied it to myself. He wasn't that sort. I put it out of mind. I looked for the telltale smear.

In an agony of difficult friendship we exchanged gifts like shy romancers. He put me up for his club as if to tell me I should now consider myself middle-aged. I gave him a copy of *Shakespeare's Bawdy* as if to tell him he could still have boyish intellectual fun. He asked to meet girls. I asked to meet interesting people. He was bored with the girls I introduced him to, and looked wan and bored. I was bored with the social people he introduced me to, and once escaped a party on Long Island through the library window. I hitchhiked back to Manhattan, frantic and drunk. We didn't see each other for a week, but then had a laugh over it and he wanted to take me to Southampton again so I could repeat my famous vanishing act. The cream that made me vanish was oil of small talk. He thought he might sell it along with excursions to Europe on Icelandic Airlines.

Ever since the peculiar thought about his wearing eye liner, I tried to conduct our meetings along with the company of ladies. Foursomes strolling Greenwich Village, four on week-

ends to Westport, that was my new idea. The old male intimacy dimmed a bit in our new occupations. He was irritated
by my increasing implication in the temptations of Manhattan, as if only he had kept our interludes of talk pure, free of
money and sex and ambition, just two friends sharing a flight
through middle space.

One night, over the final brandy, he asked, "What's it all
about? We are paper men, air men, we float and glide over this
abstract town. Who are we? We are what we are—nobodies."

"I wish you'd speak for yourself, Philip."

He gazed mournfully into my eyes. Maybe he didn't wear
eye liner, after all. It would be a sin to suspect him wrongly.
He had hard, clear, bluish whites, he had a fixity of gaze. "I
suppose I should only speak for myself," he said. "It's part of
the disease—abstraction. I want to take everybody my own
way, as if a crowd of paper figures could make one man of flesh
and soul. I apologize. Nothing personal." He waited for me to
reply. "My daughter is breaking my heart."

I had nothing to say. I was tired after the long evening—a
divorced Wellesley girl and her best friend—and the abrupt
moment of King Lear found me unprepared. We had been
amusing the ladies and it left my philosophic skills a bit
threadbare. After so much laughter, nudging, and tickling,
here came Carol. I must have looked distracted.

"Take the service elevator out," he said. "It's faster after
one. Wait, I'll show you."

I found other friends. Philip joined a Unitarian group. We
were both in search. He thought up a TV special to promote,
something about the revival of irrational religion. He asked
me if I liked his working title for it: "The Now! Churches."
Rational and irrational, he said; but in quest of some sort of
purity. Ninety minutes of stomping and glossolalia, plus Erich
Fromm and maybe Norman O. Brown—what did I think?

"Terrific, Philip."

"Sensational," he said, "*and* educational."

Also, as a remedy for that after-five feeling, that void, that anomie, that angst, those mid-century whatchamacallits, he fell in love.

In fact, despite the slow and stately stride of maturity, Philip the Pure was in love with the whole chorus line in the revived version of *West Side Story*. He had a friend whose skinny wife was a featured player and he would stand in her dressing room and look at the girls—High School of Performing Arts, Actors Studio, Merce Cunningham, readers of Buber and Frantz Fanon and *Variety*—through a crack in her half-shut door. They undressed with miraculous calm. Naked but for their eyelashes, long-limbed, cute, oh cute, they primped and jiggled and waited for the Big Chance near massed banks of hot white bare bulbs. Gradually he narrowed his devotion to just one, Sandy Grasset, and gradually she came to understand that he wanted her for his very own.

Okay, one Sunday morning after an ecumenical mass at a Now! church, she gave herself to Philip for his very own. A man deserves a Big Chance, too. But then it wasn't enough. He wanted to marry her, to keep and cherish her. "Will you be my widow?" he demanded, dropping to his knees and mumbling, "George Bernard Shaw, an early play, I have total recall."

"Wha?"

"I was quoting. Shouldn't joke at a time like this. Total visual, not oral. Marry me."

She laughed and laughed, though not at the touching whimsy he intended, and he coolly noted that one thin tape of eyelash was coming unstuck. But he only loved her the more for this single blemish on her perfection of greedy little showgirl.

"Naw," she said. "I have my career, and my afternoons I go to the New School." Her evenings, of course, belonged to the Theater. She also studied creative writing, mime (*meem*), and existential psychodrama for a time of crisis.

He stared, hair thick and white, body thumped and worked at the New York Athletic Club. "I need you," he said.

"I like you," she said. "Isn't it obvious, really clear?"

"I would hope it all means something."

"Does, *does*, sweetie. I wouldn't do . . . *that*"—and she made a pretty little moufie, as if to say dirty-dirty. "I wouldn't do that for just anybody. Not even to get a job I wouldn't. I don't have to, besides. I'm well known for not doing it unless—"

"Unless you really like a fellow?"

"Well, you could put it." She got the point a second later. "Okay, then, you be sarcastic and see if it encourages an I-thou relationship between us."

"I'm sorry," he cooed, miserable.

"Aw, come on," she said, wrapping him in her skinny arms.

But she dawdled about marrying him. He worked out a miracle plan: me. I should persuade her, me, with my inspired pleading of his case. *Who?* It was like filling out a recommendation for a foundation grant. It was not like that, but he had his peculiar notion that I could help and he arranged for me to meet her alone at her apartment one afternoon (all of us supposed to be there, Philip delayed, last-minute telephone call, a carefully orchestrated plan). By means of straight talk, full of depth charges there in the shadow of Lincoln Center, I was supposed to win him his third/fourth wife.

I felt a bit wooden and pasted together. I said, "Um, he really cares for you. He wants you badly. I think you would do well."

"Icky," she said. "He's not icky, but he is too old. Hey, how's about I make us some coffee?"

"You said yourself he's not icky," I said, "and with vitamin pills and the new statistics from the insurance companies, he's got many carefree years ahead of him. How long do you think you can dance, Sandy?"

"Three wives. Icky."

59

"But you're different. And it wasn't really three. And he's a boy at heart."

"Plus he tole me I remind him of his *daughter!* I wanna stay in show business."

"True, he'd like you to be a helpmeet, entertain, spend his money." I hoped she was listening. I'd hate to have to repeat that.

"Hey, he's really loaded?"

"Then you won't?"

She fixed me with her violet eyes in that starved, bony dancer's face. Cheekbones and eyes in the context of violet and good definition always make a fellow think profound. "How much—how much you *bet?*" she asked. First she grinned with elfin humor. Then a hilarious peel of jeering laughter as the implications began to deal with her. Blacch, another natural screamer, I thought. She looks so physical, so much body and dance, but she's like an actress, a nice suburban girl, a nice normal hysteric. Abruptly she stopped laughing. "Maybe I will," she said. "You think the kid, uh—"

"Carol."

"—'ll bug us a lot?"

"No."

"Cause I hate kids like that—the selfish age."

"No, the kid is grown up, nearly your age."

That was three fifths of a faux pas, but she didn't seem to mind. She was twitching with thought, tongue working in corner of mouth, Kleenex at eye, knees jiggling. Perhaps she was just practicing her new role of charming hostess, for she said, "Ooh, ick, the coffee's boiling over. Philip has a Chemex, doesn't he?"

On their honeymoon in Paris he suffered a ruptured blood vessel in one eye and had to go to the American Hospital. Too much drinking or love-making, an expatriate doctor commented, but I never heard that one before. That was one for

Neuilly. Personally I thought he got some dirt in it and
rubbed. And that's one for Sheridan Square.

They came back and it took a long time before they invited
me over to their new apartment (condominium, East Sixties,
excellent view of the write-off). Of course, they were busy fixing it up, but other friends got invited two, three times. I was
out, it seemed. I had been too close to the premarital exami-
nations, but I still saw Philip occasionally for lunch. He was
keeping in touch and I'd be patient. His eye was red for
months afterward, as if he had just been crying. Well, let him
adjust to conjugal life again. It took some pressure off me, too.
Our friendship would find its natural level.

One of the matters we shared was a friend, Baron Clausen, a
Danish money pirate with castles in Austria, ranchos in Mexico, and ambitions to keep his tax-exempt fingers in all available tax-free pies. His nineteen-year-old wife (he was sixty)
distracted him for a few hours each day, but then there were
the sleepless nights and days of Manhattan. He liked Philip
for the reasons of Philip's charm and savvy; he liked to discuss
himself with me. Philip telephoned me one day at an odd
early hour to say, "Clausen—you've been talking to him."

"Of course, sometimes, when he lets me."

"Too much, pal. He's been spreading the gossip about you."

"Clausen? What gossip?"

Philip reminded me of an incident involving—oh, a silly
trouble about a party and a wife and her husband. I was irritated with Philip for reminding me of it. I was infuriated with
my smiling Danish enemy. As soon as he next proposed one of
his damn smørrebrød-and-cigar lunches, I'd give him some
honest American lip. Senseless malice: why should he do that
to me? I was shaking with the bachelor's dammed-up anger. I
fretted, I sulked. I wouldn't deign to reach Clausen.

He never telephoned.

In a few days it dawned on me. Somehow Philip must have

made him angry with me, too. What had I said of him? That
he was too old for his young bride? That he was hanging about
the artists to drink their blood? Well, I might have speculated
along those lines—who doesn't speculate?

I should have had an explanation with Clausen, but the
whole thing was a nasty bore. Foolish and foolishness. I let it
pass. I forgot it. I fell in love. I let them pass, both of them,
Clausen and Philip, and moved into another of the many
worlds of Manhattan.

Only gradually, reluctant to admit the loss of friendship,
did I guess that Philip was getting rid of me this way. He
spread gossip about me among our mutual acquaintances because, well, he needed a bit of a change and he was in the
business of opinion and that's how he did things. No matter.
Another day, he must have decided from long experience, if I
need him, I'll just come with my offer. He'll jump. There's no
fun and profit in remembering history, which is mostly a series
of grudges. He had once assured me that to his certain knowledge, people operate almost entirely in the light of their present interests. "Not principles or paranoia, friend, but what
seems to be in the cards right now. I've found this to be true.
It's tough, but it's nice to have confidence in the future, where
you get what you want by talking about what's happening this
afternoon. Say, listen, it's better that way."

Wine, oysters, talk, and the dangled carrot. Also a continual
earnest labor at completing my education. Corrupt and corruption, I thought; no matter. I had other business in life. I
felt like Dick Whittington come to conquer the great city. Although Philip had the knack of making his business seem important, more important than anything anyone else wanted to
do, I found new routes through skyscraper and across plaza, up
subway and into conference room.

Sometimes the crazy orbits of Manhattan intersect or col-
lide. We remained acquaintances, but the old clubby ex-

changes were finished. We would continue toward new ca-
reers, wives, hopes and troubles on divergent paths.

I had a friend, J. Willis, a long-time Village writer, with
three stories and a poem to his credit after twenty years and
four grants, who turned out to be dating Philip's daughter,
Carol. There's a crossed path for you. Willis had presided over
his self-contempt for so long that it had become a friend to
him—a deadly enemy to the ladies he sucked dry. Carol was a
pretty thing with long blond bangs that tickled her eyes as if
she had no interest in where she was going. Willis took his
exercise on such girls and thought he was a man. If I had been
Philip with a daughter . . . but I was not Philip with that
daughter.

Baron Clausen started a foundation, incidentally, and made
Philip the president of it. Philip may have suspected me of
wanting to push into the foundation business.

Sandy was an odder girl than she appeared—girl making out
okay in Manhattan. Dancing seemed to have trained the up-
turned corners of her mouth, but there were also secret down-
turning depths. She had been supported for several years by
Rico diRico, the Jukebox King, who had known the joy of seeing his picture in *Life*, not in connection with his Wurlitzer
musical activities, but because he was a friend of friends of
folks with complex police and FBI records. Rico preserved
his friendship with Sandy after her marriage, and also with
Philip. It seemed a sporty connection for that elegant veteran
of Washington conferences on the arts and network efforts to
upgrade popular culture. (*From Shlock to Kitsch*, an auto-
biography by Philip Grove. That was his idea. Subtitle?
"Through Darkest Camera with Grant and Program.") Philip
didn't fear for reputation, since most of Rico's arrests had not
resulted in convictions.

There is a reason, or a season, or at least a cause for every-thing, as Ecclesiastes almost says. Philip wanted to produce his first movie, based on a forgotten novel about the Depres-sion. There were many curious elements in the equation. The book was written by a man, now rather elderly and a senior editor of *Reader's Digest,* who at one time had been an iron-willed literary Marxist ("The land is the people! The people is the land!" was the last paragraph and hiccup of the novel). The original story aimed to show (a) the American working and peasant classes oppressed by county banks and agents of Wall Street in jodhpurs, then (b) their gallant uprising at the iron will of the novelist; the movie script aimed to show the warmth and humanity of immigrant racketeers, who managed by means of tenderness and vigor to crash through staid class lines, thereby getting the grateful girl in the end. The suspense for her was terrific. She would have to wait ninety minutes, eighty if cut for drive-ins, to discover she was worth more to the hero than land, people, or his mama's hand-stuffed lasagna. Much more; a symbol of the transcendence of Nor-man O. Brown's polymorphous perverse eros over economic determinism; a really modern scam, actual, contemporary, today, existential, and within the limits set by the concept of redeeming social importance, dirty.

Sandy played a small part, mostly leaning against a white piano in a speakeasy, looking fearful, as if the chandelier might fall. The financing came from Rico diRico, who may have been crooked but who was not necessarily clever. The film lost money, even with a syndicated sale to TV. The Bonnie & Clyde epoch was not yet upon us. But was it real coin-operated money? Probably the lonely toy money of drugs and gambling that sought warmth and companionship in the real world of tax losses.

Anyway, it made sense for Philip to keep good connections with diRico. Perhaps he could count on cultural impetus in the future, too. I used to run into the three of them, Philip, Sandy, and diRico, at those steamy steak palaces on Third Avenue where you also find popular priests, daytime game-show emcees, and out-of-town buyers working hard at their ex-pense-account cholesterol. Once I sat with them through dessert (I was meeting an option holder from the Coast, who was late). Philip, I noticed, played with his food. He looked pale, and the broken vein in his eye had never quite mended, so that it always seemed as if he were recovering from a recent crying jag or had spent too much time with his accountant. He was hoping to do his second film, maybe this time with Sandy as the star. DiRico was considering it.

Then one morning I got a call from Philip's secretary. Mr. Grove wanted to see me at his office. As soon as possible. Very important. Of course, like all writers, I seek any possible opportunity to avoid work. I was showered, shaved, and in a cab within half an hour. Manhattan traffic jams being what they are, I needed a shower by the time I arrived and wished I had taken a subway, but my shave was still intact.

I carried it through an honor guard of new receptionists and secretaries, Itkin décor, wormwood paneling—the diRico touch. Philip began right off: "What do you do with people, chap?"

"Who people? What people?"

"The public. My daughter."

That pretty girl with the regulation straight blond hair, wan little face, dropout credentials from Sarah Lawrence, and those eye-tickling bangs. She had left J. Willis, my Charles Street pal. She had been moving pretty fast.

"I want to tell somebody," he said, "and then I want to forget it. I'm going to tell you." It sounded like a threat. Before I could say *Oh no you don't,* or *What about your analyst?,* he was on the way and all the way there: she had died of hepatitis in San Francisco.

He looked at me with his peculiar courteous attention. I was frozen with misery and confusion. He waited until he decided I was okay.

"She was taking methedrine sulfate, I think they call it. Speed. Dio-metha-something, I don't know. Affected her mind—memory, reasoning power, she was a skinny thing, not the pretty girl you met. But it wasn't speed that killed her. It was a dirty needle."

"Philip, I'm sorry."

"She was always careless with her things. Her mother used to complain, but what could I do? I wasn't responsible—could I be? That woman really cut me off from her, so how could I?"

"Philip, where is she?"

He looked at me through his one red eye, his two eye-lined eyes. "Ah, she was buried out there yesterday. What's the good?" He shook his head. "I wanted someone to know. Pass it on. Communicate." I realized he was slightly drunk. "I suppose it's better," he said.

"What's better?"

"Hey, fella, let's go to P.J.'s. You can have a hamburger and I can have a freshener."

"No, I can't, Philip."

"Okay, a small salad. I need it. I need to sit with you—someone."

"Okay, Philip."

He smiled, stood up, shrugged his shoulders in that handsome, boyish, stylish way. "What did she have to live for? Her life was a mess. Man, I know about the problems with *my* oedipal hangups. I tried as much as I could, I worried about her, fella. But that rusty needle probably just saved a lot of trouble, agony, and expense."

The secretary came in and he waved her away. "Please. I'm taking an early lunch." He waited until she closed the door.

He turned to get his coat and said to me, "Life—what is it? Let's not frighten ourselves with that question, but we got to ask it. China. India. It's time for some perspective. Carol. It's pathetic. But when you've had as much therapy as I have, eighteen years and a small fortune, one thing you learn is admit your secret feelings. Expense and worry and what good is it?"

I was out of that office in a few seconds. I noticed I was gone when the elevator door showed me lobby and street. It wasn't grief that made me flee, or not only grief.

But it wasn't as if I could shake him so easily. That conversation about Carol had gone past the end for him, too. After I left the office, he waited a few weeks and then summoned me about what he called a "reasonable" project—miscalled. "Let's just discuss," he said, "with no obligations on either side. I always find you have an interesting mind." Which meant: I'm sure you'll want to do what I want you to do. He hired me to work on a film script he was "developing." That means, speculating in. First he told me it was to be based on a story of mine, but it turned out to be based on a story by the network computer which told him what he could (a) get into the nabes and then (b) presell to television. Rico was putting up the front money and Sandy had a slightly smaller part—one scene where we would all presumably share the curve of her dancer's thighs through the magic communion of the cinema art. While I wrote, she became pregnant; no connection. "I'll be an instant grandfather," Philip announced with his shyest smile that invited you to think whatever you liked about his feelings.

However, he didn't look well. His skin had become blue and his body slow and spectral. He should have seen a doctor. He said he was on to what they were selling. His nose bled. He

67

sweated at night and Sandy slept in another room because he felt icky in bed. He refused to go to his doctor. I suppose he knew what he was doing, and buying.

One afternoon we had a meeting about the script. He suddenly closed his eyes as if thinking, as if sleeping. He lay at an odd angle, like a stick in his chair, and I caught him before he fell. He quickly came out of the faint, blinking and smiling, but his secretary called the doctor and we got him to a little private hospital nearby, in the East Sixties. No problem with the heart. Weakness, general weakness. The doctor ran blood tests to confirm what he already suspected.

There was an abnormal increase of white blood cells originating in a disease of the bone marrow. They gave him transfusions to increase his strength for the time being, temporarily. They do that to provide a breathing space. Leukemia.

Philip got the news early. He conned the doctor into telling him everything. Calm and elegant, he heard him out and asked intelligent questions and it seemed the doctor was flattered by the patient's interest. He might live as little as six months. He might last from three to five years. The suppressant drugs have variable results. When one wears out, or starts to wear out the body—the side effects are often very disagreeable—the doctors shift to another drug.

"And of course," Philip said, "by the time you finish rotating the known drugs, they may have some new ones."

"Or a cure," said Dr. Berman.

"Or even a cure," Philip said, smiling and nodding. "Thank you very much."

I suppose there is no normal routine for handling the friends and relatives. Philip told me, his wife, Rico; he told the poodle and his newborn son; he told the people with whom he did business and cab drivers and stopped just short of writing letters to the editor stating that he had six months left to live. He set up a means for sharing the experience, irony in him, horror in others. He seemed pleased and proud. I wondered if he was taking mood drugs, and perhaps he was, but the euphoria seemed genuine, rooted in the vain and frantic blood. He would call me in the middle of the night to discuss "our" script, and then his illness. He wanted to get the script finished and shot before he "went." He dwelled in an ecstasy of energy and good will, popping into the hospital for transfusions and then flying off to do rapid business with banks and studios and networks. It made story conferences difficult.

"I can't write that girl as man-eater," I would say. "She's sad, but she's not mean."

"Look," he replied gently, "let's cut the crap. I may have only six months left and I see her for what she is: a bitch-whore-destroyer."

The only-six-months argument won his way about character, style, money, whatever the day brought into his office. As some people are name-droppers, he would sit in Sardi's East and death-drop his own death to get one up on me. He was doing it all around, with agents, creditors, secretaries, and even with his wife. Ever since these two events had come to complicate her time—the birth of her child, the announced death of her husband—she had grown quieter and the silliness had disappeared. She had discovered something outside herself. She was interested, frightened, appalled. It was all happening at once. I believe she even stopped seeing Rico, though that may have been his doing, a superstitious fear. She had the eye-liner look which seemed to run in Philip's family—his daughter, too—but it gave her a bit of staring style. He may have succeeded in instructing her to care for him. For sure Sandy was going through the miseries.

Philip's production staff accommodated his various television and film projects. He used to charm them into working long hours, bending to his will; now he bullied them.

"What are you complaining for?" he would ask a secretary who needed something, such as time off, which he didn't want to give her. "After all, you have your whole life ahead of you."

She blushed.

"So do I, of course."

He got his way. Midtown Manhattan knows how to be nervous and even how to suffer, but this was one boss, handsome Philip, that a secretary couldn't handle.

"What do you mean, you don't like the project. It's changing into, okay, so kitsch. Never mind, listen, now is the time to communicate—gut level. There will come a day," he told me, "when this will be the last project I can close. I won't be able to come to the office." He smiled. "It'll be *me* closing. I'll turn into a vegetable," he said affably, "except it'll hurt a lot, fella."

I was learning to hate him.

"That's for openers and up front," he said.

And yet I couldn't pull out at this stage, could I? Just because he was slurring and jiving and bullying, and using his own death as a marketing and production tool, was that any reason to give him more trouble than usual?

The job became more complicated than most jobs. Rico and Sandy had me talking to doctors; Sandy because she was broken-hearted, Rico because he couldn't believe the happy-boy partner would really let him down at some point in their business together. Philip was piling ahead, grandiose and furious, with the energy of a pink-cheeked young producer despite his bluish skin and his death's-head eyes.

The doctor said, "Remission. Like a lot of them . . ." He added cautiously, "Mr. Grove—Philip—seemed almost disappointed when I told him his place on the curve may be rather late. It won't be another six-month deal. He might well have five years, and then what? We don't know any more."

Disappointed?

"You'll see that sometimes—disappointed."

It was a hard campaign to live up to. It was a whirlwind campaign, intended for a six-month promotion; Philip wasn't programmed for a five-year plan. Nobody could put up with his dying for five whole years ahead. Speaking as an associate, it would kill us all. Or at least give migraine headaches, anxious nightmares, Manhattan boredom assaults, creeping paralysis. "They're out to get us," one secretary kept muttering. She meant the leukocytes. We became experts on the disease, as if it were an un-American conspiracy, like Communism or Swedish art films.

He was killing friendship by falsity.

Let me be fair: he was also killing enmity by creating an eerie contempt for his suffering. He made his own suffering unreal by using it as a public relations trick. He was trivializing his own and everyone else's feeling about the primary fact. He was barring his own recognition of death the friend, death the enemy.

Bravado: manipulating his own emotion.

Worse, a public relations bravado: manipulating the emotions of others and calling them his own.

Which?

Both. I wanted to say: China, India, what is life? Your daughter dies. You die. Everybody dies; big deal. Phony trouble. But where then is the real trouble?

I tried to see through the strategy of management to the terror beneath, but felt myself failing beneath my own spite. I began to have nightmares about the emptiness within myself that made me want to destroy this man, or to take relish in his self-destruction; no, not nightmares, black insomnias full of shooting dreams like meteors and murky under-earth movements. Because I found myself hating him and hating myself, I was tied to him by a pity suspiciously like self-pity. What in the past gave him such energy and resolution? How could the mask fit so seamlessly, and leave him so malignant and joyous? He was a mystery to me, and a fearful one.

I visited him whenever I could. I let him work his will upon me. Submissively I awaited new indignities. Confusion. To live with the confusion made the life of New York seem avid, arid, abstract, and horrible. We spent our workday lives in those radiant East Side glass tombs. It was as if I had some wasting disease.

I entered his office one lunch hour—the secretary was out—and found him crooning over a photograph of Carol. He was bowing and rocking and his face was broken. When he saw me, he brightened up immediately. "I didn't hear you come in!" he cried happily.

He had not heard me come in. It was the truth. I had found him alone, entirely alone with his grief and regret.

And it was double the pleasure, double the fun, when he realized that this scene had just come naturally, it was a happy accident, it gave the touch of life and truth to his act, it was sincere. He profited handsomely from his own incontestable sincerity. The incident was proof positive. The secretary had gone to lunch and left him unprotected. I had walked in with no appointment. Who could find a flaw in the deep feeling which I had discovered despite the deep feeler's intent to keep it absolutely mum?

During this same sincere period in his life, Philip was using the opportunity to "speak frankly"—to bad-mouth friends, to encourage confidences and then to betray them, immune to reproach. He stalked like the white death in our midst, swaddled in graveclothes, clutching at our sleeves and murmuring, "Hey, I'm dying." We wanted to shake him off like those midtown alcoholics who beg for sympathy in the lounges. But he was not dying on time. The months passed. His friends wanted to say to the sleeve-clutcher, "Aw, go away, will you?"

One day I said to him, *"Don't."*

"Don't what?"

He was spreading silly rumors—oh, silliness—such as something, well, on the order of being mean to my former wife. In fact, that was it. Exactly. Mean to stepwife. Now, what a stupid story! Who would ever do a thing like that? But that was what he said—mean (me?) to that dark lady of my miserable twenties.

Of course, I'd have liked to be meaner than I was. As mean as I managed to be, it barely saved my skin. But he tried to tell people I wasn't nice. And you know what? They believed him. People are funny about believing what they are told, especially when the delicious news is coming from someone as credible, as mortally ill as Philip; and especially if there are some really nasty tidbits.

"Don't what?" he repeated with great earnest concern.

"Don't voice your opinions as if you know. Don't tell people you think I'm this and that and wait to have them pick up on it and then tell me what they say and then tell them how I react—just *don't*, Philip. Okay, gossip if you have to, but I'd rather you wouldn't."

"I have no time for small talk, buddy."

"That's not what I'm asking you."

"Wait. You cut the crap at a time like this." He put his hand on my arm and squeezed it gently. He made my gaze meet his. He gave me a long look from dark, sad, beautiful, almost girlish eyes. He squinted them slightly and looked deep into mine. "You fail to appreciate how this changes a man's life," he said, retreating, hurt, leaving me to meditate on his soft turning away of my irritation. He had become a master of the pronoun *this*, a word with a subject and predicate, a dense clause of unspoken explanations and commands.

"Okay, Philip," I said, "I don't suppose I should try to educate you."

"I just try to call the shots how they are," he said. "I've said and done things in the past, things I regret. Carol. Well, you know. Now, with what's left to me, *this*, I'm just trying to be as straight as I know how."

"Okay, Philip, you've explained."

"I want you to understand me, pal, you above all. I've opened up to you. You've seen the worst. I don't even mean I intended it that way, that's just how it worked out. You're someone I really trust and count on."

That's a hard one to answer if it's only the eve of battle, but when it's leukemia time on old Madison Avenue, this country boy from Cleveland, Ohio, found he was losing the argument.

"Thank you, fella," he said, "for understanding where I live."

At first it only seemed like giving him his way on script changes because of *this*, but now it was letting him get away with undoing the little world in which we all moved. Digs, jabs, pryings, and do everything he wanted. Finally one six o'clock after a long session of mixed work and philosophy, I yelled at him, "Goddammit, don't! I don't care! I don't care what's happening to you."

"You don't want to say that," he remarked serenely, coming back into his office to hear me out.

"You have no right!"

He pulled the drapes and stood staring into the swollen orange-gray light of the late-afternoon Manhattan sky. Then he turned back to me, huge and spectral in the altered glow of our glass section of the glass tomb.

"Let's discuss a moment," he said happily. "You've brought this up before. I know I've changed, even as to manner. I feel I have a special emergency built in, a sense of crisis, and it gives me an intensity, a certain clarity and directness—"

I walked out.

I didn't see him for several days. Everyone brings confusion for everyone else. He brought too much of it. He left messages for me, but I took off for Easthampton.

Then Sandy called and got through to me. Her voice gave a correct but incorrect message. "He's in the hospital," she said.

"A relapse? What's up?"

"He may die."

"So soon."

Again the confusion. He had crept close in my life, and lent me moments of power. What right had I to judge him?

"Pills," she said. "They pumped his stomach, but I'm not sure . . ."

He recovered. They gave him blood, they kept him in the hospital for a few days, and then they released him, as good and as bad as ever. He had only taken six or seven Seconals. He apologized to everyone individually, including me. It was just an impulse, he said, a silly one, to spare us all the trouble.

"I'm a little foolish and desperate," he said. "I'm sure I'm being a little, ah, extreme, but who is to say what is proper behavior at a time like this?"

"Philip."

"Please forgive me—please? For the sake of old friendship? You once had a good feeling about me. Will you hold on to it, friend? I know I've done some bad things. We were friends. Try to remember, okay? Please?"

Despite all this busy play, it was finally about to happen. Philip's body began its mortal closing down. The rhythm of trips to the hospital, ameliorations, remissions, transfusions, new techniques, interventions, failures, hopes, desperations, was now a familiar matter. Accelerations did not change the pattern. Hope and despair provided a kind of vividness; then the vividness, like an amphetamine, wore out its host. Sandy became a stilled, sick child with a grin like the beginning of tears and a strangled voice reading the packaging of Philip's old habits: "Hiya, fella." She had learned other things from him, too. "I think he's a little better today. You're going in to see him, aren't you?" She uttered her grief and made his demands for him and slid through the day stricken by the smiling horrors.

Their son was invisible. He had disappeared almost as completely as Carol. Well, this was no time for a baby.

For every man there is a last trip to his office. Philip made that final visit, knowing it was final, and walked out without taking his briefcase. He left his appointment book open, three lunches scheduled for next week. He walked with the stiff gait of a sick man under tight control. He told his secretary he would be back after the weekend; she knew he would not be back. He had drawn into his diminished body. The writer would miss his oysters at the Algonquin; the agent would miss his *scampi* at Fontana di Trevi; the expense account had drawn to its end.

I wonder if many men in business put an exact close to the work by which they think to define themselves. Well, nothing is eternal, not even a great tax gimmick, not even a good East Side address. But Philip made no plans for his uncompleted projects. He left no provisions. He walked out. It was dead to him—the public relations, the TV series, the movie. Someone else could do it; someone else could not do it. He felt nothing for it. Rico might move someone in to try to hatch the eggs, but Philip ceased to fret about it. It was as dead as Carol, and about this retreat from work he was as dry and cold as, it seemed, he hoped to be about his own death. It was no longer what he used to call a plus factor in the daily round.

I came to see him. He was propped in a hospital bed with a lever sticking like a key out of his back. No, there was a thin mattress behind his back, and then the crank. His eyes were burning out of the bluish skin. "They shave me," he said. "I can still shave myself, but this way I have strength left over to waste." He grinned. "I got to figure out what to do with the strength left over from not having to shave myself."

"How are you feeling, Philip?"

"How do you feel when the know the end is near?"

"I don't know," I said.

"You will someday, I trust, fella." As if to soften the malice, he quickly added, "I try to get Sandy to take the towels home from this place. You know what it's costing my estate?"

"I can imagine."

"Oh, boy. Imagine on through."

A nurse was standing in the doorway. "It's time," she said.

"A treat or a treatment?"

"Mr. Grove, it's time now."

He grinned at me and said, "You mind waiting? I'd like to talk to someone when I get back."

"What are they going to do to you?"

"Stick needles. In the veins, that's okay. In the bone to get at the marrow, that hurts. Would you wait? Do you mind waiting?"

The attendants wheeled him out. I waited. He didn't go far. There was an adjacent laboratory. I could hear a distant creaking through the walls, Philip howling with pain, and then abruptly nothing. I was soaked in my clothes when he returned. He looked stunned and goofy. His pajama top was unbuttoned. His chest was covered with unhealed needle marks —deep scars and lesions. He was panting, but quiet. He tried to button one button of his pajamas, but his hand fell away, exhausted. I thought maybe he wanted to sleep.

"No, don't go."

I waited.

He said, "What do you do when you *know?*"

I couldn't answer yet.

"They keep making experiments, I think. Pieces of marrow they drag out. I don't heal any more, either—the skin—not that it matters. All for sweet research. I'm happy to stop healing."

I had nothing to say.

"Relax and enjoy it, I guess," he said.

The nurse came in with two pills. She held them to his mouth, a glass of water in her other hand. She was a black girl with good country looks, a prim intelligent face, an opulent intelligent body in the rustling uniform. He shook his head to the pills and took them in his hand. "My friend'll give me the water," he said. I took the glass. His hand closed tightly over

77

the pills. "Stay and talk . . ." He meant me. "No, you can go, nurse. Thank you."

I had nothing to say, but I said it: "That must be painful."

"I'm sorry if it bothers you, pal. I found these tears in a test tube. The doctor gave me the sample, and I sprinkle them everywhere. It's convenient. Too bad I didn't have them when Carol died." He closed his eyes. "You're right," he said at last, "relax and enjoy it."

"I didn't say it. You said it."

"I thought you said it."

"*You* said it."

"Am I getting confused? Now, there's a nasty."

He was stretching and wiggling, and the sweat kept starting on his upper lip. He wiped it with his sleeve. I stifled my panic. "Can't they give you something for the pain?"

"Yes, of course, they did."

"Why are you suffering so?"

He opened his fist. The pills were soggy and crumbled. "I didn't want to get dopey. I wanted to talk to you first, before I take them."

"Take them!" I said.

He shrugged and put them in his mouth. I held the glass to his lips. He drank.

Yes, I wanted to turn away. It's not so easy! I wanted to take all the opportunities he gave me to trim the recognition of decay and death with disgust at a performance. I assured myself that his refusal to complain of pain, to confess his mortal fear, was just another matter of style; he knew it would capture me; it was the unspoken in art, the hidden dream of time in a melody, an esthetic trick like his other tricks. But no, his discretion was real, I think—the foundation of style and comeliness within all his cunning chic. He tried not to frighten me with his body so that he could teach me something with his soul. His selfishness may have been very deep, as his style was most pervasive. But his intention was also to make me learn from him. I could complain and strike back. I couldn't follow my itch to flee. I couldn't be honest and impulsive that way. I couldn't simply walk out on him. How nice it would be to withdraw to criticism. He gave me grounds. I had to follow my yearning in another way.

"Thank you very much," Philip said.

"For what?" I saw the bottle of sedatives by his bed and remembered what the doctor had said: "I give them the pills and let them make the choice. I warn them: 'Too many and you sleep forever.' But they just wait, usually until they have no choice. Stubborn—most men are stubborn."

"For entertaining Sandy, I mean taking her to the movies, talking to her—I mean everything, friend."

"Nonsense."

"Please try to be a little more gracious when I'm being grateful, pal."

My own history with him is not very pretty—a history of falling in with his schemes, taking his money (never as much as I expected), letting the con give me coffee nerves, and then walking out with cold parting shots and angry resolutions. Well, I couldn't just walk out on him any more. He was in the thick of battle. He—not his words, not even his deeds, but Philip himself, the person hidden beyond all tricks—was telling a part of the truth, like all men, and more of the truth than many. Good-bye to the con. He was suffering. I learned some sour facts about myself from him; that's familiar enough in these days of prideful self-examination and self-laceration; but what was more common, traditional, and yet surprising, I was learning something about him. He struggled for control; he sought to master himself. He no longer thought of killing himself. The rest of life was precious to him, and not merely something he could use. He smiled handsomely, histrionically, and yet he was truly brave in his way.

The disease was marching through his body, consolidating its gains around his organs, receding, sending out marauding scouts, voraciously living off the country, blood, lymph, liver, spleen. First he felt weakness and dizziness, like a rapid elevator to earth, then seasickness and landsickness; remissions, illusions; then pain to breathe, pain around the heart, his body poisoning itself, drowning in its own fluids. This animal suffering he did not include in his public performance. He did not know how to use it; yet he was suffering atrociously. The horror of inexorable, irreversible pain is a great incitement to drama. He refused it. He suffered and left the suffering apart, as if it were the last holy object in his life.

His lungs filled with fluids. The doctors were making taps, inserting drains. They strapped him up like a sick tree and drew interesting substances from the trunk. "Did I tell you I was raised in Vermont?" he asked me. "Maple-syrup time again. Listen, we learned to say very little in Brattleboro, we learned to hide, and when I got garrulous those years in New York—"

"New York'll do that to you."

"I know. That's what I wanted. I never got good enough at it, was what I'm getting at . . ."

He was in torment, and reconciled to the fact that this time he could not pass it on as gossip or conniving. Could there have been some joy in giving up the mission of promoter, of user? No, but relief at defining the area of no copout. Something. Anything. There must have been, I pray there was, some brain flash of discovery and relief. This was not borrowed pain, picked up on the free-lance market. It was his own, his personal creation, he had world rights to it. Once, or sometimes, or steadily through the new and terrible routines of his nights and days, he must have received the message, he must have gotten through to himself. Oh, surely he would have agreed to do without in return for ease, but it was offered anyway—that brain flash, that ebb of sea over the meshed debris of depths, that withdrawal, clarity, and renewed confusion. An accurate, silent, perfect recognition of himself! And still rich in confusions.

He had stopped leaving his room. The transfusions were no longer perking him up; his body said no to the cortisone and mustard and cell suppressants; the organs, the whole system was disoriented.

Now what? How long?

Last week propped lightly in a chair with book and glasses; sometimes shaving himself, sometimes dressed.

Now wearing pajamas and shaved by his wife or a nurse, saving the strength for sitting and talk. It was too much trouble to turn face and lift chin. He should let the gray-mottled beard grow.

"I'm going to sleep," he said. "Wait. Wait a sec." He was working something out, his lips moving, racing the pills in his blood. He smiled as if it were a game. He nodded. He had found what he was looking for. "I'm carrying it by myself for the rest of the way—ah, that's nonsense. Forget it. I'm sorry."

"For what? It's unnecessary."

Behind drugs and coming in after drugs and without drugs at all, in the spaces wrought by disaster, he was finally exploring a territory which was his alone, bordered entirely by Philip, traversed solely by Philip, private beyond any despair or consolation.

"It's soon now," he said.

"Might be."

"First I'll sleep."

"That's fine."

"I'm finished promoting my last asset," he said.

"Shush, Philip."

The panic had left me. I too was calmed, as if for the first time Philip was present in the room with me. The games were done and there was no more advantage.

"There was something I wanted to say before I got confused

by one thing or another, but that wasn't it—the romance of my little situation. Not that. Oh, not that, buddy."

"No hurry, Philip."

"Yes, hurry, pal." He winked. "Didn't I do some bad things to you? I seem to remember. I can't remember."

At the last minute, I was thinking, death might come to him as the friend he had always sought, or another enemy, or as an ecstasy of distraction; or merely as a new campaign and project—there was no reason to expect more of death than of life.

"Didn't I?" he asked anxiously. "Bad-mouth you one time? Put you on?"

"Never mind, Philip."

No, none of these. It would slip over him as it slips over animals and men—a diminution, a withdrawal and an acceptance. He would be here like other men and then he would be gone.

"It was someone else then."

"Forget it."

"No, it was you *and* someone else. Plus a lot of others."

"I said forget it."

He shut his eyes. "Next year at this time I'll be a better person," he said. "You wait. This same time next year." There was an almost girlish, peaceful look on his face—eyes closed and mouth in a sensual, smiling pout.

I sat there, watching him, trying for my own sake to try to carry something away with me; and for his sake, too. Despite the drugs and vanity, the money and power and the cleverness, the common paraphernalia of hospitals and the special vaults of Philip's character, his body and soul were falling from him just as other men's do, and I had to meet my own abiding distrust of him in coming to see that he had a soul like other men's, like mine; and he did the best he could for his daughter and his wife, and if it wasn't enough to suit me, it was still all he could do; and finally he held the monster close, as every man one day must.

He seemed to be asleep. I tiptoed out.

"Bye-bye," he said. "Take care, fella."

I looked back, but his eyes were shut and I suppose he was sleeping.

THE LIFE CONTAINED
IN NOVELS AND
THE NOVELIST'S LIFE
1

Who am I? How am I to live?

A decent person discovers his identity through his actions as a man, not through some actorish feeling of his own pulse and measuring of his fever. He doesn't say, "Today the temperature is ninety-eight point six inside"; he says, "Today it's warm enough outside so that I can do my duty and take my joy, maybe." The novelist is also a man, afflicted with some trouble in defining both his pleasures and his intentions, and needs more than most men to be firm in these endeavors, rain or shine, hot or cold.

Thus, if we happen to turn to the sociology of novelists, we find confusion, silliness, and desperation—a greater dosage than is conventional in the larger population—in addition to the occasional instances of power and energy. As in Elizabethan England, the moiling crowd may squeeze out of itself a few genial darlings; but it is at least distracting that so many jerks seem to be required to keep up the pressure on the masters. And there surely is a mob pressing about the dream of meaning and truth. For example: the Zen novelists-as-thinkers ultimately communicate an odd effect—the soft sound of one hand washing itself. The spectacular novelists–as–self-advertisers seem not to be shouting in order to make an indifferent audience hear them; they have been emotionally deafened by anxiety; they yell for the same reason that a deaf man yells, trying to hear himself. The inside-dopester novelists ultimately seem to share all the same inside dope: it's sex, illicit and perverse, which makes Hawaii or Washington or Inner and Outer Space cause so much ruckus. The solemn pursuers of Form mainly invent the mere typographical look of novelty or the appearance of thought—like the frown of the television commentator, who shows that he is serious by furrowing his brow. The moralists who practice the art of black humor make us, indeed, laugh, but leave us the fretful sense that one joke—the world is stupid, and that's the end of the joke—cannot properly be stretched through hundreds of pages. And so on. As soon as we find categories and schools, we also find mechanical anxieties and resolutions, automatic nostalgias, gods in machines.

The novel is groping for its way in a time when novelists have considerable popularity. This apparent paradox accompanies both a vitality and a desperation to use it; there is great good luck abroad in the vocation of novelist today—chance for failure and glimmer of enormous opportunity. Part of the interest in novelists and even sometimes in the product of their lonely labors comes from the fact that, as always, people need solutions. We want answers to the prime questions. Why are we here on earth? What can we do about our lives? How can we assimilate joy and grief to the daily routines? How can we assimilate our daily routines to a vision of the privilege of being human and to the mounting infinity of injustices? He who will die is each one of us—how can we reckon with our fate?

These are the classic questions which priests, philosophers, political thinkers, journalists, poets once helped us consider. Now faith in these gentlemen is at an all-time low. Either they seem to be mere instruments of the scheme of things or they seem to be paltry and vain. We may not learn from history, but the dossiers of the great drag heavily on the will to believe.

85

The novelist, on the other hand, with his empirical grasp of daily life, appeals to the practical mind in quest of impractical solutions. The novelist seems to know what is going on; at least, he supports his description with dramatic detail. When he is wrong, as Dostoevsky or Tolstoy were wrong, his complex errors are not fatal to his complex truths. He supplies fresh evidence, his booty carried off from the days and nights of his life, his working and his sleeping. The newly literate and increasingly fretful public would sometimes rather listen to the avowed creator of fictions than to the presidential press conference with its taped exhortations and its promises to shrink painful piles without surgery.

What does the novelist give us and what does he seek to give us?

What is his aim, what are the gifts and responsibilities of his mission?

What does the form itself provide? How do the souls of novelists respond to the needs of their audience and the enticements of their art?

Does the novelist sing as the bird sings? (Answer: No.) Then, how can he prepare himself for mastery of his intention? Will he suggest surgery?

2

NIETZSCHE said: *We possess nothing but the metaphors of things.* Plato said: *A desire is always a desire for something.* If we put these two remarks together, both of them revealing ones, we discover an arena of overlapping contradiction. Reality needs to be dramatized for it to become real. This is a task for the novelist, bringing his good and bad news of the world to the world. He supplies the metaphors of things. The transient, vague, evanescent longings which help to define us as human—which do the job as much as our thinking and deciding do it—must also be made into somethings, into projected images. Again the task of the novelist, aiming his hope, memory, nostalgia, and will toward an image of coherence and mastery.

A desire is always a desire for something. But history has altered the claims of instinct, even if the greedy beast remains crouched within. Much data-processing equipment has flowed under the bridges. One radical alteration: men used to want food, clothing, housing, the pleasures of sex, and wanted in vain. Now many, probably nearly all of the novel-reading public, take their plentitude of food, clothes, warmth, drink, the body's gratification. Not all, to be sure; but at least those who traditionally have expressed these yearnings in the form of art.

And so now there remain, flourishing in the dark, those nameless and nicknamed desires: for meaning, for power beyond power; the nostalgia for the infinite; the metaphysical hungers which must increasingly preoccupy us in the sight of the hopelessness and brevity of our lives. Probably the more relish we take in life, the greater the consequent melancholy. Love seeks to accept this burden and is not adequate. Earthly power and dominion surely fall short. Wealth, fame, indulgence are futile. I have argued that the novelist seeks to master his experience and give it shape; this is true enough, but he can only succeed to an extent, for a moment, in time alone, and his mastery ceases when he puts down his pen. The rest of the time he is wishing for mastery. There is still Sunday afternoon and the sleepless midnight. The condition of mortality is our delight when we defy it and ride with it. And the rest of our days it is our anguish.

To the degree that he is a philosopher, the novelist yearns for solutions, total visions, completed systems; to the degree that he is a scientist, he is bemused by fact and structure, the day-to-day play of events; by his nature as a poet, immersed in revisions of reality, he forever looks backward to the fantastic exaltations of adolescence—nostalgic, piecemeal, clinging to hopes and fragments, sensual, frivolous, undetermined, grateful for murder and willing to perish for the truth he knows not

87

of. When all these qualities are joined, we discover the special idiocy of any artist, but perhaps they lead to a set of dilemmas especially characteristic of the novelist, who deals directly with passions and goals within the thickness of life here and now, on earth and in society. He inclines toward endowing the metaphysical goals with the character of sensual evenings, strolls on the beach; he inclines toward endowing the strolls on the beach with universal significance. These confusions comprise a part of the risk and glory of the novelist. They mean that he must continually struggle to swim out of his dreamy evasions and consolations into the "real" reality. And he must learn how his desolate optimism about the body, about friendship and love, about things and pleasures, give him a key to meaning. He is corrected by the real world, which puts a spine against his evasiveness; his childish energy—give it another word: lust—feeds his appetite for understanding; he must modify both pleasures and solutions and make his search sociable rather than abstract.

All this is rather morose and weighty. I mean something quite practical by it. Professor Irwin Corey has a most philosophical argument in favor of hatred when he points out that without hatred, there is no joy in revenge. The novelist says something like this for most emotions. Without trouble there is no joy in solutions; without solutions, there is no joy in making fresh trouble. The novelist whirls about like the Marx Brothers, making both solutions and trouble and taking great joy in the activity.

In addition, the visionary poet who boards in the crowded soul of the novelist has a vocation to make the invisible visible, and perhaps sometimes to make the visible invisible—that is, to submerge the real in the possible. (I say "possible" rather than "ideal" for reasons of American modesty about grand assertions.) Part of the novelist's mastery of the real world comes from his control, his godlike riding above and ordering; this includes tyrannical suppression of that against which his taste revolts. It may be seen as mastery, as I choose to see it; but also as a flight, which is the view of the good chap who averts his eyes from the artist as a sick, disappointed child. In any case, the world is not left the same.

Ernest Renan was contemptuous of those who refused to sign a loyalty oath to Louis Bonaparte. Their refusal betrayed an anemic conscience, he believed, remarking, "It implies that everything that is done and everything that happens ought to be taken seriously."

Yes says the artist, with his dreadful playfulness: *My words are serious, they can revive and they can kill.* Focused on the job at hand, he really means it, though afterward he knows, like Renan, that this cannot be true; everything is not serious in life, and survival demands modesty. Love-making, which most contemporary novelists take most seriously, is clearly an act which is made to be revised tomorrow morning; it has a joyous lack of finality. When the novelist takes this act for total, he is wishing for timelessness, oblivion, and death. E. E. Cummings said that the poet is only a true poet during a few hours of his lifetime; the rest of the time he is a would-be poet. Most of the life of everyone, including artists, is a preparation, a revision, a set of mistakes, hopes, expectations. Our triumphs, our claims on immortality, are rare. I am outraged by this—isn't everyone? But if we think this outrage through, we can return to the basic truth in Renan's cynical remark, though perhaps without the time-serving cynicism. Art is too serious a matter to be taken seriously. The triviality of pleasure and play may be the best model for freedom and the highest human duties and delights. What makes possible this shift in judgment is the element of focus: the true artist dreams without distraction, in focus, with a breath-taking will to make his vision clear and true; and in those rare moments when he is up to his intention, he suffers the redeeming illusion that his words can destroy, can resurrect; in short, that they are serious —they entertain.

To support these moments of inspiration, which are physical, erotic, in a sense mindless but with a blessed strong throb, and to give them depth, the writer needs a "causal connection" with his experience and with society. He must both take effect and be responsible. If he lives apart, with the sense of being a passive onlooker, his books will be about passive onlookers victimized by godlike or devilish doers, about the betrayed sensibility—we know that story well; or he will withdraw into cool contemplation, which is often a nice name for indifference. Later on I will argue for the obvious means toward this causal connection with the American experience— work, *other* work. For the moment, let us grant that the novelist seeks, whatever else he seeks, to bring the discord of the human destiny into some meaningful pattern. To expose injustice or stupidity, Madison Avenue or race prejudice, is the paltriest expression of the writer's job of synthesis. He must also see important people within an important world. Vision, talent, ambition, intelligence, rage, generosity, love, these things moving in the confusion of life in society. He also needs some sense of a strong relation to the prime matters of life and death. He cannot be a mere ideologue, intending to inflict his scheme on his readers, though the ideologue has an advantage: he *seems* to know, and some readers will therefore credit him with knowing, and his work will have the energy of conviction. But fiction is one of the last legitimate strongholds of the Raid mentality. The novelist pounces on reality with a bandit individual fervor; his passionate and sardonic eye spies out the way he and only he can see the matter, and makes someone else, the reader, a terrified herd of readers, go his way. He has a radical need and a special power to coerce. He seduces and lays waste and, like Moses, strikes the rock to bring forth sweet water. He promises the Promised Land, elsewhere, soon, over there. But when it is clearly in sight, he may be on his way toward another love.

Many dangers are in the Raid mentality. For the pure bandit—terribly frightened, needful, vain, demanding of the public—the only reality comes of fame and power. This produces shrill self-assertions, not genuine personality. For a public avid for genuine personality and selfhood, deprived and rootless, the stylized mask of ferocity may be more convincing than the living face of strength. This is one reason that the contemporary confession has become so fashionable. It imitates intimacy by offering up more desperate weaknesses than thine. It says: "The emperor has no clothes and is therefore better dressed than anyone, because nakedness is purity and truth and threat and my nakedness is lewd and horrible and marvelous and *look at me.*" It is confused and flatters everybody's confusion. The writer becomes a mere performer; he is a ghost writer, but the writer for whom he ghosts is himself. "This book is written by me, as told to me."

There is a curious detachment in all this concentration on the (apparent) self. It appeals to keyhole curiosity, it dissolves concern, it allows the reader to go away with the paltry pleasure of having participated in an orgy without committing himself to anything. Such a writer violates his mystery by telling all his secrets, but makes no use of the powerful connections supplied by intelligence, imagination, and awe, those elements which deepen the mystery by employing it to create a communion in possibility. His confessional roar may seem to be personality because it is so quirky. Certainly the sense of self is an important element of personality, and the quirk is a way of pointing to the self. Compassion for oneself precedes compassion for others and probably provides the model for love, but in the fullness of growth, self-love takes its proper place as a subsidiary of respect, sympathy, generosity, the capacity to love others. In the writer, this must lead to a skilled concern with the unfolding world. The novelist wants to unfold it himself.

With all the similarities in the demands made on imagination, there remains a primary difference of readiness and stance between the writer and the reader. Surely all appreciation involves a re-creation, a participation in the essential act. But the reader has a security system which the writer lacks. The writer takes a risk against which the reader is insured. The reader knows that the destiny of the people in the book he holds in his hand is already decided. He does not yet know it in his own heart, he has not discovered it, he has not made it part of his own soul and history, he has not produced his own synthesis in time and place and in the light of his own intentions: nevertheless he holds it in his hand. But the novelist, inventing as he invents, does not know the fate of his people. Perhaps they have no fate at all—mere dribblers—and his book will never be finished. But perhaps they will be unique, lovely, magical. His passion to discover the destiny of his characters is an essential element of the energy which convinces the reader of his reality. This conviction of value, the necessity, dread, and love in which the novelist is somehow enmeshed, gives shape to the mystery of personality which the reader craves to share. Its power comes from these elements and others. Beyond craft, the mystery of personality seems to be what matters.

We commonly accept two adequate reasons for reading fiction: the dream of evasion from reality into another, more vivid world ("entertainment"); and an analysis of ourselves and society by the artist-as-surgeon, the artist-as-trained-observer. Neither covers the matter. We take the personality of the fictional character within ourselves as we take the ceremony of the host; we find reality by touching another, by becoming another. We communicate (this is very different from transmitting information); we enlarge our actual humanity by including the imaginary others. The act is symbolic and practical, like love-making. And naming it is an impossible way to express its power, exactly as the expressed desire to make sacrifices is a world away from the acts of devotion and sacrifice.

At any rate, it is not evasion and knowledge we seek, though we also seek both knowledge and evasion. It is a link, a joining, a sense of mystery shared. The novel is not a popular sociology, a more subtle psychology, a moral fable, a graceful distraction, though it may partake of these enterprises; and the novelist, rushing to save himself by saving the world, may be motivated by ambitions in these areas. At his best, the novelist is in touch with his own mystery and puts the reader in touch. He is in touch with the mystery of the reader's personality and puts his readers in touch with one another. There is a ritual of communion.

The novel of low seriousness deals mainly with information, what we want to know about Hawaii, Washington, homosexuality, Southeast Asia, the early-warning system, the advertising business, the movie business, the Nobel Prize, the celebrity's scandalous career, etc. The truly serious novel often sets out to explore an apparently minor problem. The subject often seems to be the novel itself, a research into form, as in *Ulysses*, or into style, as in the books of Gide, or a pedagogical, philosophical translation, as in Santayana's *The Last Puritan*. Joyce, Gide and Santayana do more than this, and thus we continue to be interested by them once the form, style, or set of ideas has been consolidated into our vocabularies. What is the more that they, all three, give? And what is the typical novelist's incentive? The poet can celebrate his beloved's sweet disorder, the painter fixes on canvas a shape and color he wishes to define for others, the musician travels in his abstract but sometimes hummable realms.

I think that nostalgia is the word which sums up the impulse (not the aim) of the novelist. This is not a prescription, but a description; an observation about the practice of novelists, not an order to be followed. Nostalgia for a better state, for an elsewhere, another time. If we think of Flaubert, Proust, and Henry James, we see different ways of handling this boyish emotion; irony seems to be its chief container, the maudlin held at bay by elegance and self-judgment. When other aims seem to be predominant, as in Joyce's experiments with new forms, what defines success is nevertheless traditional, the successful dramatization of the questing soul.

We seem to be less thinking, rational, decision-making, political animals, as we so often tell ourselves that we are, than nostalgic and dreaming ones. We want more. We desire that which we cannot define. It is perhaps undefinable. The novelist defines the area of undefinability. Of course this is absurd, paradoxical, oxymoronic. No wonder our impatience with him, and his impatience with himself. And no wonder the job of definition must be done again for each changing social weather and time, each age and condition. A most private desperation is being poured into the most sociable of the individual arts. We peek through the keyhole to find a party in progress, but are expected to keep broody Rostov or anguished Anna firmly in mind at every instant. Old Karamazov wants something more. All want more. What is the *more* they want? How easy if it could be reduced to lust, power, riches, fame. Gatsby looking out toward the blank gray horizon of Long Island Sound tells us as well as any protagonist what he and the rest of us are looking for. For the we-know-not-what. For structure against chaos. For warmth against the chill. For a way to join our each and lonely mortalities with something complete and permanent.

3

Now please let us bring the discussion down to a very practical and anticlimactic small detail: *Should writers work?* The suffering of love and nostalgia is a kind of labor, to be sure; at least it hurts, gives pleasure, and is sometimes instructive. Work sets goals and accomplishes ends; nostalgia, however sharp at midnight, also follows a pattern followed by others. The sufferer, for love or a dream of childhood, industriously plays out his role. But it is not the same thing as work. It seldom gives an active model of work. However universal, it is a private and broody commitment. The lover has a predicament, not a job to do. Should a writer also work?

The question engages us in paradox, for surely the poet's or storyteller's imaginative re-creation of experience, with love and judgment, is one of the hardest jobs on earth. The writer does work, and with greedy intensity. The origins and nature of his subject are one thing; the demands of form and communication are quite another. And yet his work is also play and indulgence in fantasy, a mere dream of work at the same time as it sets about exploring the limits of nature, the limits of society.

This definition of the writer's labor presents not only a curious intellectual paradox, but also a set of dilemmas for those who seek through art the deepest truths. In a world in which literature is asked to do much of the hard job of synthesizing a view of life—religion and philosophy are dimmed out for many of us—the novelist needs to find a meaningful connection between his own work and the work of others, a practical implication in the habits of civilization. It is at great cost to his art that he removes himself from the abrasive facts of life in society.

Surely one of the primary aims of fiction is to rehearse real life, the heroes of novels carrying the burdens of others as they exercise their ardent private wills. The reminiscence of life in the world forms an essential part of that purging of pity and terror of which Aristotle spoke. The hero is in some way exemplary; he lives for others and others live in him. But is the American writer equipped to imagine the burdens of others? Or does he often carry these burdens as actors carry the suitcases in movies, very lightly, the prop suitcases filled with air? Most American writers just don't know enough about the world. They may observe accurately, they may read and study, but they don't *know* in their bones, where an artist needs to know. A remedy for this deficiency might be to take another

95

job besides writing, some corollary to the continual lonely wondering as judge and dreamer, observer and stylist, clasping ideal Time and imaginary Soul to the clogged bosom. A prophet must also come *out* of the wilderness.

A frequent weakness in the ripening of the man of letters is that his responsibility tends to narrow as his success widens; he thinks more and more of self, of family, of career, of his place in a future biographical dictionary; his subject matter becomes that of fantasy and memories, psychology in its narrowest form, with mastery of craft his chief rage. He makes his way into an aristocratic isolation while outside his study the world grinds along without him. Society indulges him; he finds irony or pathos or mere rhetorical stimulation in the continually desperate history unrolling beyond his window. Naturally, he is intelligent enough to suspect the danger. He frets. He signs manifestoes. He speaks at rallies. But these remedies are mere dramatic gestures. They do not finally give the organic connection with society—the sense of causal responsibility—which an artist requires.

Many serious readers have complained that the best novelists simply don't know enough about the workings of society and power. They are called "best" because of technique, language, sensibility, and that modern gift for making marginal differentiations, but it is left to the mediocre inside-dopester novelists to inform us how we really live in the world here below. The researched-up commercial product like *Advise and Consent* or *Hawaii,* the Sloan Wilson and Evan Hunter factories, does not reflect a causal responsibility any more than does the tricky or obsessed fantast flopping about in his own psyche.

American writers seem to have divided their tasks. The most talented tend to isolate themselves in formal pursuits, in abstract ideas, in memory and psychology. The worst do the work of the world. The best have no choice, being committed to isolation, both because this is a constant temptation and because the opportunities to live otherwise close down early. The worst are cunning enough to see their chance to sell spicy pictures to the customers hungry for reality.

The lack of responsibility on both sides poses a practical problem for those readers who want to see life truly. It certainly poses a moral problem for writers who aim, at least before they are spoiled, toward the highest realms of persuasion and utility. And it is a nagging issue for those critics who are not satisfied with the inside-dopesters and yet are not eased by mere style. These readers seek to explore the world as it really is, but recognize that many of the novelists who set out with the purpose of giving a fair picture are simply inadequate as minds and sensibilities. The trivializing of experience fails; abstention from the real issues fails.

Is there an avenue of escape for those who matter, the writers blessed with energy and tainted by genius? Might there be some alternative in a rhythm of composition and worldly labor? In France, for example, governmental and diplomatic jobs attract some writers; in England and France, journalism still appeals to the literary mind; in America many teach, but can they do anything else? Teaching certainly provides a causal connection, with plenty of politics and the chance of usefulness and a weight of responsibility. There should be a choice of other occupations for sweet variety's sake. But what happens to the writer who is interested in, let us say, the foreign service? He may flunk the security test; he is a bad risk. Will the great corporations seek to use him? For them he is a dilettante; he is undevoted to the Cause; and anyway, is he just going to write another exposé? (Alan Harrington's *Life in the Crystal Palace* deals brilliantly with the difficulty of marrying a corporate career with the life of a writer.) The law and medicine now require more specialized training and experience than a writer can give to another job; there is nothing graceful about the "liberal professions" in America—the competition is keen and deadly. There are not many openings; the fabric of society does not welcome the man who wants to spend part of himself in a job, the essential part in literature.

The obvious advantage to writers of having another job besides writing is the practical one of "research"—that is, broadening experience. They can see human beings in society, struggling for and against one another, doing the work of the world; they can commit themselves to sharing the trouble and then go away to write about it. A less immediately practical but subtle and persuasive advantage is connected with the moral consciousness of the time. Writers feel guilty and left out in a period of rage and despair. Even a job that involved no contact with people in office, factory, field, or school would give advantages in reckoning with one's bad conscience. It is in the area of moral involvement, of commitment to the contribution of work, that many writers now feel a deprivation. Publicly they claim: *What I do is of the greatest importance;* but inwardly they think: *Words, words, merest words.* They envy the leaders of men, the promulgators of laws, the inventors of techniques and products. Perhaps they mourn a simpler but imaginary history. They feel strangers to the times with their little lights, their words, their attentive ears and twitching nerves. Success may be sweet if it comes, but the success of isolation is not what they seek.

American writers in particular, precariously pampered, poor one day and rich the next, praised and panned, discovered and buried, need to escape the never-never world of the literary life. If they enter the common society of labor, of responsibility to hours and co-workers, to rush-time traffic and committees, bosses and underlings, they may return refreshed to the isolation of their art. If real writers could have real jobs, they might be able to master home truths in a more compelling way.

At the level of moral commitment, they would also earn a gain in common humanity. It depends on their own felt concern, their willingness to give up a comfortable insularity; it also depends on the society's coming to give up suspicion and permit the writer a dual role. Since this latter is unlikely to happen on a large scale, such a solution probably demands that individual writers see the way out of isolation themselves, and scheme their way into the structure of power. There is no institutional support for it; the individual must make his own estimate of possibilities. The rewards are worth the trouble. We need the writers to tell us about power; the sociologists do a poor job. We need the writers to tell us about how people work together, love, tear down, create, destroy; the psychologists don't do it well enough. We need sensible translations of the tensions of American politics; the official speech or press conference is a symptom, not an explanation. The writers need to know about the real world in order to make models of the real hope of mastery of the times.

Besides teaching, what else do American writers normally consider when they think of work? Journalism—remember the foreign correspondent in the trench coat?—still appeals to the fantasy yearnings of the young, and perhaps it is still a good way to know the world, despite Hemingway's warning. The Peace Corps or VISTA might do for a few whose family and financial commitments are under control. But bullfighting, exploring, and idealistic soldiering are for a very few romantics, and the time is not friendly to them. Advertising writing, scriptwriting, the various ways to merchandise a talent with words seem to produce nausea in writers; these machines are psychologically very risky, close to the natural function and yet plugged in directly to the control of money rather than that of the imagination. They give experience of the real world, but they insult the mind.

Are there viable ways for that specialized nonspecialist, the novelist, to inform himself of the world's business and give of himself to the world's needs through doing a normal job of work? There should be, despite the difficulties; there are, despite the resistance of a society of specialists; we must invent our own openings out of our special talents and needs. Each writer's character, like every man's, has room for serious occupation besides writing. The person who loves is precious; the person who lives for love is absurd. If writing is a writer's only serious occupation, the writing itself will suffer. Part of his life's effort is to find his causes, his principles, his skills in the world, his willingness to sacrifice; they constitute part of both the fuel of his heart and its reward.

The writers who can find some rhythmic way of advancing and retreating—into the wide world, into their studies for work—might open the windows and let the novel breathe. The writer becomes a specialist only at a heavy price. To be a "man of letters" is to perform too narrowly. Work in the world brings in a bit of cash, and it also brings in the world. Perhaps the young writer should not seek independence and freedom "so that I can have time to write." His project for the future might be the reverse—to find a significant job—if he means to distill the largest significance from his lonely and committed fantastic journey.

A SURVIVAL

1

HOLDING his two sons by the hand as we waited to board an Air France flight from Orly Airport near Paris to New York on June 3, 1962, a short, plump Frenchman frowned at the fiery ribbon flailing into the sky at one end of the field and turned to me with the remark: *"Cent personnes viennent de mourir."*

"No," I said. "It must be something with the fuel."

A moment later the ribbon flung itself higher; then abruptly it whipped itself out; the flames gave way to black billows of smoke. No noise came to us behind our glass in the air-conditioned departure room. In slow silent motion, trucks and fire engines swept out and wheeled across the field.

"We won't depart for a while now," said the Frenchman, leading his sons away from the window. He was right about this. He was wrong about the number on board the flight chartered to carry a touring group from Paris to Atlanta, Georgia, by way of New York. There were one hundred and thirty people incinerated in an instant, without a sound for us who were in plain sight of the accident, but behind glass. The pilot of the Boeing 707 had begun the cycle of takeoff and then, suddenly, too late to stop, had begun to brake the plane for reasons unknown. The black of melting and exploding tires seared the field. Two stewardesses survived. They were in a tail section which was thrown free.

Within the terminal, there was apparent calm. Baggage was being watched, newspapers rustled, candy munched. The plump Frenchman, who had accepted at once what he saw happening, retreated with his two sons, holding their hands. The boys were dressed *à l'anglaise* in Eton suits. Their father was wearing a worn tweed hunting jacket and a *casquette* and walked with a slight waddle. Watching their backs as they retreated, I decided that the sons would grow up to be taller than their father, who had lived through a long war.

Others who, like myself, had seen the accident with their own eyes began to ask themselves what had happened out there on the field: "A gasoline truck blew"; "The brakes didn't work"; "That last plane seems to have run into a little trouble." And a few minutes later: "I hear there were two people injured—local personnel." "Everything is normal, isn't it?"

We had seen it and not quite seen it. If my fellow passengers wanted to talk among themselves like this, I decided not to add any comment. At that moment I saw no duty to be a truth-enforcer. When asked what I thought had occurred, I shrugged. "Isn't there something peculiar going on out on the field? Do you think there'll be a delay?"

"Yes. Maybe."

I also began to wander about the airport in a state of hallucinated clarity, a condition which was to last all day and part of the night. I would not say that I was out of myself, but merely that I was very busy. I have never been hypnotized; I think this was something like a hypnotic state in which I remembered things I had barely perceived and would never otherwise have known I knew. Apparently I had noticed the passengers who had boarded the charter flight. We had shared the waiting room. They were all from Atlanta and I had been aware of the concentration of Southern accents after a few months away from home. Now, like cards turning up, one after another of these people showed themselves to me. People I had not seen I suddenly saw. Valises with hotel stickers, clear as nightmare. Voices, querulous and soft; worried travelers; Southern voices. My single previous impression had been a

vague peripheral one of Southern voices: now the faces returned. Flipped up like silent cards, one after the other; and
tennis racquets, suitcases, packages, ribbons, pennants, hats,
straw catchalls with souvenir stickers and tags.

An announcement: "There will be a delay of all flights."

"Why?" people asked.

"The field has been blocked. There has been some trouble
on the field. The field must be cleared."

Many wondered why the field was blocked. Though almost
everyone had been told that an airplane had blown up, some
had not yet understood. Some who had seen a jet airplane ex-
plode were sure that it had been a gasoline truck, a fuel flame-
out, an engine. They had asked the question but not listened
for the answer. They had seen the event but not allowed
it to be recognized.

"Why can't they use another runway?" asked a worried
businessman.

"The wind," someone answered. "You have to take off
against the wind. I was in the Air Force. Or maybe *with* the
wind, I forget now. I was in the service during the war."

"Why do we have to wait? How long? I have an appointment first thing in New York. I'm being met. My friends worry
a lot, specially they buck the Sunday traffic out to Idlewild."

There was no official announcement that an airplane had
exploded, killing one hundred and thirty people. The bureaucrats behind their counters told various stories and the fretful
bureaucratic faces looked no different than usual—just fretful.
Some looked strainedly genial. The crowd of delayed travelers
decided, as a group, not to understand what had happened. It
was impossible. It had not happened. Like cards, the faces and
bodies of the dead kept turning up toward me—tennis racquets, suitcases, packages, ribbons, pennants, hats, straw catchalls—as I strolled the terminal with my fretful or genial
face, seeming to be looking for something. I was first indulging
the cards turning up in my head, the faces now beginning to

grow very familiar to me, but then seeking to find the means to deny them. They were not relevant. My flight was delayed and someone was waiting for me in New York. The way we sometimes hum to ourselves a song as an anti-song, to rid ourselves of a melody grinding away in our ears, I strove to remember some lines by the poet Thom Gunn:

> Much that is natural, to the will must yield.
> Men manufacture both machine and soul,
> And use what they imperfectly control
> To dare a future from the taken routes.

In the meantime, Air France was receiving passenger complaints. The terminal was jammed with backed-up flights. The chief complaint seemed to be: "Aw, this was supposed to be a meal flight. I didn't even get my breakfast. When are we gonna get fed?"

Met by death and disaster, the tourist felt hungry. In his defense, let it be said that the disaster seemed curiously abstract from within that air-conditioned, aluminum-and-glass, Scandinavian- or Detroit-designed building. There was a pure ribbon of fire whipping into the air, true; and then a dense black smudge; and perhaps the cards of faces turning up one after another in other heads besides mine, Southern flush on Southern faces; but we were viewers and spectators and bystanders wounded in our own ways. Many of us felt ravenous. "They advertised the complimentary luncheon. The travel agent told me personally champagne. They call this Air France service?"

Laboriously, like a hurt organism shaking itself and returning to the habits of life, Air France took cognizance of the emergency. The silent trucks had slid back and forth over the field. There was very little more to do out there. Soon the flights of other airlines, El Al, Alitalia and Pan American, began to head down the cleared runways. Mystified, Air France passengers were still delayed. An announcement came over the loudspeaker in several languages: "All Air France passengers will please go to the terminal restaurant for a complimentary dinner."

This was about two hours after the explosion.

There was a starved rush toward the little dining room. No one bit or scratched, but there were intense struggles for place, with delicate use of elbows and cold eyes. Those who could not be seated at once stood outside, gazing magic wishes at the fortunate eaters inside.

By this time, of course, almost all but the most bewildered knew what had happened to the Air France Boeing 707 with one hundred and thirty passengers from Atlanta, Georgia. It was long past their mealtimes by now. Like me, some of them must have called up memories of those passengers we had all seen in the waiting room, people like us, in transit, in grip, waiting to board their flight for Atlanta via New York.

Still nervously strolling, trying to get out of sight of the cards turning up in my head, I passed the crowd waiting to be admitted to the restaurant. Apparently I stared at a woman waiting outside with her weeping daughter. Food smells— roast beef, French bread, wine and coffee—were flooding out of the crowded room, along with the angry smell of nervous human beings. No animal, not even the caged lion, smells worse than the human being in distress. The lady at whom I stared said to me in French, with a heavy accent, with furious apology: "It's for my child! I'm not hungry! Do you think I can eat? The child is hungry!"

I hastily apologized for staring.

"We have a long journey from Turkey. I am taking my child alone. She is a little upset by the trip. My husband always sends us away for the vacation. Did you see any good plays while you were in Paris, sir?"

What happens when a group of human beings is struck by disaster? They recoil. Then they survive as best they can. This is natural and, surely, admirable. It is one of the reasons why a novelist, recently dead, felt convinced of the worthiness of human beings to prevail on earth. We are tough and responsive at our best. But this was a different enterprise of survival on June 3, 1962, in the airport at Orly. The famous novelist's admonition to dignity under disaster did not apply. The catastrophe had struck others, not ourselves. We were as near as we could be to it without being hurt, and we were not hurt. A rose-fever sufferer informed me that for the first time during his tour in Europe, his nasal passages had cleared. We were insulated from the world by glass and technique; we breathed filtered air; we were soothed by a melodramatic and comfortable framing of the event. There was no way to participate, to help the victims, even to help ourselves. Any emotion at all seemed in excess of that required. Were we really there? We were present on the scene, that's all. We were not responsible.

Perhaps panic, like a slight fever, clears the sinuses. Perhaps some, like me, went into a dreamy trance of total recall, remembering faces, remembering voices we had barely heard in our abstracted personal arranging of a departure. Perhaps some had reacted by leaving the airfield to take sea passage homeward; perhaps some even prayed. The Turkish lady took her child to dine. I wandered the huge building, poking into corners, looking for something to do.

2

Now I must ask you to recall the happy reputation of the French girl. There is a myth about French women, a sentimental asperity which is ascribed to them, and I believe there is some justice in the myth. Passing through Orly a few months before, with ten hours between planes, I had tried to check my valise for the day while I went to Paris. The checking facilities had been removed because of plastic bombs which were then being hidden by terrorists in places like checkrooms. "Do you mean I have to carry all my stuff into town for one day?" I had demanded. *"Oui,"* said the impassive clerk. But I had struck up a conversation with an Air France hostess, and in the time-honored way had teased, flirted, and conned her into keeping my suitcase in her personal locker. It is the sort of thing a well-brought-up French girl might do for a stranger who speaks nicely to her. The rules of the game are one thing; the good nature of the French girl is another. I offered to open the suitcase to show her there was no *plastique* in it, but she just laughed. I thanked her for her kindness, went on my way, and picked up my belongings that evening.

Now, two months later, I met that Air France ground hostess talking with a group of irate passengers. They were delayed; they wanted to know when they would get out; they wanted to know what was being done for them. I watched her face, a little ordinary, soft and sweet, however, very serious in response to their questions. She looked trim in her blue uniform, with legs slightly more plump than is the American ideal. Patiently she explained and answered. I greeted her and she remembered me. I remarked that she looked tired and asked her to sit awhile with me. I told her that I was waiting for my flight to go out, that it had been the one scheduled directly after the chartered Boeing 707.

"Mon Dieu," she said. *"C'est affreux."*

My God. Frightful. We signaled sympathy to each other. In order to have something to say in the silence that followed, I made the banal remark that I found the behavior of the passengers in the terminal disconcerting.

"What can they do?" she asked me. *"C'est affreux.* No one can do anything." And she kept on saying, *"Mon Dieu, mon Dieu,"* chattering a little like a schoolgirl, troubled and holding back tears. *"Mon Dieu que c'est affreux."* Her face was slightly swollen. She was very tired. She kept jumping up to perform various tasks, but each time returned to where I was sitting. Since we knew hardly anything more about the disaster than that it had happened and that we happened to be present, there was little we could say to each other besides "My God it's awful." But this catastrophe led to talk of other disasters, and she spoke to me of her personal involvement in the Algerian national tragedy as we just sat on a leather couch in the middle of an enormous waiting room. She said that she wished she could do something for the Algerian *pieds noirs* then flooding into the capital. She tried to make them comfortable as they arrived; coffee, biscuits, civil answers to their confused questions. What else could she do?

Nothing.

What else could anyone do?

"Nous, des individus, vous savez . . ."

Individuals.

She talked on sweetly, mildly, with that French sweetness men have always loved in the French girl, chic in her natty blues, without a perfect figure, with legs a little full and a heavier crease than we ordinarily approve of at the place where the calf joins the knee. Saying: *"Mon Dieu qu'ils ont souffert, les algériens, les arabes, les français. Des morts, des blessés."* Suffering, death, wounds. With her good French education in words, with a simple vocabulary appealing to God and to the sense of horror and justice, she spoke of the miseries of the Algerian refugees. Her eyes were red-rimmed beneath the adroit mascara because she had been working, not weeping, fighting back the tears, not weeping over the fate of the one hundred and thirty passengers bound for Atlanta *dans l'état de Georgia.*

"Ça se trouve où?" she asked me.

"Dans le sud."

"Mon Dieu."

Behind her voice, I heard the murmur of small talk in Southern accents of the departing passengers. *Much that is natural, to the will must yield.*

Now I must apologize for an embarrassing admission. I thought of asking her to come back to America with me and be my bride. This thought was very pressing and insistent. It was a foolish impulse, but I had trouble putting it down. Every argument that I could think of at the moment was in favor. Whatever force was turning up the cards in my head, showing me the faces of people I had not known I had seen, was also asking me to make a new fate for myself. I did not know her name, but she helped me to know where I was: on earth. Within an aluminum-and-glass, air-conditioned building, but on earth. Despite the desperate eaters—the last of them were just then being served their complimentary dinner by Air France—the Turkish lady, the surly waiters, the glazed bureaucrats behind counters who refused to answer questions or told their silly official lies, the police and the porters, the busy and the irascible, there were points of anchorage on earth. We had joined our eyes in private feeling. We could touch reality together, and we could answer it back. This is very like love.

When she went off duty, we said good-bye casually, like old friends, and then shook hands. "I hope to see you next time," I said.

"Next time."

I had never asked her name.

3

For nearly twelve hours I wandered in that station, looking for those Southern faces which I kept finding everywhere in my head, consoled for their loss, unconsoled, straggling. Hours ago I should have arranged to get myself on another flight. The one for which I had been scheduled seemed to be particularly delayed by its proximity to the accident, but I was not thinking systematically. I was straggling.

Near midnight I went into the men's room. It was empty

except for me and one other man. He was an African and looked like a once-tall man who had been artificially shortened, wizened, blue-black, gnarled and distant in his Western clothes. The collar of his shirt was so large that it fit like a shawl about his neck. He was wearing blue serge and a wide white satin tie of a cut that looked vaguely zoot, vaguely Soviet. He had a serious, puckered-up, shrunken face and was applying himself to washing his hands with many tentative motions toward the hot water, cold water, soap, towels. Like a careful pilot he played with various manipulations of strange nozzles and apertures, buttons and cranks. Washing the hands is not uncomplicated if you have arrived in this Scandinavian-modern, Detroit-modern outpost from a primitive land. But he knew what he was doing. He was washing his hands—that was what he was doing. He succeeded. He dried them approximately by snapping them at the wrists into the sink, ignoring the paper towels, sprinkling little drops into the basin. Then he recognized the towels for what they were and plucked out one. He was intelligent. He knew exactly what to do with a towel and wet hands. While I was still thinking about the one hundred and thirty human creatures on board the Air France charter flight, I had grown very tired. My legs ached from walking. I was now watching another survivor and grew interested in him. At last finished with his hands, he bent to his shoes; I thought to tie them, but no. He took them off. Then he rolled down his socks and removed them.

This sawed-off Watusi, this elongated pygmy then gazed dreamily at me and began walking barefoot across the tiles of a men's room at the airport of Orly at midnight. He stopped before a urinal. He rolled up his pants legs. He put one foot in the urinal, leaned on it and pulled the lever. Water flushed over his foot and ankle. Then he removed it, put the other foot in, leaned on it. A steamy tumble of water. He sighed.

I had entered the men's room with one of the least complicated of purposes in mind—to urinate. But how could I now?

A diplomat from one of the "emergent African nations" would return to his tribe to tell of air disasters and of how afterward he saw a white man, a North American, urinating in the footbath.

I held my counsel. I sneaked around a corner to perform the act shamefully in another, concealed footbath. Remembering the booklet that came with my passport, in which the State Department informed me of my responsibilities as an American abroad—I was an American, a representative of Americans, practically an ambassador, I should pee with care—I had an impulse to giggle like a child. I had restrained my fire when I saw the whites of his eyes. I had proved my patriotism and saw myself grinning in the mirror when I washed my hands afterward, snapping the water into the basin.

Then, lightened, chipper, I hurried up to the Air France counter to begin a long argument about getting on the very next flight to New York. The father protecting his tall sons, the girl, the African, and even my own rapt hypnosis—that turning up of the cards showing the faces of the dead—had finally brought me back to the efficient actions of life. Like the Turkish lady and the other ardent eaters, I had found my own way to thrust aside the travelers from Atlanta with their suitcases and straw bags containing the overflow of souvenirs, their jokes about touring together, their Southern affability, their anxiety as they hastened to the difficult voyage ahead of them which we all must make one day soon.

A DAY WITH
THE BOGEYMAN

1 LETTER FROM HAITI

On THAT day in November 1963, I may have been the only
tourist in the Republic of Haiti, which had enjoyed a brief
flowering as a visitor's paradise before the crumbling into near
chaos of the Duvalier regime. Now the predatory *tontons
macoutes*—or "bogeymen"—wandered this desolated tropical
paradox, their guns cradled sleepily in the crooks of their arms,
gaining revenge for history through small extortions, frequent
beatings, occasional murders. On the theory that they owed
everything to him, and that his fall would result in their
slaughter, and that therefore they could be both trusted and
indulged, the *Chef de la Nation*, François Duvalier, had dis-
armed the police and the Army and developed this militia of
his personal pets. They fed on the scorched poverty of the
land. The beauty of sky and sun, bay and mountains, now had
its traditional accompaniment of idle violence. The time of
human sacrifice, absent in Haiti except as legend, had returned in a parody of a European fascism under the so-called
Government of National Renovation.

The Minister of Tourism heard of my lonely visit at the
Grand Hotel Oloffson—I had once lived for a year in Haiti—
and sent word by a police spy, who was ineffectually disguised
as a journalist, that he would like to take me on an outing—a
pique-nique. At the appointed hour, ten o'clock on a Sunday
morning, the minister's Buick drove up the curving, palm-

lined driveway. We were six in the car—a German diplomat whom I shall call Bruno; his pretty young wife, Gretchen; the police spy, Bienvenue l'Aurore; the minister, whose real name is Nevers Constant; a young Mexican girl; and myself.

This is not the occasion for an analysis of the current troubles of Haiti—hurricanes, floods, famines, a police state staffed by anemic policemen, a decaying society and a mad ruler. But please imagine our picnicking group driving through a dusty, weary Port-au-Prince, a city denuded of cars, beset by bored gangs of armed thugs and a desperate population. Monsieur Nevers Constant, the Minister of Tourism, seemed to believe that if he could convince me, his Emissary Tourist, that Haiti is a tourist haven, the rest of my compatriots would find their way to spend their dollars under the brilliant tropical sky of Dr. François Duvalier. The Mexican girl, a very thin blonde with very long hair and perhaps the skinniest legs in the Caribbean (including both Central America and the Greater and Lesser Antilles), kept scratching the mosquito bites on her calves and complaining that no one had yet taught her either English or French. In answer to my question about what she was doing in Haiti, she replied, "I am throwing myself into the diplomacy." Although this sounded like a peculiarly dramatic form of suicide, it turned out that she had come to study French at the Institut Lope de Vega.

The German diplomat explained that he was on a cultural mission for his government. "Loffly pipple! Vriendchip!" (Henceforth I will try to avoid transcription of his accent.) His wife, a delicate Berliner, added blushingly, "Honeymoon! *Lune de miel!*" She blushed for me in English, and then turned to blush again in French. The couple were visiting nineteen countries in three months, and then would report to some central clearing house for reports on Latin America in Bonn.

The police spy, Bienvenue l'Aurore, had come along as my special companion. He was detailed, apparently, to the task of talking to me, making me feel happy, and keeping watch on my activities. Occasionally he would make a verbal jab at the government and then wait for my reply with a radiant, enticing smile. I was usually able to dodge him. He had a short span of attention.

And there was the minister himself, a very fat man with a pendulous lower lip, a nasal speech that sounded as if he had inherited a bad cold three generations back, and the habit of falling asleep suddenly, in the middle of a sentence. He drove. When he felt himself falling asleep, he drove very slowly. Otherwise he conversed in a laborious, thick-throated French.

2

First M. Constant drove us downtown to visit his recent accomplishments in reviving the tourist trade. He had erected enormous neon signs with such legends, in French, as I AM THE FLAG, ONE AND INDIVISIBLE—FRANÇOIS DUVALIER and MY ONLY ENEMIES ARE THE ENEMIES OF HAITI—FRANÇOIS DUVALIER. "The tourists will love that," I assured him, crammed by his side with his pistol pressing against my thigh.

"They're coming next week," he said. "Lots of them—hordes. Beautiful schoolteachers, millionaires, artists *en retraite.*"

"*Ah oui, Excellence,*" cried Bruno. The German was qualified for his intercultural labors by studies in both Spanish and Portuguese, but he had not learned a fluent French. Therefore all his initiative and skill at improvisation came into play in order to communicate the proper emotions to the minister. When he saw something good (neon signs, paved roads, smiling faces), he cried, "*Ah oui, Excellence, oui! oui!*" When he saw something bad (hurricane damage, slums, children without shoes), he said, "*Oh Excellence, tch, tch, tch.*" If this did not adequately sum up his emotions, he would think further upon it, shaking his head from side to side. "*Excellence! Tch! Tch! Tch!*"

The minister, breathing thickly, drove us past certain selected monuments so that the *oui*'s were brought to outnumber the *tch*'s.

For example, there was the neon sign which faced the empty harbor, empty of tour boats, empty of freighters, empty of fishing boats, empty of everything but the brackish water of the harbor. JOYEUX NOËL 1964, announced the neon sign, making an error of a year in its calculations.

"Maybe they mean next year will be a happy year," said Bienvenue l'Aurore, once again essaying the role of *agent provocateur*. Once again I gave proof of maturity—strong and silent.

A workman was tinkering with the sign, attaching the electricity. His family stood about in the little park in the center of Boulevard Harry-Truman, admiring him because he had a job and also because there was nothing else to do. The minister blew his horn as a signal and then stopped the Buick; they all came to attention; he barked out ministerial orders and advice in French concerning the installation of neon for the *Rénovation Nationale*. He then smiled graciously and bid them rest. I asked him why he spoke French and not Creole, since few other than the educated élite understand much French. "Creole is a joke for children," he informed me. "Personally I don't understand it. All Haitians speak French—the French of Paris, not of Canada. Canadians speak execrable French, don't you find?"

I found it useful once again to apologize for my own French. That always broke the ice.

"*Bon travail, mon ami!*" he called to the workman.

"Hokai, *M'sieu Minist'*."

As we drove away, he explained that beautification and city planning were his two ideals in life. Beginning in a few days, on December first, recordings of Christmas carols, in English and in French, would be heard at this spot, beamed especially to the tourists, whom he wanted to feel entirely at home in Haiti. Also, the police would arrest all beggars, prostitutes, peddlers, and anyone passing without shoes or identification papers or otherwise giving evidence of sinister missions. All the tourist had to do was to point out a Communist and the authorities would take care of him. "Not like in Cuba, eh?" he asked, nudging me with his pistol.

He then abruptly fell asleep while the Buick glided past the slum of La Saline, in which uncounted thousands of Haitians live in houses made of rubbish and banana leaves, with no jobs and practically no chance to find one, waiting for epidemic, starvation, or fire to carry them off to a better place. Patrolling the area were small gangs of armed *tontons macoutes*, the official Duvalier ruling class. The *tontons macoutes* are as common as pigs, dogs, or roosters on the byways of Haiti. They collect tolls, inspect and search, and live by incursions against their neighbors, against visitors, against anybody their eyes light upon. They confiscate what pleases them. As an experienced cop-hater, I was astonished that I found them even more ominous in their rags than a uniformed fascist corps would be. There was no real hierarchy; there was no appeal; there was no arguing with them.

"And this is the new jet airport for the tourists," said Minister Constant, abruptly alert, blowing his horn to have the guard open the barbed-wire gate. True enough, a landing strip was being constructed here on the edge of Port-au-Prince. We drove up and down with grand freedom.

"*Ah oui, Excellence!*" cried Bruno.

"Is airplanes," said Conchita, the eighteen-year-old Mexican diplomat.

"How sweet of you, how gentle, how nice, to come all this way," said Gretchen to me.

"Haiti is like home to me," I said.

She asked, "Is the United States of America like this?"

"And our new jet airport?" demanded the minister.

"I love that too," I said.

"It will surely be finished next year," he promised. "We are strictly ahead of schedule."

"*Excellence! Oui!*"

I was grateful to Germany for having given birth to Bruno, since he took the burden of responding off my conscience. He responded enough for everyone, sometimes uttering a single *oui* or a *oui* in series, sometimes clacking his tongue to indicate the full compassion of tongue-tied Western man for the troubles of this little Caribbean nation with its confused tradition of Africa, of France, of colonization, misery, overpopulation, and perverse grace and hope.

Conchita, the Mexican girl diplomat, was scratching her calves. Little flecks of blood appeared. I said, in English and in French, "Don't scratch, *ne grattez-pas.*" But she scratched away and asked me, smiling like a beatnik statesman stalling for time, "Hanh?"

"Moustiko bites, *tch tch tch*," said the German.

"No malaria!" cried the minister. "Due to Haitian science, no malaria! You take pills?"

"*Oh Excellence, oui! oui!*"

The minister was beeping the horn to awaken the guard at the fence of the jet airport. We had been locked into the landing strip. Now we needed to be let out. I was ready to throw my arms about my head to protect myself against an early jet arrival, but we were released in time, and dipped and bowed on to the road leading past Damiens toward Duvalierville, our next destination. Damiens is the agricultural college, a little matrix of political manipulation and serious technical labor at improving livestock, stocking waters with fish, experimentation with the possibilities of raising food commercially in a land which never knows frost. Along the roads the begging and the starving turned to gaze at the black ministerial automobile. I chatted with the German diplomat's wife about Haitian painting while Conchita malevolently stroked her mosquito bites. This was her Mexican scientific answer to the problem of insect control. I wondered numbly in the midday heat how a Mexican had gotten so blond, so thin, so morose in her first diplomatic endeavor.

3

As REPRESENTATIVE by default of all American tourism, I received sly questions from the minister. The reputation of Haiti had suffered from recent official murders, destructions, expulsions of priests, prosecutions of the élite class; American aid had been cut off and Americans were being advised to stay away; pressures were being applied. The *tontons macoutes*, the Chief's personal creatures, that gang of marauding and extorting militia, had particularly blackened Haiti for visitors, who desire at least an appearance of tranquillity and reliability. Since taxes were not collected in the usual ways, they were now collected in unusual ways. A group of *macoutes* would enter a businessman's office and beat him until he paid. Or they would set fire to his house. Or, in milder fashion, they would extract tolls on the roads or, soliciting, door to door. In their tattered pants and their "I AM THE FLAG" T-shirts, with their bands of ammunition and their M-1 rifles or submachine guns cradled loosely in their arms, they inspired a pervasive feeling of unease.

"Soon the tourist will come to see our National Renovation," declared the Minister of Tourism. "Soon?" he repeated to me.

"That would make Haiti more prosperous," I parried, with all my dormant skills at statesmanship being awakened.

"But a bad propaganda in the *New York Times*," he reported.

"I know."

"*Tch tch tch.*"

"We had to build a new society, didn't we?" asked the minister.

"*Oh Excellence, oui oui oui!*"

"And there were malcontents, vain malefactors, the pigs of the unborn." (He used a Spanish phrase.)

"*Oh Excellence, tch, tch, tch.*"

"So," concluded the minister triumphantly, "the National Assembly has voted a budget of twenty-two thousand dollars in order to place advertisements in the *New York Times* which will tell the truth about Our Protector, the estimable Dr. François Duvalier."

Timidly I remarked that the chief problem lay elsewhere than in the *New York Times*. I wished, in this world of sleepwalking misery, to see twenty-two thousand dollars worth of rice distributed to those rendered homeless, their gardens destroyed by the hurricane; to the children with swollen bellies and retreated eyes who lay in the compounds in front of their *caille-pailles*, the Afro-Haitian house of straw.

"No," the minister sternly corrected me. "We must fight evil with evil."

I remembered my place, noticed Bienvenue l'Aurore breathing tensely at my side, and fell to watching the road again. It takes a long time to misunderstand people. I was too abrupt a nostalgic revisitor to Haiti to have the proper critical judgment of the hunger of others, the proper stoical acceptance of the bogeymen. Occasionally the car would be stopped by *macoutes* who would cry, "*Inspection!*" The minister managed to avoid having us searched by crying out in return, "*Le Ministre Constant! Le Ministre Nevers Constant!*"

"*Ouais. Passez.*"

We passed, inching by the gasoline drums with which they barricaded the road. Instead of rolling them out of the way, they gazed at them to indicate partial intention. They sat on crates or lounged in the ditches and said, "*Ouais.*"

4

ABOUT an hour's drive from Port-au-Prince along the Saint-
Marc road, we poked our way into one of the major achieve-
ments of the Duvalier regime. This was the new town of Duvalierville, built on the site of an old Haitian peasant village,
Cabaret. Cabaret had been leveled by bulldozers—houses,
trees, bushes and plantings. While one should not romanticize
the traditional settlement of *caille-pailles,* those straw-roofed
houses built of mud and banana leaves, the town had its own
relevance to the conditions of Haitian country life. Duvalierville is a parody of Brasilia, cement blockhouses with butterfly
roofs, a cement cockfighting pit, a cement stadium, a cement
police station, and a grill of streets going nowhere, frazzled off
into the surrounding mud.

"Why was this town built here?" I asked.

"By the will of the people," said the minister.

"Who will live here?"

"The deserving. They will pay no rent."

"How will they be selected?"

"By the census," he said enigmatically.

This halted my questions for the moment. The German diplomat said *oui.* We drove in and through and back down the
streets of Duvalierville. People in the streets were slow to move.
Even the dogs and the black, skinny Haitian pigs were in no
hurry to escape our wheels. The sun beat down without respite
on the denuded fields. Where once palm trees and banana
bushes had grown, there now were cracked patches of clay and
running ditches. "Soon electricity! Purified water! Example to
the Haitian people of the benevolence of the Chief!" cried the
minister.

Bruno was in ecstasy.

Conchita wanted to know when the picnic began. "That is a
pig?" she remarked disdainfully. "In Mexico the pigs and dogs

have separate identities. The pig is fat because Mexico is an advanced industrial and agricultural nation."

There was the dank smell of wet cement in sunny air. A beggar came up to show his gums and ask, *"Ba'm cinq cob"*— "Give me five cents."

When we had examined Duvalierville, and had seen the huts in which the former inhabitants of Cabaret now awaited their further disposition in a nameless compound, we then headed back along the bay toward Ibo Beach, a resort for upper-class Haitians and tourists. This was the former Isle Cabrit (Goat Island), a sandy spit in the water which had been fortified by an enterprising Haitian engineer, reached by motorboat from a place on shore. We disembarked and hurried to our model *caille-pailles* to change into swimming suit, spearfishing uniform, skin-diving equipment. The German diplomat was abruptly transformed into a submarine and went crawling across the bottom, examining coral and marine life. I saw little of him for the rest of the afternoon, although occasionally, like a whale, he spouted. There was the usual aimless pattering of a day at the beach, sleeping in the sun, dips in the salt, drinking of rum and tradings of worn-out, frazzled newspapers and magazines. The minister held my hand tightly to his, *tutoyed* me, and told me about his trips as a representative of Haiti in Washington. "Oh, Lyndon is my good friend," he cried, "and Laddy-bird, too, you know? I have dine at their house these many time. You know his friend Marty? You know his friend Joe *Quelquechose?* Oh, I know him well, he is a friend to Haiti, my deep personal friend."

"Personally I don't know him," I admitted.

"Joe, Joe, Joe—" he snapped his fingers angrily. "What's Joe's last name? It come to me later."

Conchita tried rubbing rum on her mosquito bites. For some reason no one else seemed to be much bothered, but she was swelling and bleeding and suffering. The word "allergy" was passed about in French, Creole, Spanish, English, and

German by the various guests at the picnic. The minister suggested that if she swallowed the rum instead of rubbing it into her wounds a greater benefit might ensue. He winked at me. Though he was a minister in the Government of National Renovation and Social Justice, he knew how to unbend.

"You don't know Lyndon?" he insisted.

"I live in San Francisco," I apologized. "I don't know many people."

"*Tch tch tch,*" said the submarine, emerged from no place to set a conch to dry in the sun as a souvenir. He was wearing flippers and puffing. He stood in the sun and beat his chest, and winked past the minister to his wife. Abruptly I decided he was not stupid, just a hypocrite. His wife was too pretty for him to be stupid; there is no law that prevents a hypocrite from having a pretty wife. I could be on the right track, logically. I could also still be in error.

"My husband doesn't like primitive art," said Gretchen, "he is a doctor in economics yet. You say 'yet'?"

"Still."

"He is still a doctor in economics, but soon I will teach him to love the primitive painters of nineteen nations, one of them Portuguese, one French, and the rest speaking Spanish."

5

ONE of the odd facts about Isle Cabrit is that it seems to be isolated from humanity. In Haiti, one of the most densely populated lands in the world, privacy is nearly unknown; dense crowds of workers, strollers, beggars, children, peddlers, shoeshine boys, prostitutes, babies, herdsmen, travelers, farmers, philosophers, thieves, police, militia, and others perform their business or their avocation in public, on the road, wherever you are performing your own business or avocation. But this island was an island, and a strip of water lay between it and the mainland (which, of course, is a larger island). Except for the barmen, waiters, beachboys, other tourists and visitors, and our hosts, we were absolutely alone; except, that is, for the fishermen sailing a few yards offshore; except, that is, for the crowds clustered on the beach, straining their eyes to try to make out what peculiar ways wealth and power invent to fill the hours. In this peculiar Haitian isolation—this relative isolation—the minister poured out his philosophy of life, his history, his hopes and dreams, and his repertory of sexual techniques which he had tested on his wife and a respectable series of mistresses, none of whom could ever resist him. I listened because I was fascinated and also because he was a *tonton macoute.* He carried a pistol tucked into his two-piece bathing dress. He droned on and on in his congested voice, coughing occasionally with emotion. "I take you back five years. It is Carnival. She is a tourist, a schoolteacher from Chee-k'go— you know Chee-k'go in the Illinois?—and she is beautiful but soon the holidays end. *Ah, la pauvre Haïti,* you have lost your fairest bloom. She send me greeting cards every year. She cannot forget me. Don't scratch, please." That last remark was directed to the Mexican diplomat.

"Now you tell me about your love," he said to me.

Having read widely in Erich Fromm, Karen Horney, Smiley Blanton, Theodore Reik, and Wilhelm Reich, not to speak of Freud and Ovid, the poets and the novelists, I felt qualified to speak and yet strangely timid.

"You are a man!" the minister urged me.

I blushed and could not gainsay this observation.

Fortunately again, as in the matter of his friend Lyndon Johnson, he was distracted by other events. One of the cooks had caught a lobster. He had earlier caught several lobsters. He brought it forward to be inspected by the minister. The minister turned it over and approved it as he might have approved the vintage of the wine. Now lunch was being laid out alfresco for us—avocado salad with tomatoes and cucumbers from Kenscoff, lobster and ham, cheeses, Creole rice and beans, plenty of rum-sodas and Cokes and charcoal-broiled steaks for the Americans. I chose adventure by taking lobster. "It's really crayfish," stated the minister. "Soon we will export them to the States because they don't know the difference. We who have the French inheritance enjoy a more sensitive palate, that's a known fact."

At the end of a long day in the sun, we loaded ourselves into the motorboat to be carried back to shore. The owner of Ibo Beach looked ready to weep; the minister had signed for the food and drink and the government does not pay its bills. But the rest of us were satiated with sun, crayfish, swimming, talking, and old copies of *Match* and *Nouvelliste*.

6

DURING our drive back to Port-au-Prince, there were occasional moments of silence. The car skidded past potholes, went honking through crowds, plowed through debris. Bruno felt obliged to keep up his end (*"Oui! oui!"*), and sometimes addressed me in English, since the minister also understood it. "Iss vonderbar," he declared, "iss fery vonderbar, iss only zmiling vaces in zis country."

At that very moment the car was brought to a halt by a troupe of *tontons macoutes* with their weapons cocked and their eyes cold and malevolent. *"C'est le Ministre Constant!"* bawled our host.

"Inspection."

"Le Ministre Constant!"

"In-spec-tion."

They made us stand out, they searched the car, they searched us, they kept the guns leveled on us. Illiterate, careless of law, they were uninterested in the minister. He was just another rich man from Port-au-Prince to these nameless ones. The Mexican girl began to weep with fear. When she bent to scratch a bite, a *macoute* waved his rifle at her and ordered her to stand up. Her tears ran; she was afraid to scratch or wipe. The German's wife, pale and icy, stood silently watching while *le Ministre* Constant argued in Creole. He was sweating and nasal and dismayed. They did not know him. They asked him to open the trunk of the car. They tapped the spare tire. They prodded the cushions. They walked about while we stood under guard, and they discussed how else to prove their patriotism. At last they accepted a toll from Monsieur Constant and allowed us to get back in the automobile. But they still kept their guns on us. I asked the minister not to move while they pointed their weapons our way; I did not want us to be shot for a misunderstanding. He agreed, shaking with rage, and spoke in Creole, *"Nou capab passé?"*

They stared.

"M'Minist'! Nou passé?"

Finally their leader turned on his heels and strolled off. He was followed by the others. Monsieur Constant wheeled past the gasoline drums in the road, accelerated, and we were off down the road to Port-au-Prince, the capital, and the known world beyond it. After a moment of silence, the German spoke:

"Excellence?" He repeated it to make sure that our host was listening. *"Excellence? Tch tch tch."*

Haiti is a part of my dream life. I have lived an essential fraction of my time in that fantastic nightmare world. (What does it mean to say "fantastic nightmare"? I also swam, played tennis, raised children, worked at a job, danced the meringue, paid homage to sweet ladies—"fantastic nightmare" is only words about a life which was merely ordinary, like all lives. And yet it was also a fantastic nightmare.) Since ending my life in Haiti, I have visited it again, though now I must stay away until the government changes.

These stories are two of the many I've written about Haiti. (A friend and magazine editor said to me, "What can we give you to stop you from writing about Haiti? Money? Can I get down on my knees? Please?" "A Haitian Gentleman" was printed in the Hudson Review; "Max and the Pacemaker" was printed no place before now.)

Haiti helps to strip off the skin of those who know her. The craziness of Haitians and those who love Haiti is an emblem. The horror of the condition of Haitian life now, under a tyranny that seems to disturb no one, is a warning of what might happen to all of us. And Haitian endurance and joy are a consolation, though the time is surely past when we can accept the suffering of others as a moral gain for ourselves.

A HAITIAN GENTLEMAN

A STORY

My FIRST and a coincidental meeting with André-Pierre Vilaire took place on a Panama Lines vessel, steaming southward along the North American coast from New York to Port-au-Prince, just ten years ago. I was bound for Haiti for a year of study in this odd paradox of an Afro-French nation in the Caribbean; he was simply bound home. I watched him pacing the deck, impeccable in a starched white tropical suit, appearing quietly distraught, the lid of control tightly fastened, an elegant tall black man with narrow features and no interest at all in the vague efforts at ship spirit on board the S.S. *Harding*. The other passengers—the ship was about a quarter full—were mainly dependent families of men working in the Canal Zone, so I couldn't blame André-Pierre for his determined abstraction. After he was pointed out to me, I sought an occasion for conversation with him; he was one of the people I had been told to look up in Haiti, and the description I had been given made him seem a curious person. He was the friend of a world-famous harpsichordist whom he had met at school in Paris years before; he was the lover of an actress then popular on the New York stage, and it must have been to see her that he came to New York; he was a prosperous Haitian lawyer; and he had that typical élite Haitian inheritance of divergent ancestry poured onto the African roots—French colonists, a Jewish peddler (grandfather), and a Dutch businessman from Curaçao—so that in his family there were those who sought to pass abroad as exotic Frenchmen and those who, like proud André-Pierre, flaunted their blood and color. To be sure, André-Pierre could not have passed, as one sister did, but also it was not in his nature to try; he even stretched out his long legs in a deck chair as the ship entered tropical waters and seemed to be searching the sky with his closed eyes for a deeper suntan.

He did not invite conversation. He ate alone; he read popular magazines negligently, and then flung them down; he walked incessantly, as if counting for a record number of turns around the deck. There was no tranquillity in the man, though his striking appearance made one think that such a person should be content to let the world admire him. While the ship bucked and plowed through icy Atlantic waters, he wore dress suitable to New York in winter; on the day the weather broke, and the tropics announced themselves with a humid calm, he began to wear that archaic starched suit which had been crafted for him by his rue du Centre tailor.

Also on that day, as if abruptly feeling at home on the ship, he greeted me cheerily. My problem of how to introduce myself to him was settled by his introducing himself to me. He seemed delighted by my tale of having his name in my notebook—the small-world syndrome; he couldn't place the "mutual acquaintance" who had given me his name, but he was accustomed to being noticed by American women and did not think it odd that a dim stranger should describe him as her friend. He shrugged and turned his hands out. He did not dwell on it. *"Mes-z-amis!"* he said. *"Quelle vie, eh?* You do not know what you are finding in Haiti. I warn you, you do not know!"

I told him I had read almost everything in English and much of what was published in French about his native land.

He laughed richly at this. "You do not, do not know, my friend! Cannot possibly!" My pedantry delighted him. When he threw back his head to laugh, he radiated the charm— teeth, grace, open joy, desire to share it—which had led my friend to describe him as "the handsomest man in Haiti, perhaps the handsomest man in the whole world." I pitied her, since he had not even noticed her enough to recall her name; but this indifference to his effect upon others was also a part of his grace.

André-Pierre Vilaire was an atypical member of the Haitian élite, whose traditional business is cultivating lust and indulging pride, whether or not the occasion supports the fantasy. He was a little aloof from women, despite his famous love affair—or perhaps because of it—and he was barely curious about the ladies who stared after him. He made no lists and catalogues of his conquests, as other Haitians did. What he loved passionately, with a suffering and unrequited ardor, was politics; he had a desperate vision of Haiti, of the possibilities of life in the sovereign republic of Haiti, and frustrated by the succession of corrupt governments over a graceful, miserable people, he could shout and rant like a deceived lover. He talked of presidents, generals, colonels, and ministers with despair, with spite, with grinding hatred. With his hand on his heart he quoted "Haiti," by the murdered poet Massillon Coicou:

> Et pourtant elle est riche; et pourtant elle est belle:
> L'océan captive vient baiser ses pieds nus;
> De son plus vif éclat le soleil luit pour elle;
> La nature s'épand dans ses yeux ingénus.

Perhaps Coicou had indeed plotted against a corrupt regime, but have we the right to destroy (he asked me) the heir to Musset?

I answered no as loud as I could, but envied his raging pride. He pleaded the case of *la belle Haïti* with me as if I were her father; her sky and her sea, her sun and perfume seemed to absorb all the lust in the man; he spoke as if I were familiar with the intrigues of Cap-Haïtien and the Capitol. At first this was as strange to my palate as cassava or *griots*. With the passing days, I began to share his dramatic sense of the quarrels between mulatto and black, between Army and bureaucracy, between peasant and city dweller, between vodun and the Roman church, between Francophiles and those who believed that American technique pointed the way to the future, among the admirers of Mexico and Jamaica and even the isolated circles of Marxists. These desperate struggles took on an intimate, playacting quality, since the élite class was so small that André-Pierre had relatives in almost all camps. He wanted to shoot his cousin. He had once been forcibly entertained for a weekend in the dread Fort Dimanche prison, of which another cousin was the commandant. He had a nephew in the Cabinet and was convinced that the current government, that of the most illustrious General Paul Magloire, would again imprison and perhaps torture him.

Sometimes, however, he relaxed briefly and other matters could occupy our turns about the deck. He talked about his student days in Paris, when he had fallen in love with the daughter of the mayor of Marseilles; he had taken a doctor of laws degree. He believed Anglo-American jurisprudence to be more humane than the Napoleonic Code. The judge—the *juge d'instruction*—begins his investigation with the clear dream of revenge. This necessarily corrupts; it allows too much to the human; it gives privileges to passion, and passion in authority is the enemy of justice. ("They shot Massillon Coicou! They crucified Charlemagne Peralte! The best of us have been immolated!") He paced, he put his hands behind his back, he calmed himself before four o'clock tea on the deck. "I am the victim of my history—agreed? *Mes-z-amis!*" He shrugged and accepted his history, eager to change only the future.

I tried to lead him to talk about his plump Marseillaise, but he was uninterested in sex, it seemed, and uninterested in the handicap of his color. In the circles in which he moved abroad, he was more special for his good looks than for his espresso color, and both bored him. He never discussed the actress, other than once to remark that he had a friend in New York— "I am a man sometimes, am I not?" After knowing other Haitians, I found his refusal to gloat over prowess and success a miracle. He was unique in this and other ways.

And then suddenly one morning we lay at anchor in the sweltering harbor of Port-au-Prince, the ship pointed into the long, low, curving line of the shore, tiers of city rising into misty hills toward Pétionville, Kenscoff, and the faraway pine forests of Furcy, and the cathedral sticking out of one tier with its candy colors, and a confusion of customs and police and naked boys in hollow-log canoes, screaming at us to throw

coins into the bay. I stood with André-Pierre and watched the
flashing bodies cleave the water, come up gasping, the coin
grasped between teeth, and then tucked into the cheek for another plea, "Aie! Aie! You! American! *Encore! Encore!*"

"My daughters will be here. You will stay longer in
douane. My son will come with the pickup and take you to
your hotel."

Busy with his homecoming, André-Pierre eased my arrival
in Haiti, and then excused himself. Of course he had much to
do. Later we would take up our friendship again, continuing
that shipboard good luck of intimacy which is often estab-
lished but seldom sustained in the "real life" of land and habit.

My image of André-Pierre, from what I knew of him and
from his manner on board ship, was of a very rich man, living
elegantly, with aloof and indulgent manners toward his wife,
children, and servants. He played tennis. He liked to lock himself in his den and build shortwave radios. But my conception
was wrong. His house in the Canapé-Vert section of Port-au-
Prince was modest and undistinguished; his Syrian wife
suffered from his snappish temper, as did the servants; he indulged his two daughters and two sons, but they too got on his
nerves. He would give them candy and tell them he had a
headache. When he was nervous, he sniffed from a Benzedrine
inhaler. He was allergic—to bougainvillaea? burning charcoal?
bananas? to which of the many fervent smokes and smells of
Port-au-Prince? Once I saw him dance the *meringue,* and that
only for a few moments to entertain a foreign visitor, and
never again. "Frivolity! This people destroys itself!" He had
given up dancing, he said, as a protest against the corruption
of Haitian life; in any case, it bored him. Sometimes he would
go with friends to the Choucoune, where the blare of the or-
chestra eliminated all but the thought of the *meringue* or the
mambo and the girls, and he would smile and nod; his friends
received his smile, his mirthless laughter, his self-deprecating
discontent; he would not dance; he was there only to confirm

what he already knew. "*Mes-z-amis!*" he cried, laughing with chagrin for Haiti, "in such a world to dance?" And then he would tell me how President Stenio Vincent—or was it Lescot?—had stolen the bounty paid by Trujillo for the fourteen thousand Haitians slaughtered in a senseless pogrom.

My early sense of a man exotically endowed by fortune gave place to pity, even to irritation; but in that familiar way, even his weaknesses contributed to our friendship. He snapped at his dowdy Syrian wife. He listened impatiently to the prattle of his daughters, and his sons sulked and avoided him. His law practice dwindled and there was less money for his trips abroad. He never mentioned the famous actress. Finally, in an access of gossipaceous curiosity—in Port-au-Prince sex and politics were the consuming passions of the few who had enough to eat—I brought up the subject. André-Pierre listened pensively, with a bruised thoughtfulness. "You know of her?" he asked. "Hm. Yes. Well, you know, my friend, at my age—"

"You're young yet." (He was forty-eight, with gray flecking the short curly hair which softened the angular planes of his skull.)

"But in this difficult life, *nos tristes tropiques* . . . So you've thought about her all this time? You've been curious all this time? *Mes-z-amis!*" He laughed softly. "Sometimes you seem so young, like all Americans."

Sometimes André-Pierre seemed very young to me, open to the world like an adolescent in his bruised idealism. Each new abuse of power by the Magloire government outraged him afresh; he collected dossiers on grafters, cheaters and trimmers; he invited fellow dissidents to his house, all of them risking a beating, imprisonment, or worse. They knew it; their meetings had little point other than to declare to each other their opposition; they knew it and they met anyway. Since most business was connected with the government, which was supported mainly by aid from the United States, André-Pierre lay under a financial interdiction. He had few clients. He was slipping down; he could not afford to spend. But sin made him howl, and this howling gave him something like joy, and it cost nothing but the danger.

An incident typical of the Haitian toy politics of the time took place about one of these clandestine meetings in André-Pierre's house. Word of the gathering had gotten to the police, and André-Pierre knew that word had gotten to the police. To persist seemed a suicidal folly. His friends decided to hold their illegal meeting anyway. They would be arrested and take the consequences.

That week I had a friend visiting me from the States. He was an oral surgeon, familiar with the mouth and jaw but unfamiliar with the dreamy games of Haiti. I decided to give him a lesson. We drove his rented car to Canapé-Vert to watch the police raid. We stood in the street, waiting for trucks and sirens. This was adventure aplenty for a seventeen-day vacation; the cops would be carrying submachine guns. Within a stone-hot afternoon, with dogs barking and cocks crowing and donkeys crunching the grass, and the skinny black Haitian pigs darting and foraging in the ditches, and the shoeshine boys clacking and the sellers of lottery tickets shouting their lucky numbers—amid all the ceaseless animal teeming of Port-au-Prince—we stood at the corner and waited as the half-dozen conspirators entered André-Pierre's house. They peeked over their shoulders and dodged inside. We were watching dead men in tan suits, in starched white suits from the tailor on the rue du Centre, with briefcases, smiling. They were men who had no need to imagine their own death—they were stepping forward to welcome it.

My friend and I loitered. We felt blindingly Caucasian on that nameless street in Canapé-Vert.

Twenty minutes later we heard motors. The police roared up in black Buicks. They sprang out, and then the major in charge caught sight of me and my oral-surgeon friend. The oral surgeon was a stranger in town. To the major he was not an oral surgeon—he must have seemed a dangerous, lounging creature. Could the American embassy or the FBI or the Secret Service or the OSS or the CIA be interested in this case? Why were we watching? Who were we? There was an abrupt halt and a council among the raiding police. They peeked at us as we stood gossiping together in our Keds.

What if they made a mistake?

What if it turned out badly?

Internationally?

My friend blew his nose in a Kleenex—was that a signal to Foster Dulles? To Edgar Hoover?

The police decided to take no chances. Because of our presence on that corner, they piled back into their automobiles and drove away. An oral surgeon and a student had become factors in Haitian political maneuvering.

For André-Pierre the incident again demonstrated the absolute inferiority of Haitian political life. He seemed to regret being spared. After all, to be arrested was only an inconvenience. In those amiable days of the mid-nineteen-fifties, the murder of political prisoners was not yet very common. Haitian coffee commanded a high price on the market, and more important, the one known Haitian Communist commanded a lot of anti-Communist dollars in aid from the United States. The government was corrupt, but the people were optimistic. There were enough beans, enough rice, plenty of mangoes and bananas. The songs about the sun of Haiti and the pneumatic Creole maidens and the joys of carnival, *rara* and *bamboche* seemed more real than the grinding habitual poverty of Haiti's uncounted, unconsidered millions of peasants. "We could tell the truth," said André-Pierre, "except that things are real to us. We get hungry, we want things, we can't tell the truth."

·   ·   ·

André-Pierre was bored by vodun, as a Southern planter might be bored by hillbilly music. The *loas* of vodun, and the *bakas* and *loups-garous* and zombies—the beasts of the Haitian hills—he had put away years ago, along with his childhood. If others believed, then others were foolish. "I have a degree from Paris, do you think I need to spend time on chicken-worship?" This sounded snobbish to me; I was fascinated by an exotic religion, folklore, and language; but on the other hand, hillbilly songs had found me a snob in the Army. André-Pierre had grown up surrounded by sounds of the drums in the hills around Port-au-Prince, and ceremonies often blocked the road when he had business elsewhere.

Once he had business in the dying provincial town of Saint-Marc and I drove there with him, over a pitted road, through miles of barren mountains and gray sisal plantations, sometimes descending toward the blue and white waters of the bay which washes that island. In Saint-Marc itself, the ruins of colonial architecture, thick walls and abutments, were surrounded by huts of mud and straw; the remaining coffee was loaded onto decaying docks, into iron-sheet sheds; sleepy peasants and a few sun-struck, white-suited old men wandered the seaside square. I saw one gentleman in a starched white suit, carrying a *coco-macaque*, the knobbed stick of the bourgeois, beating his way with tiny, arthritic steps across the street to the customs house. "Why does he dress like that?" I asked. He wore a high celluloid collar and button shoes. It was sixty years ago by his costume.

"He sees no reason to change his habits," André-Pierre said.

"It couldn't have been very comfortable when lots of people had those habits."

"They dressed like that in Madagascar, Martinique, Guadaloupe—in the French colonies."

"But Haiti has been independent for a hundred and fifty years."

André-Pierre then smiled as if his next remark answered all

135

my objections. "It's my first cousin." He honked the horn and stopped the old man. He shook his hand in formal greeting. When I was introduced and took his hand, I felt the soft and womanly hand of a man who had lived in Saint-Marc all his life and not yet done very much work. He did not take us to his house. He lived on pride; his starched clothes were his home, and he slept in what was little more than a hut. "Haitians are like that," André-Pierre said of him, said of many. "We are crazy—agreed?"

My friend's cousin would continue until the end of his term on earth taking his daily walk on vague business across the central square of Saint-Marc, expecting deference from the peasants and soldiers who thronged the square, carrying bills, passes, receipts, orders, little slips of paper, and living on a few dollars a month—the rent of his land, the transfer of a few bags of coffee. He knew the town was dying; but he also knew he himself was dying, and he and the town awaited their fate together.

In Cap-Haïtien, Jacmel, Jérémie, and Saint-Marc, my friend had relatives, or relatives of relatives, who lived like this. Once flourishing provincial centers, now the tramp ships only occasionally stopped in these places, unloading a few cases of Dutch chocolate, kerosene for the lamps, candles and medicine and mail. In Port-de-Paix, the one town of size where my friend knew no one, I was the first foreigner to visit since a woman anthropologist nearly ten years earlier. But when the mayor asked whom I knew in Port-au-Prince and I named André-Pierre Vilaire, he said, "Oh yes! My wife's cousin is married to his niece!" And we played chess by flaring lamplight through a long evening which ended, I think, with my getting bitten by the mosquito that gave me malaria.

During the French colonial times, wealth poured through these ports along the crumpled shoreline of Haiti. In André-Pierre's youth, fortunes were still made by landholders. In 1954 there would still be a Café des Poètes or an Au Bon

Boisson where, among a display of coconuts and dusty bottles, the old men might gather at dusk to drink their coffee by candlelight and discuss the future of Russia, the United States, Haiti, and Jérémie. A cousin to André-Pierre informed me that Haiti would be the third force to mediate among the other two great powers. But first, he said in this town without electricity, without sanitation, inhabited by illiterate and half-naked peasants and a few spirit-wounded Francophiles like himself, Jérémie would die. It would be killed by the predators of Port-au-Prince. He raised his fist and shook it in the dim air of six o'clock. Cursed Port-au-Prince! *Jérémie la douce*, as all the world knows. He ordered more coffee for both of us, and candles. As I met the friends and relatives of my friend throughout Haiti, I felt that I knew André-Pierre better. Kindness and courtesy and the deepest isolation.

On the drive back from Saint-Marc, he honked furiously at a vodun funeral procession on the road. The mourners scampered and dodged, carrying the coffin zigzag as they ran, in order to keep the evil spirits from invading the body. Only evil spirits travel in a straight line.

"Fools. Idiots. Poor deprived people," said my friend. "Evil can move in as crooked a line as you and I."

When my mother visited Haiti, I expected the response of bewilderment. She had a conventional mistrust of Negroes, based on the habits of Cleveland, Ohio. ("Don't drive through Woodland Avenue unless you lock your doors, they'll jump on the runningboard.") But I underestimated her empirical character. She was charmed by André-Pierre; she was too old and too married to allow herself to fall in love, but she turned a bit girlish in his presence. Patiently he explained Haiti to her, controlling his exclamations of chagrin before the iniquities of the government, and later explained to me his affection for her: "My own mother, Christ rest her soul, was

half-Jewish. She was a black nigger, but she had a nose—look
at mine and see the shadow of it." He apologized for smoking
in my mother's presence. She advised him not to use the nasal
inhaler because it would not be good for his passages. They
discussed, knee-to-knee in deep mahogany and wicker furniture, and saw eye-to-eye in some mysterious way.

André-Pierre poured himself into generous good-feeling
with my mother; his striking appearance was a mere happen-
stance of his character; he did not depend on it. Sex occupied a
trivial place in his life. Most Haitians had as many women as
they could afford—a wife, one or several *placées* (semiofficial
wives, whose children were often recognized by the father),
plus mistresses, occasional unfocused affairs, drunken mount-
ings. Their pride lay in possession, and unsanctioned possession was a demonstration of freedom. André-Pierre dwelled in
his fierce dreaming against the government, his friendships,
and little more. His pride was in being right. "*New-York, c'est
fini,*" he once told me. The word *New-York* meant that famous actress; I envisioned a devouring love affair occasioned by
sacrifice and passion and a dream of perfect attainment. Now
he understood that there was no perfect attainment.

My mother kissed André-Pierre good-bye at the airport
when he surprised her by appearing to see her off. "He's not
the kind who'll jump on your runningboard, is he?" I asked.

"Hanh?" she said, oblivious to the indoctrinations of my
childhood. "He's such a beautiful man—I mean, he came to
the airport to say good-bye!"

During the nine years after I left Haiti, my mother asked
me every time I saw her, "Have you heard from Andrew Pe-
ters?" I did hear from him at first, with the following messages:
One daughter was married. Then a son was married. And all
the time, the situation grew worse. In veiled ways, in case his
letter was opened, he wrote with the intention of a drowning

man: *Help!* He reported Roman Catholic marriages for all his children—to please his wife, to please them. "I attended," he noted ironically, as if he had a choice in the matter. Once he telephoned me from New York, but I was then living in San Francisco. It was the only time he visited the States during that period; earlier his habit had been to make the trip every six months. Money was becoming extinct.

During the past few years of the Duvalier regime in Haiti, I heard from André-Pierre not at all. My notes were unanswered. Was he alive? He would now be in his late fifties. Would he still have that graceful tread when he walked, that lean power in his gaze? And would he survive?

When the chance to revisit Haiti came, I was afraid of the news. Bad times lay heavy on Port-au-Prince—danger, morose suspicion, gusts of terror. Since the telephone system no longer operated, the only way to make contact with someone was to go seek him out. I directed the cab driver to his office, *"près maison Morisseau,"* and found it boarded up. He no longer had an office in town.

It took me three days to find him. Most of his family were either dead or in exile. Almost by accident, I heard that he lived alone in a small house up the mountain in Pétionville, that he had suffered serious trouble with the government, that he had been imprisoned and hurt in an abominable way. The man who knew where he lived said with a grin, "He is obliged to be a philosopher one hundred percent. No more jigajig." This man was a *tonton macoute,* a member of the private militia of the ruling dictator, François Duvalier, who called them his "bogeymen" and let them roam the nation, administering the terror. He wore a pistol stuck in his belt. It pleased this *macoute* to hint at the injury done Monsieur Vilaire.

When I found him, in the makeshift house in a courtyard where he lived, almost his first words sounded an echo of the *tonton macoute* who had snickered about the change in him. *"Eh! Mes-z-amis!"* he cried, stepping toward me in the door-

139

way with delight, but not with astonishment, as if it had been nine hours and not nine years since last we had met. Then he put his arms around me and leaned back, squinting and grinning, as we performed that ritual mutual inspection of the damage and gain given by nearly a decade. Well, he was older, the tight skull a little less precise in its lines, the close hair nearly white now, but not really so very much changed except for a brutal scar at the side of his head, crossing just at the long line of his left eye. It looked as if he had been hit a glancing blow by a *coco-macaque*. "Oh!" he said. "They nearly expropriated my eye. It was infected, but you know my African blood, I thrive on disease. It healed without a doctor seeing it." He looked proud and then he shrugged. "Well!"

He was in a bathrobe. He wanted to dress for me, but I begged him not to move. When I found him, he had been eating rice and beans out of a bowl. On the table along with his lunch were bottles with Spanish labels on them—drugs from the Dominican Republic for indigestion, for calming, for stimulating. With a delighted smile he told me that he now lived alone in this "baraque"; his entire family was in the States, wife and children and in-laws. "But they won't give me my passport. They let me out of Fort Dimanche, but they're still afraid of me," he said. When he stood up again, I saw that he was as tall as ever, though with the soft weight added to his spare frame, the soft flesh flowing, he seemed less towering.

In ten minutes he told me his story. He had been held for five months in prison by the Duvalier militia. He told me with a smile. He had been brutalized, beaten, disgraced in the imaginative ways invented by a people slow to violence but with violence deep in their nature, as it is in the nature of all peoples. He showed his teeth delightedly as he explained what was happening to Haiti. Upon his release from prison—his eye had been damaged slightly, he had been forced to eat abominations and his stomach had been ruined, his manhood had been damaged—he went straight back to his conversations with the opposition, his sedition, his rebellion, as if nothing had changed. "*Ah, mais oui!* Now I must be a philosopher. But of course I cannot travel anyway. And no money. Listen, this country is beyond disaster, my friend. Listen, we know grief now, grief pure and abstract. Listen"—and I listened as he described the regime of a ruler mystically devoted to control of the apparatus of the state without any rational aim. The continuation of control by means of terror and grief meant a thousand instances of corruption, hatred, torture, and murder. Even the famous gaiety of the Haitian countryside was in ruins. Any stranger, even any friend could be a secret *macoute.*

The afternoon passed as he spent his pity upon this suffering nation. Then abruptly he paused and thought of his visitor. He gazed at me, confused suddenly by the time that had fled. "Are you happy, my friend? And you? Are you happy?"

"Pierrot, how can you ask that? What a question!"

"Ask *me,*" he commanded.

"What do you mean?"

"Ask it me!"

His skin had a grayish tone under the espresso brown. "How do you feel?" I asked.

"That's not the question—agreed?"

"You can't enjoy being a martyr. Are you accomplishing nothing, Pierrot? What are you after?"

"My daughters are lovely. They became lovely girls. You knew them when they were awkward, but now they are lovely. They both live on the West Ninety-second Street near Riverside Drive."

"I'll see them when I'm in New York."

"But ask me! Ask me the question!"

Amid the desolation of that house of concrete blocks, with its debris of equipment, shortwave radio and inoperative telephone, photographs and piled-up magazines, bare bulbs hanging and disconnected refrigerator and a mess of half-naked children playing in the compound outside, I gave him his question: "Are you happy, Pierrot?"

He stood up with the tail of his bathrobe flapping. "Haiti has no future! I have said it and said it a thousand, thousand times! Now everyone sees the proof. We can no longer save ourselves. The power is gone. The sky is falling about our heads." He paused for a moment and flashed his delighted grin. "To your question: *Yes.*"

MAX AND THE PACEMAKER

A STORY

PORT-AU-PRINCE has become an amputated town, throbbing in upon itself. Grief muffles the rhythms of this Caribbean port city—tourists gone, trade vanished, a crazed dictator pressing the Haitian millions into misery. Still, amid desolation and dismay, the smell of ripe mangoes is good, sun and salt are good, the sway of Creole girls as they go about their day is a happy reminder of time that was and time still to come—why not?

Or so my friend Max Liptzen the Fish Importer explained to me. Someday the walls of the Fort Dimanche prison would be torn down and *bamboche* would take the dancers once more. And then, he said, the living will regret giving up life before they have to. "This is a country for people with juice in them. Let's squeeze the juice, kid."

Convinced by Max's argument on a particularly sweet and humid evening, I wanted to pay a visit to the house of flowers known as the Flamingo, just beyond city limits in the district called Carrefour. I suggested the expedition partly to distract

Max, who was one of the few foreigners to remain in Haiti after many years of the capricious and brutal regime of François Duvalier. The phrase "house of flowers" is a sweeter name for what in other places is called BAR! DANCE!! GIRLS!!! A place for talk, dance, and putting away the cares of the world; also a place for catching an assortment of penicillin-resistant diseases, nostalgia, *Weltschmerz*, and weariness with the self. Max needed distraction for the long night stretching ahead. He didn't answer me.

Because of the general decay of life in Haiti—roads, electricity, telephone, police—Max had given up his house and was rattling about the Grand Hotel Oloffson, as was I. The tourist business was moribund. We became rapid easy friends, in the fashion of travelers on shipboard or marooned in hotels, but this night was a difficult one for Max Liptzen: news by cable that his mother was dying in Brooklyn and the next flight out of Port-au-Prince was two days away. He needed to survive until then. A broad-faced, deeply tanned man—that mahogany weathering of the dweller in the tropics who has retained his northern love of the sun—Max had played football for the Texas Aggies (scholarship), spent the war in the Marines (sergeant), wandered New York looking for a crevice in which his lazy, free-swinging spirit might pass its time, and finally cast himself up on the beach in Haiti. There he found play for his talents—a bit of business, a bit of monkey business—and lived easy and hard, married several times, and gave the world a number of children in assorted colors. Two of his children were now in school in the States, living with their separate mothers. And now his hair was thinning, too much salt water, too much sun; and he blacked what remained with a Dominican product guaranteed to restore youth. The heavy shoulders were sloped with flesh; belly pressed over and around belt, no matter how he worked at the Royal Canadian Air Force exercises. And his mother, to whom he remained faithful as only a lazy, playful New York boy is faithful, was dying far away and out of reach.

"I thought heart is for men?" he asked. "Isn't it usually cancer for women, or the sugar diabetes?"

"Well, not much difference any more."

"Not much difference between men and women?" He threw his head back and roared at his joke. The ritual laughter was called up by the idea of a joke; nothing to do with his feelings.

"No, I meant—"

"She's only sixty-seven," he said. "Can't they put in one of those pacemakers I read about in *Time?* For the heart? I get the Latin-American edition. Aren't there lots of things they can do if it's only a young woman like that, just sixty-seven? I bet they're putting in one of those new pacemakers."

During the afternoon, after receiving the cable, Max took a long shower. Tami ben Missa, his current companion, a plump Syrian widow who ran a souvenir shop on the Boulevard Harry-Truman, reported that he had wept his heart out. "I saw it myself," she said, as if she had seen his heart. "It was sad to me. It made me sad." She was familiar with tears, too; she had wept when her husband died, leaving her defenseless, and she also wept when the little purple worms crawled out of the mahogany salad bowls in her shop, leaving a powdery dust on the shelves. Mortality in all forms betrayed her. Normally the tourists were supposed to buy the mahogany before the worms found their way through the grain. Now there was no telling when they would buy again. And in the meantime, out of worry, she was getting fat; and because of Max's grief, she had again, for the third day in a row, dipped into the jar of imported peanut butter with the imported crackers after eating her lunch of measured calories. Max was no good to her at times like this.

· · ·

After tears and shower, Max went down to the pool and lay with his leathery face and heavy, still-muscular body quivering under the Caribbean sun. Later, a reddish-bronze heap of flesh in the kerosene light of evening, stuffed with crayfish and avocado salad, he finally replied to my suggestion. "Come on, kid, *my* treat for an evening at the Flamingo. Come on, I'm inviting. Come *on!*"

He drove like a taxi driver, with that Haitian habit of turning off the ignition on slopes in order to save gas, and accelerating around curves in order to test the nerves. Working through Port-au-Prince in the evening was like fitting together a jigsaw puzzle. Besides the usual confusions of a town that has grown from a colonial port to a monument to human fertility—shantytowns of banana leaves woven through mud, suburbs of crates and boards, exurbs of piled debris—the Duvalier government had put roving gangs of *tontons macoutes* on guard against invasion, sedition, and unexplained loitering. The *macoutes* blocked off streets at random to confuse the devils; they stopped our car to demand, "*Inspection! In-spection!*," which meant: "Get out, let us feel you for weapons, pay up." When they searched us, huffing with excitement, they showed by the way they felt us and pinched us that it was spite, not civil caution, which sent them into this profession. We paid a gourd (twenty cents) in order to pass on.

Few fun-lovers ventured out at night. Bars were closed or deserted. The Casino—bankrupt, run by the state—was empty. The ever-present crowds which live in the street—students studying beneath street lamps, the homeless, the wandering, those who live "under the same sky like you do," as one beggar said—watched us pass and stared without the Haitian eagerness which I remembered from other times. The smell of Port-au-Prince, charcoal smoke and refuse and strong humanity, followed us down the rutted streets to the waterfront, and then a sea breeze swept through the covered jeep as we headed out toward Carrefour.

"These are some great girls," said Max. "Why is it I can't stand them more than once or twice, the same girl? You tell *me* that."

"I suppose you don't care much, pal."

"I don't understand how if they put that pacemaker thing in the heart—how they do if the battery runs down. Do they use a transistor?"

"They must."

"That cruddy wife of mine in the Bronx, do you think she'll bring our kid to see her?"

"Maybe it depends on how sick—"

"Hell, it's a beautiful country, isn't it? Just look at it. This could be paradise."

"Yes."

"They use transistors for everything now, even radios, haha."

And then he fell into silence and tended to his driving. True, the solemn processions, the glowing blue-black of the seaside road, the flicker of fires and kerosene lamps and candles, and the pervading human warmth of evening, give all who visit Haiti for more than a few days a special nostalgia for the night hours on this heart-testing, desperate island.

Just past the third set of barricades on the Carrefour road lay a clump of woods, palm trees, banana bushes, and a grove of mangoes. Abruptly Max turned the jeep down a mud road. In the lurching dark I could make out the dark shape of a house. It looked like the underside of a shipwreck in the churning sea of night, disturbed by birds and branches and swelling clouds. Our headlights caught the sign:

LE FLAMINGO

Welcome Friend and Visitor

La Bienvenue

The Flamingo Welcome You

"The Flamingo Happy Whorehouse and Discussion Club seems pretty dark," said Max. Irritably he honked his horn. A watchman came running on one foot, ambling on another, limping along.

"Go home! Go home!" he cried.

"Where are the girls?"

"No! No! No! Go home, please, I beg you, dear sirs."

"What's happened to everyone?"

The watchman struggled with a feeble grasp on French and sailor English, translating from his native Creole. "*Pas* clients! All lonesome! No do-do! Everbody in movies! Now you be nice and go home, please! No make trouble and break up joint!"

Max discussed the bad news with himself. The ladies had all been loaded into the truck for an outing. Well, he'd be a . . . It wasn't even a dirty movie at the Rex, it was just "Les Hot-Girls de Paris," a French striptease nudie picking up carfare in Port-au-Prince on its way to South America after the burlesque circuits of Ohio and Indiana.

For perhaps weeks there had been no customers, no drinkers, no kidders and talkers. The American tourists and sailors had long since disappeared; the thirteen-year-old virgins were growing old and weary for lack of practice at the trade of being thirteen. Even the local businessmen and diplomats hated to go out at night. They were tired. There was no one looking for the Flamingo; there was no one in Haiti. So the girls were sad. But not too sad to enjoy a nice movie, and the boss had piled them into the tap-tap for a treat.

Max had been sad, but not too sad to visit the girls. That's what they were there for—to improve the sadness. And now they weren't there.

I was sad for Max the Fish Importer, whose mother lay in Mount Sinai Hospital gasping for breath while her favorite and youngest son, straining all his muscles to reach her, was held up by Pan Am scheduling. In the golden age of tourism in Haiti, there had been two flights a day out of Bowen Field.

"But!" cried the watchman, recognizing misery and a possible tip. "But!" It turned out that the Flamingo Annex down the road, another house of flowers, carried on during emergencies such as a mass visit to the movies. He had barely explained how to find it when Max, in one clean, athletic motion, gave him a gourd, put the jeep in reverse, and sent us, spinning mud, back onto the road toward the Flamingo Annex. It was called the G. Washington Bar & Girl, honoring the U. S. naval cruisers which used to put over in the bay of Port-au-Prince. The good old days when a Bar & Girl did good for the Good Neighbor Policy. In those times, fantastic snowfalls were seen by tropical Port-au-Prince—a thick blanket of white from the passed-out sailor suits containing passed-out sailors sleeping it off on the lawns of the G. Washington, the A. Lincoln, the Flamingo, the S.S. Lollypop, the Voodoo-Club, and the Choucounette, where lonely men gathered to console themselves for the absence of those they loved.

The G. Washington Bar & Girl had none of the undersea grace of the Flamingo. It was an annex and little more. A decaying wooden house with the minimal grace of filigree and shutter, eave and pointed rooftop, it had been converted into a giant sounding board. Warned by the sound of the motor, it began to throb and pulsate as we approached. We saw lights flashing on; first the string of colored Christmas bulbs across the yard and porch, then the jukebox, then the bare bulbs in the rooms, and then the jewels in the eyes of the naked boy who ran out to greet us and hold an umbrella over our heads. It was not a wet evening. There was no rain. But an umbrella for dignity and to keep the dew from our hot brows.

And the girls were all over us like the dew on a plant left out to make its own way in nature. They ran and glittered. They took eager possession. They were gleaming, black, round, brown, and tan. They were loosely gowned in rope-secured frocks. There is a small town in Haiti which is famous for two qualities: the relatively light color of its inhabitants (its white colony did not leave after the revolution of 1804), and the single-minded intentions of its women. Many find favor in the bars along the Carrefour road. The best of these village girls have high rumps, jolly natures, and avaricious hearts—they are self-respecting whores. The jukebox boomed out its Chubby Checker beat; the ladies, who take their English neat, were mouthing the memorized words; Max was buying surcease from sorrow, rum and soda; and to keep from being hounded by a pack of ladies, I had chosen one of them to be my very own. I discovered, as my head filled with smoke, that I was dancing the twist.

"Tweest! An' tweest again!" my partner sang. "An' tweest wan more time!"

All this for us? I recall thinking. Naked bar boys running, girls chanting, sweat rolling, rum bottles clinking. On the wall the portrait of Dr. François Duvalier, the swollen owl's face in black horn-rimmed glasses and topped by a homburg, like a voodoo priest, gazed down unblinkingly upon us. "The Great Protector," I said to my dancing partner.

"*Ah oui oui oui*," she said.

"Everyone has him on the wall," I said.

"Of course, he is the Great Protector."

I led her toward him by the arm, making as if to press her face against the photograph. "I've seen him on lots of walls," I said, "but I've never seen anybody kiss him."

She collapsed with the giggles. In Creole she reported my remark to the other girls and the bar man. The girls howled. One cried out, "He never kiss me either," and the shrieks of laughter mounted afresh. The bar man frowned and brought me a rum-soda on the house.

Max said without conviction, "You want to get me expelled?"

"Tweest again?" said my date. "An' we tweest again?"

The jukebox took off in stratospheric answer to her question. I went along for the ride. Watching her deal with the problem of weightfulness, I nominated her for lady astronaut. When the record was over, we held hands back to the table, where Max was deep in conversation with another girl, a girl of about fifteen with a healthy high pout to everything, rump, breasts, lips. "We talk," I said to my lady.

"No no no! We go upstairs!"

"Talk!" I said.

"No"—and then with sudden suspicion: "You seeck?"

"No."

"You t'ink I seeck? I no seeck. Fresh young t'ing. Inspection by *docteur* evair mont', and no jigajig busi-ness zis mont'. *C'est la pagaïe.*" She gazed at Max, who was busy downing one rum after another and talking, talking, talking to his lady. "He seeck?"

Perhaps unnerved by the music, the noise, the expectation of direct action, I told her that his mother was very ill in New York and that he was awaiting the plane to take him there. She advised me to advise him to go upstairs with his lady in order to while away the hours of waiting. This is the remedy for most problems, especially the ones for which there is no other remedy. But when the girls knew that we had come only to drink and talk, they made the best of it. They drank. They talked. Max was getting very drunk as he explained to a lady who spoke about twenty words of English, all learned from sailors, what the pacemaker does, how heart surgery has developed in recent years, and where New York lies in relation to Port-au-Prince, Cap-Haïtien, Jacmel, Jérémie, and Port-de-Paix. Further north it lies. The pacemaker can lie to the north or the south of the heart. But it keeps the heart going with an electrical impulse conforming to the heart's own rhythm, the rhythm of a mother who loved her youngest son though he gave her no joy, only a succession of daughters-in-law and grandchildren—the grandchildren scattered, the daughters-in-law scattered, the son lost in a strange land with a business that bore no looking into. A fish business, but what kind of a fish business? A fishy business, she always said.

The girl sitting with Max asked him, "You like maybe my sister?"

I was telling my own lady about the United States. I was keeping an eye on Max. When she asked if I would take her to the United States, and I said maybe, she laughed scornfully. She didn't expect to get taken to the United States by a man who bought drinks but paid her no serious attention. She didn't even expect to get taken from Carrefour to Port-au-Prince, or from the Flamingo Annex to the Flamingo. She expected very little from life, and knew she would get less than she expected.

Then suddenly Max turned away from the girl listening with her elbows on that wobbly table and began to talk to me. "I've been married four times," he said. "My mother is dying. I make about seven–eight thousand a year here, but it goes as far as twenty in the States. Maybe about that far. And in the good years I made more, sometimes twice as much. But I could never keep up the support payments too good. My kids don't see me. I can't visit them much on what I make. I can't bring them down here. My mother, I always wrote to her, though. We kept in touch. We kept in touch. How can I keep in touch now?"

I asked if he would like to go back to the Oloffson. I offered to drive.

"No," he said.

Tears began to flow down the furrows of his sunburned cheeks.

"Yes," he said.

The girls followed us to the door. He was having trouble keeping on his feet. He was cursing the government of François Duvalier because Pan Am only flew out of Port-au-Prince three times a week.

Now I saw the same tears that his Syrian girl friend had

discovered on his face. But he was not ashamed of them. I was a stranger to him; the girls were strangers; they chattered and clucked and helped to push him into the jeep, just as if this were their customary job—to pack away a weeping American. "I been married four times!" he said to one of them.

She understood a little English. "In one night?" she asked. "Oooh, you beeg man. You come back when you feel better, yes? *Gran'bamboche*, we marry you four time in one night."

There was the smell of charcoal smoke and rotting mangoes on the road.

Max asked me, "What if my mother knew how I spend my time?"

I told him not to worry about it.

He turned to me again, seeming nearly sober in the darkness, first sticking his head out into the midnight coolness of the bayside road. He was giving thought to what the girl had told him. "Listen," he said, "if you're really in love, there's no limit. You know what it's like—really in love? Listen, if it's true love, hell, you're a man all the time. 'Be a man,' you say to yourself, and you're a man, just like that. When she looks at you with that look because she loves you. When you want to." He ran his hand through his thin hair. He looked at it in the dark as if the blacking might smudge his fingers. "My mother used to fly down sometimes for the home games," he said, "you know, in Texas there. Of course, the school paid her fare. They knew I liked to have her in the stands. I played better with her watching me."

"I know."

"Listen!" he said. We were stopped at a barricade by the ragged militia known as the *tontons macoutes*. They pointed their guns and shined their flashlights over us. Max held himself with dignity and let me do the talking. I paid the toll. Then he continued, dead sober.

"Listen," he said, "this is how I spent my whole life in this place. Since the war. Since 1948, that wasn't so long after the

war. Since after I got done bumming around. I figured out
how to import fish in barrels from Canada. Started with Nor-
way, ended up with Canada. Dried. Salted. Industrial quality,
it won't kill you. Okay, it made me some money. I didn't have
to work much. Just organize it a little. Listen, I got married a
lot. Kids all over. A couple brown kids, too. Now I can't fall in
love any more. Ma gets her pacemaker, maybe she'll be all
right, okay? You think so? Oh Christ. Oh God. I get out on
Pan Am, Montego Bay, Idlewild, my brother meets me.
Straight to the hospital and she'll ask me—oh God in heaven,
keep her alive. But I don't know how to answer her. You
know, kid? What I started to tell you about falling in love:
This is a place for hiding out. That's all it is." He paused once
more, trying to make his discovery for me so that he could
make it for himself. "It's like this when you're in business all
alone, like I am. You bite a lot. I'm a tough fellow. You
get bitten. So my mouth been bitten by lots of girls, but
no one has bit *me.* How do I answer my mama when she asks
what I'm doing? How do I lie to her when she's needing a
pacemaker? But how can I tell her the truth?"

M arriage-and-divorce, seen as a unified entity, were the last frontier for a generation of silent and apolitical men. It was the moral equivalent of war. And the children of these battles were the element of tragedy, though the word "tragedy" is too strong a name for the deed. Pathos, juvenility, selfishness, a breakdown of social form in the light of personal need—these are the real elements in the long afternoons of child visitation and discussions of support.

The divorce reform law in California now calls the deed "dissolution of marriage." Divorce has been abolished, because it has a reputation for being unpleasant, to be replaced by friendly, charming, agreeable dissolution of marriage.

Now wars and politics again engage men, and the oedipal box of divorce no longer encloses us. "Poisoned air" is not a metaphor about broadcasting; it means the air we breathe. Divorce is no longer a piece of strange. "Togetherness" has been interred as a magazine promotion (the word came from Kahlil Gibran's The Prophet). The children make out somehow. If there are to be apocalypses, the suffering of visiting rights for divorced fathers will be obliterated along with all other suffering.

Nonetheless, the throughways and the bright malicious spirits of children and the random dislocations of America provide the landscape against which some distraught souls live out their time. Amid grander designs, footloose arrangements and pious communal structures, men still endure this Sunday kind of love.

"I WANT A SUNDAY KIND OF LOVE"

A STORY

DAN SHAPER had the court-given right to spend Christmas vacation with his children. He drove in this midwinter weather from New York to Cleveland through the wintry length of turnpike—slush and flats of New Jersey, sudden black mountains of Pennsylvania with their marred white tunnels, then slithering down through Ohio foothills—and not a stoplight after Manhattan until he approached Cleveland, his arm still embracing the wheel. He stopped for coffee at a Howard Johnson's, the coffee given by a pimply waitress, and then in the men's room studied the machine which, for an investment of eleven cents, cranked forth the Lord's Prayer engraved on a penny. A dime for labor, one cent for material.

He drove on until, again shaking with fatigue, he stopped at an identical Howard Johnson's, was offered coffee by a girl who had pimples in the same place, and retreated to possibilities for stamping the Lord's Prayer on the same or a similar penny. "Lest We Forget," the placard advised.

Like the famous drowning man, he thought of the ten years of his marriage, but with this difference: the marriage was the drowning, and afterward came the gasping and choking recovery. (Was that an unmarked patrol car behind him? Sometimes they used Edsels.)

Then he thought of Paula and Cynthia, love like lust eating at his belly, and his daughters saying, "Why do you have to stay away so long?" He bit hard into memory as if it were a plum. It was a black rock and his teeth hurt. And then he thought: "I need a wife of my own, wife and children with me every day. I need someone standing with me in the mirror." And thought: no other children could replace Paula and Cynthia, who were born of his first youth when he was a skinny boy, amazed that he could create plump living flesh.

And then thought: another coffee, another doughnut to keep him going. At least his stomach could take it. If the limits of love had been defined by pride and lust, left and right, his stomach could not still have taken doughnuts; but it still could. There was a new rock 'n' roll version of "Jingle Bells" on the radio. Fathers like him all over the world were flying, driving, training in to claim their visiting rights with their children —their stomachs jerking with excitement, hope and strain in their eyes, love and guilt and pride and an aching foot on the accelerator. Merry Christmas. God rest ye, merry gentlemen. "And now the Chipmunk Song, that newest Christmas classic . . ."

Shaper switched stations. He was near enough to Cleveland so that the pushbuttons now brought him the stations for which they had been set.

> For he shall reign for ever and ever
> He shall,
>   He shall,
> He shall reign for ever and ev-ev-ver.

All over America the fathers were returning to the scene of their defeat, their abdication, their flight. Some of them were thinking, like Dan Shaper: "Thank God I escaped! Thank God! I might have been caught forever!" Some of them were thinking, like Dan Shaper: "Regret, I should have tried once more, regret forever."

It was the late evening rush hour when he slid into the

frayed edges of Cleveland. Neon and colored lights and sudden frosty forests of ripped-up evergreens beckoned to Christmas shoppers, while the men in vacant lots pounded their mitts together and promised "a nice tree, missus." Under a shelter marked in great letters $2.98! a woman sold teddy bears as large as teddy bears ever grow, and she had a portable coal stove to give her good cheer. The light changed; traffic urged him forward, down the outskirt slopes of the Alleghenies which lead into the flattened industrial town. Through the front vents of his car Shaper breathed the chilled exhaust from the tailpipe ahead of him.

If he could arrive at his friend's apartment before eight, he could call Paula and Cynthia. Or he could stop and call from a gas station. But he liked to talk with them, even by telephone, only when he was clean and shaved and combed, and the shaking fatigue of the five-hundred-mile drive eased by a drink. Then he could lounge at his ease through the first breathless words.

Cynthia, who was eight, would say, "I can say more things in Spanish now! *Buenos días*, Señor Daddy!"

"Señor Daddy too! Señor Daddy too!" would come Paula's protesting wail, twenty desperate squirming inches from the telephone.

"Shh, I'll let you talk. Wait till I'm finished, Paula. Daddy?"

"Yes, honeybear."

"We'll be ready tomorrow morning. You pick us up at nine. We'll be out on the front porch." She was very experienced at these arrangements, busy and bustling to get herself and her sister ready, experienced buffer state between her mother and her father.

"Now it's my turn!" came the distant wail.

"Now do you want to talk to Paula?"

"Yes," he would say.

"All right, Paula, now you talk."

And as Paula wrestled for the telephone, Cynthia's voice receded, becoming childish once again, all arrangements done, repeating merely: "Daddy. Daddy. Daddy?"

He sighed, emitting frost. He was not yet on the telephone with them. He was four blocks farther into the traffic; he had shifted gears four times; he had dreamed again, but it had only gotten him a few hundred yards deeper into Cleveland. There was another lot, festooned with lights, selling rootless and truncated, sap-frozen Christmas trees.

Driving through Cleveland on one of the many nights before Christmas, under fouled industrial skies seen through his greasy windshield, Shaper felt slush under his wheels, a flying soup of snow and dirt and salt, corroding the metal underbodies of automobiles; salt in the greasy air splashed up at nightfall into the traffic, wiping its film across the windshield, rhythmic swish of salt and glass; on the radio, once more God rested his merry gentlemen, followed by the Chipmunk Song. There were snowed-in, secretly salted sheep in the used-car lots. Hunched against the weather and the hurrying shoppers, the 1952 Studebakers and the older Fraziers ($100, nothing down) waited, and the sharp later models waited, too. GIRLS! ARE YOU HARD TO FIT? (A shoe store.) THRILL TO THE GLORY OF THE OPEN ROAD! (A driving school.) And THE ELBOW BAR, THE KNICK-KNACK-KNOOK, STEVE'S PLACE, STEAKS AND TEXAS-BURGERS!

DON'T ASK THE PRICE—YOU NAME IT! EVERYTHING GOES!

CHILI! STARLITE FOOD! DAY-OLD BAKED GOODS! (Slightly used apple pies? Shaper asked. Outgrown marshmallow cookies?) RED HOTS!

Where was that chicken store he remembered? CAPONS FOR SALE! "What's a capon, Daddy?" Cynthia had once asked him.

Answer: "A capon is a very tender chicken, given special treatment, nice and soft, honey."

At last he reached the apartment of his friend, Martie Grant. Warmth and greetings; this friend always saved his life. There was an amiable steam on the windows. His visits were special occasions; hot buttered rum and how are we doing? In answer to the question, Dan answered, "I dunno, chappie. Maybe I'm making out."

He had already called and the arrangements were fixed about seeing Cynthia and Paula on their front porch in the morning. He talked with his friend until they both grew drowsy, and then one more hot rum and a couple of salty crackers, and then to the sack. He made out: he fell asleep. That was all right, chappie, when what you need is sleep.

The children, thick in mufflers, were waiting on the porch when he drove up. They had been playing, waiting, talking; cocking their heads, they watched him turn into the driveway as if interested in his style as a driver.

"Hello, Daddy," said Cynthia very shyly.

"Hello, Daddy," said Paula.

He understood and said with shyness equal to theirs, "Hello, children. Let's get into the car."

Then out the driveway, down the street and around the corner; and then he had to pull over to the side of the curb, crunching frozen snow, when they flung their arms about him: "Oh Daddy, Daddy, Daddy!" It was as if they had feared that their mother could see through the walls. But they did not believe, as he sometimes did, that she could follow him around corners with an angry eye. There was now a swarming mass of daughters greeting father, and then, tousled, flushed, he patted them both and felt pleased by the happy tears all around.

"Okay. Now, what should we do?" he asked.

"Plans!"

"That's right, I have plans. Now listen—"

"What? What? What are we going to do?"

"A trip to the moon for lunch. Then Bermuda. Then a snack. Then quickly across two or three oceans for dinner, and then we'll—"

With relieved howls of laughter at so much eating, so much travel, they said, like happy little girls everywhere, "Oh, Daddy! I don't believe you."

"All right, then I'll have to show you."

And he would show them, would, *would*. If he had to take them to both the moon and Bermuda. Focused on his daughters, he believed that he could infuse them with his energy of feeling for them—right through the snow and ice and his yearning thrust across turnpikes.

"Why are you looking at me, Daddy?"

"I want to look at you, Paula."

"I outgrew the dress you gave me for my birthday already. Mommy says you never buy the right size."

"Tough shit."

"What's that?"

"That's the word for failure to calculate how fast a little girl can grow."

Slowly a smile appeared on her face. She had learned words on the playgrounds already. "Daddy, you're teasing. But when are we going to the television?"

He had promised them a tour at a local television station. It was part of the prolonged animal act of his "visitations"— legal poetry—where he challenged himself to amuse them without going to the movies. He had arranged to watch a local television show, a teen-age "dance party" with genuine rock 'n' roll celebrities and night-club performers doing a spot of afternoon propaganda with the Saturday kids. Two days later it was time and they were having a little meal, their version of oysters, soupe printanière, turbot, sauce Beaumarchais, poulard à l'estragon, macédoine de fruits—in other words, cheeseburgers with malted milk. "Oh, good, good!" said Cynthia, her dewy eyes shining.

"You like my cooking?"

"I like your *ordering*, Daddy," Paula said with great interest in precision. "*Gracias*, Pops!" and she flew up in an infestation of the giggles.

"Tell me about your Spanish class. Do you want some double bubble?"

"Bubble gum is for babies. We're too big," Cynthia said. "Now give us Chiclets."

"That's what we always have," Paula said. "Sometimes we have sugarless for our teeth."

"Sugarless and chlorophyll," said Cynthia.

Dan nodded solemnly. Paula's malted milk repeated warmly and she grinned. Cynthia was frowning with a sudden thought. "Mommy says you only buy us junk," she said.

"But," said Paula, "but I like your junk."

"Daddy, we like your junk." And Cynthia's smile for him, radiant up toward him. The word *junk* would always be a mystery for her, a beautiful and complicated word, like *serendipity* or *communion*. "Now tell us a story."

"Yes, Daddy. A once-upon-a-time story . . ."

The story concerned a prince who wanted more than anything else to be loved. Naturally, a magic potion came into the matter, and thus everyone loved him. But the once-upon-a-time prince remained unhappy because the potion had no effect on *him*, since for happiness to come of a love potion, it must above all make the once-upon-a-time prince love those who drink of his potion.

From that dreamy oblivion of the child which is so much like indifference and contains so much caring, Cynthia looked up at her father and said, "I know you do, Daddy."

"Know I do what?"

"What you said."

"What did I say?"

She laughed, thrilled because he had forgotten—he had not heard himself—the words had slipped out like his breath. But now he heard, he felt, he even saw himself repeating, "I love you, honeybear."

The waitress in the diner came up and said, "Mister, you must be a teacher to tell stories like that. My brat won't listen to any goddamn thing I tell her."

"My father's a lifesaver," Paula said. "He lives in New York. He knows how to save people's lives."

She had been much impressed by his efforts that summer to teach her to swim; she had overcome her fear of the water. Dan smiled because she remembered so well that he had been a junior lifesaver at the age of thirteen.

"Daddy," said Cynthia, "that magic potion made me hungry."

"*Thirsty*," her sister corrected her.

"Hungry *and* thirsty, Paula! Can we have, can we have . . . something?"

"Something! Something!" cried Paula.

They ate again, and this time Dan told a magic story that had no love and food in it. It was a poor magic story, of course, but the children did not object, scattering material ketchup and actual rootbeer on Formica. They liked his poor magic stories, too, and found food therein.

"You promised to take us to the TV station."

"Wait till he finishes the story, Paula."

Pout. Reproach.

"I know. I did. I will," he said.

Reversal of pout and reproach. They blinked at so many intentions. "Let's go," he said, and that was easy to understand.

Snowsuits, rubbers, hats, mittens, and a farewell to the nice and nosy waitress who thought it swell that a father took his daughters adventuring on a Saturday afternoon. Then salty slush, feet and wheels, and Shaper put his hand in his pockets to tip the boy who parked his car.

"You give everybody money," Cynthia observed.

"I sure do." But her face was bland. She was not kidding. She had noticed, was all.

"Can I have a penny?" said Paula. "For Chiclets? A nickel?"

The Saturday-afternoon dance party was a teen-age program which featured night-club stars visiting in town, and kids sucking from bottles of pop and dancing the Chicken or the Fish to records which were put on between the performances, interviews, and commercials. The disc jockey who ran this stew of "live entertainment" was called Fat Ed because he weighed nearly two hundred and fifty long and loose pounds and liked the sound of "Ed." He also wore heavy horn-rimmed glasses with a straight, wide flange of black plastic on each side pressing against his ears; pointed shoes, which made his fat little feet look like frog's flippers; and a smile like a frog's, separating his wide expanse of jowl from an equally generous slab of nose. He was an old acquaintance of Dan's, which in show biz means a lifelong friend or enemy. Since they were not in competition, it was friend and friendly-like. Thanks to this, Dan, Paula, and Cynthia could huddle together beneath the lights just out of camera range and watch the party doings. A shuffling band of stage personnel mystified the girls with their rushing of cameras up, their hustling of people to and fro, their muscular chaos of co-ordinated indecision. "This gets sent into the box at home," Dan elaborately whispered. "You mustn't talk. You can whisper back when I whisper to you. It's what you see in the box."

With florid elegance the deejay introduced Hennery Ford, middle-aged girl singer now appearing at that famous night-spot—"What's the name of that place, doll?"

She told him.

"Reet, Hennery doll. Say, you been in Miami Beach?" She nodded.

"That's great, Hennery, soaking up all those sun vitamins— Poor old Fat Ed, I have so many heartfelt responsibilities of live entertainment, I just don't have time—But now this here chick, she is—man, I mean the greatest. You know it, dontcha, kids?"

"We know it," screamed the studio visitors, heated by coke and awe.

The hot, stuck deejay wiped the acres of black plastic on his glasses, leaving the lenses fogged. He returned the folded handkerchief to his breast pocket. "Do you *know* it?"

"We *know* it!"

Busily Cynthia whispered to her father something which he did not hear. He answered, "Don't worry, they don't know anything." She smiled quickly, relieved.

"All right!" shouted the deejay. "So now she has chosen to sing for us one of her favorite hit tunes, a religious type love number with a rock 'n' roll beat—it'll live forever, and here's 'I Want a Sunday Kind of Love.' Hennery?"

Microphone, spots, SILENCE, hushed approval, and the sweaty operators rushing cameras in and out. Miss Ford, a wizened, peeling girl of about forty, stood smiling in the light, swaying slightly as her chapped and oiled lips opened over the words:

> I want a Sunday kind of love
> Like the kind I feel Above
> I want a Sunday kind of love
> From that One I'm thinking of—

Her mouth stretched over the sounds, her body swayed, the music shrilled forth; but she did not sing. The voice of Hennery Ford came from a record while the body of Hennery Ford mimed the gestures of singing.

"What did you say?" Dan whispered to Cynthia.

"But she isn't singing!" Cynthia whispered in shock and horror, discovering another instance of the world's corruption.

"She's very foolish," Paula said primly.

Later Dan would explain to them about idealism—how everybody wanted the song to be perfect, the way Hennery had recorded it originally; about pragmatism—how art is the politics of the possible; about mass media and the way of the world—that's how things are. In the meantime, this eight-year-old daughter had found public corruption condoned, and some of her disdain was directed against her father. "I want to go *right now!*" she said.

On the way out, Dan explained, "She has chapped lips like that from so much traveling. Maybe she has a cold, besides the change of climate." *Kachoo*, he said sympathetically.

"God bless you," said Paula, sure that her wish was His command. "I don't like that song. I like 'I'm itchy lak a man on a fuzzy tree, I'm all shook up.' "

"Paula, that's not right. It's 'Ah'm itchy *lak* a man on a *fuz*-zy tree, Ah'm all—shook—*up*.' Daddy, let's go someplace else and you tell us a story about magic potions."

"Magic potions!" cried Paula.

"Again?"

"Tell it," said Cynthia, grinning, "just by moving your lips and we'll say the words, okay? Paula, what word am I saying?" And her lips squirmed over the enormous adult teeth that always surprised Dan, since it was still baby-teeth time when he stopped living with their mother. Her lips, glistening and pink, formed and re-formed over the teeth.

Paula watched, peered into her mouth, pulled back, solemnly imitated the gesture, and at last said loud and clear, "Fake! Fake! You were saying 'Fake'!"

"That's what my lips were saying," Cynthia said. "But that's what I think of 'I Want a Sunday Kind of Love' and Miss Hilary Ford."

"I guess you're right," said their father, obscurely troubled, as if somehow the children were judging him and putting him on the same side as poor Hennery-Hilary. Adults move their lips to music offstage; silently they pretend to sing; and what about Dan's willed gaiety with his girls? And did they not sense how terribly he sometimes flagged, their real father in town for a spree with them? Was he really so enthusiastic about milk shakes (magic potions) and the art museum (fairy tales)?

"It's the way of the world," he said.

"Singing like that?"

"Everything." But Cynthia patted his hand with one of her peculiarly adult, maternal gestures. It was like her salting his eggs. She wanted to be good to him for no purpose but that she was his daughter, and so she imitated the anxious gestures of her mother with that second husband whom she hoped to please and be pleased by. Logic, thought Shaper. (She had dumped a gagging amount of salt over the flattened yolk.) My daughter learns the gestures of love by monkeying around. She broods over my stepwife's gestures with the man who replaced me.

He ate egg. He wiped his mouth. He drank water and took toast. Another snack.

He would have liked a son, he suddenly thought—why? He asked himself why it came to him with such wrenching despair now, when Cynthia was so tender, Paula so sweet with their ideal, often absent, *real* father. All that rose to his mind was an image of the Square Deal Club football team, when at age twelve he had tackled a full-grown boy and, it turned out, broken his collarbone. Glory and shame and sudden hot tears making him sneeze. Well, why not have another child, more children? Why not have a wife again? He called for coffee; the girls called for milk, and dimes for the jukebox. Outside, the sky had turned black for these last days of the year. It could snow and snow and snow. He held Paula's hand and remembered his own grandfather shaking his hand, holding it, holding to life by an arthritic claw. The way ancient aunts kiss and uncles clutch, he thought, is how I hold my daughters.

It was time to take the children home after this last afternoon of his visit. The sky had clouded over again and there would be fresh snow as he aimed himself toward the highway. "What's the matter, Daddy?" Cynthia asked.

"I dunno, chappie. The weather. I'm sorry I won't be seeing you for another month."

"But you'll write to us," Paula said cheerfully.

"Yes. Yes."

A look of faint disdain and resentment crossed Paula's face, and her eye just passed to her thumb. No, she would not suck. She was too old for that. She would speak instead. "You don't come to see us often enough, Daddy. Mommy says we should call you 'Dan,' and we should call Mike 'Daddy.'"

"So," said Cynthia, statesmanlike, "we call you 'Daddy' when we're talking to you, because you're our *real* daddy—"

"And 'Dan,'" continued Paula like Mister Bones, "when we ask Mommy when you're coming to see us. She don't like us to ask."

"*Doesn't*," her sister corrected her. "You should say: 'Mike and Mommy *don't*,' but 'Mommy *doesn't*.'" She finished this moral and grammatical lesson by putting her finger in her mouth and ferociously pulling at the cuticle with her teeth.

He talked, sang, made rhymes, joked. Paula smiled, but Cynthia huddled against him as he drove. She stared with sleepy cunning at the panel showing gas, mileage, speed. Dan parked before their house and told them he had his suitcase all ready in the trunk. He was spending his last minutes with them, and then he would hurry again toward New York. Then there was silence. Somehow he had asked a question and Cynthia must answer.

She closed her eyes briefly, a gesture of restraint like a much older girl accused. She had a wide, unmarked forehead over the struggling lashes. She closed her eyes, planning. Her mother was training her excellently, but she still loved her father, she cared. Her *real* father, as she explained. And since she cared, really cared, this prematurely adult, scheming gesture of closing the eyes did not mean all that it seemed to mean. But still it meant something. She was angry because he was leaving so soon again; she was hurt, she wanted to touch and hurt him; she cared and was confused; she had something important to say and did not know how to say it. There was an item of information which would have to stand for all this. She opened and closed her eyes once more before she spoke; she squeezed something back into her brain behind the wide, hot, childish forehead. "Daddy," she said, "I didn't get your last letter."

"What do you mean? I'm afraid you don't get all my letters. How do you know about it at all?"

"I just know."

"What do you mean?"

"Rosalie"—the maid—"she said there was a letter. She said to go get it when I came home from school."

Cynthia shut her eyes again. "It must have got lost," she said.

Paula said, "I want to go inside." Dan said good-bye to his younger daughter, carried her across the snow to the door, kissed her. The wintry door opened for her; his invisible former wife took her back. Dan climbed back into the car with Cynthia. They sat awhile in thickening silence. "The letters I sent to you are supposed to be given to you," he said.

"I know, Daddy."

And they looked at each other like grownup lovers fleeing parents and family. Child, he thought; child of mine.

"I really love you awfully much, honey."

Impatient and a child again, she said, "I know. Why don't you ever wear black shoes, Daddy?"

"I like brown ones."

"Brown ones?"

Muffled in coats, they sat together in the front seat of the car as if there were more to say. It began to snow in little flakes colored yellow by industrial smoke, ragged-edged, yellow and faded. The fog of coal and steel and the fog of humid winter held the snow suspended in air, and then let it fall. He ran the motor to keep warm. The snow came down all over the city of Cleveland, and when the wiper of his car worked it left a smear, wiping the glass back and forth. He sat with his daughter before the house in which his former wife, her mother, lived, and explained to her why he wore brown shoes; why he did not wear rubbers; why some singers are fake and don't really sing; why the snow melted faster on the street than on the grass.

"Write to me anyway," she said.

"We'll figure something out, Cynthia."

"Will you?" she asked.

Fresh snow had shadowed his earlier footsteps by the time he took her to the door; evening had come. Half an hour later he was on the highway leading into the turnpike, which falls with hardly a pause through three states back to Manhattan. There in the new year he would like to find a wife and have children again.

T he true secret international underground is not Communist in these times. It is the Bohemian, whatever it's called this season. You can begin a sentence in North Beach in San Francisco, continue it in Greenwich Village or Chelsea or Saint-Germain-des-Prés, and finish it in the Molodezhne Café in Moscow. And it's a language which the artists understand, maybe, and the dropout non-flower children, but to the good bourgeois of the United States, England, France, or the Soviet graystate, it is wasteful play. I have written about Bohemia in New York, Cleveland, Reno, and San Francisco, in Havana and Port-au-Prince, in Greenwich Village and London, Paris, Rome, and Moscow, and this seems to be an undersea nation to which I belong. Beat and hip, sad and hopeful, mean and generous, in the years since World War II, Bohemia has become the conduit for friendly communication across time and distance—sex, drugs, music, clothes, styles, contents, art and nonart, utopias and boarding arrangements. The communication doesn't always say nice things. But it's ours.

In San Francisco there are third-generation marijuana smokers.

As to these stories, The First and Last Beatnik is an old man now. The boy who loves an Older Woman will be an old man someday. Let them know each other.

SONG OF THE FIRST AND LAST BEATNIK

A STORY

BACK in 1957, in San Francisco, my friend the Famous Beat Poet wanted me to meet the champion beatnik of them all. This was during the finest rage of the holy barbarians, when North Beach, Chinatown and Telegraph Hill lay aswarm and abuzz with bongos, guitars, sandals, chicks, poets —and journalists watching everything—and San Francisco's Finest watching everyone. It was the golden age of the mimeographed manifesto and one girl for every ten geniuses, except when the tourists came out on weekends. Remember the beards? Remember red wine? Remember the revolutions? Remember poetry read to jazz?

Howard, one of the great men of the time, stood guard at his station on the sidewalk in front of the Co-Existence Bagel Shop on upper Grant, aslant on Telegraph Hill, revolving like a beacon in the fog. He was a tall, gangling, grinning, shambling young Negro possessed of that curious compulsion called logorrhea. He couldn't stop talking. He mumbled, he chanted, he discoursed; he was surely very strange with his baroque-sculptured, empty ears and hard-working mouth. But what he said had an odd off-wit; and unlike most madmen, Howard seemed to know what would please his hearers. He repeated a good story and discarded a bad one. He picked up the clues. He kept the faith that there are others out here.

When my friend the Famous Beat Poet introduced us, Howard said, "Howdya do. I got the water if you got the bucket."

To communicate was the beginning of misunderstanding. We stood in front of the Bagel Shop and talked. I listened. Someone mentioned the law. "Oh yes, oh yes, oh yes," he said. (I had heard that he was a disbarred lawyer.) "Tell you something right now. The man in the courtroom with the long hair is always the defendant. You better cut your hair, boy."

"I'm not on trial."

"Not so's you'd know it," he said, "but we are all on trial. Oh yes, oh *yes*. And for to be a prosecutor a man has to eat those *mean* pills all the day long. You get them in the little capsules. And that's another thing about the practice of the

171

law. I was a dee-ay once, just starting out, an assistant dee-ay. But I'll tell you, friend, I was guilty of moral turpentine, I wiped out stains."

For just a moment he stopped speaking, leaving his mouth at the ready, and I saw the foam of saliva which all this talk stimulated. With an elaborate lean and smile he peered up the street toward a pretty, very young blond girl in tooled cowboy boots and jeans who was strolling toward us. At the same time a finny police car swung around the corner, and the cops pulled over to study the action. Fins had just come in. The girl moved to lay her head against Howard's shoulder. He dodged away. "Lisa Subterranean," he said, introducing us. "That's a funny name, ain't it? And this is my friend's friend, his name is . . . " Oddly enough, he had remembered my name. He listened even while he talked and kept his eye on the policemen. Lisa again tried to snuggle and he danced away as if she were stepping on his shoeshine. "Listen, honey, you see those fuzz over there? Let me explain it to you, as if you didn't know. Contempt breeds familiarity. All right, so be nice. I do not want any trouble. In my *mind* there is no trouble. So you run along home now and put on the coffee and I'll be there as soon as I finish cutting up a jackpot with this here friend of my friend—okay now, baby?"

The girl ambled off. The cops looked sad. One blew his nose noisily, wadded up the Kleenex, and dropped it in our direction. The other one took down his clipboard and sat writing nothing. Howard smiled at me and said, "Sometimes I think I got the bucket *and* the water, but the most of the time I just got the water, and it run through my hands."

Howard had several wives and many children; he had many girl friends; he was chosen more than he chose. He was a renowned expert. Self-selected disciples fell by the Bagel Shop and chose him to eat with them; he ate. Girls came by and chose him to befriend them; he gave them a meaning in life and a revenge against parents. He was a maestro without a baton, a guru before krispie gurus came in packages from India. But what he really liked was to converse, just the simple flow, as birds sang in those distant mornings before DDT. It was his art form—like sneezing for a frustrated cop. Later there were those who claimed that Lenny Bruce was a better talker than Howard, but in 1957 Howard took the single's championship at monologue, standing and indoor, strolling and outdoor. He also carried sugar cubes in his pocket, stolen from the terrace of Enrico's Coffeehouse, to feed to beatnik, Italian, and Chinese kids on the street. And it was said that he had written a children's book, *The Cultivated Young Person's Garden of Hemp*, but this was probably an example of the heavy exaggeration of the Grant Avenue scene in those days. *On the Road* had replaced Senator McCarthy as a source of awe.

In 1960 the Bagel Shop was closed down (hassles, energy loss); the fickle beatniks were exchanging their guitars and bongos for washer-driers; an interval of complaint was passing, and the period of protest, peace march, Peace Corps, and civil rights was on its way. The few beatniks still shambling in the streets were morose, lonely and astigmatic; they did not see that they were the sediment left by history. The San Francisco police, the end of the Eisenhower epoch, and the dynamics of their style had done in the holy barbarians. But there remained, of course, the nuts, the nostalgia-ridden, the rearguard tourists, and the traditional bohemians who assimilated some of the beat ways. So there was a certain continuity, anyway—bookshops, coffeehouses, jazz, chess, and Howard. And other elements—sketch artists, sandal makers, jewelry makers, future in-writers and out-patients, perpetual students, would-be sex fiends, drinkers and smokers and health-food addicts, livers on the cheap. And Howard carried on.

But Howard also moved forward with the times.

Howard had taken to painting and religion. Since the sidewalk outside the Bagel Shop was now much changed (a dress
shop had replaced the main office of the Beat Generation), he
began to paint as he had once loitered, forgathered, and talked
—with an intense passion which was both random and focused. Knowing nothing about painting, his style owed much
to "Prince Valiant" and other comic strips; but his subject was
pious. He planned a mural, depicting the Stations of the
Cross, which he hoped to wrap around the nave of Grace Cathedral. Bishop Pike must have turned him down; he per-
sisted, and found a storefront church in the Fillmore district—
"The Moh," as it is sometimes called—which is San Francisco's Harlem. The bishop of the St. Booth Church of God in
Every Soul, Inc., gave Howard the space on his walls. Howard
had to supply the paint, but in return would be allowed to use
the washroom for cleaning up afterward.

He painted the Stations of the Cross with Prince Valiant
Romans and peasants out of "Peanuts" and a Christ who
looked a little like Eddie Fisher. But of course this summary
description cannot do justice to the passionate glow of his intentions. He worked all day, every day, and for nearly a year.
Judas was white, Pilate was white, Christ was dark, and Mary
was black. Howard gave up his girl friends. "The flesh is willing," he said, "but the spirit is weak." He still took sugar from
Enrico's for the babies. He talked softly to himself, giving in-
structions, sketched cartoons and then projected them onto
the walls, and painted as if paint could save his life. Lord
knows how he ate. I think he borrowed some of the babies'
sugar.

Sometimes I went to visit him as he worked. He wore blue
jeans sawed off at the bottom, and padded about in bare feet.
He was speckled with paint in his hair, on his arms, and on his
grayish, horny toes. "Don't you get tired, standing up and
reaching at the wall all day?" I asked him.

"It's easier'n sitting down if you have hemorrhoids or piles, and I have hemorrhoids and piles," he said. "I wish you wouldn't bother me with jivey questions like this was a courtroom. You see that Judas?"

"Yes."

"Negative. You don't see that Judas."

But I did. Judas was white. "What about that Judas?" I asked.

"You don't see him because I have trouble getting the expression. I ain't very good on the expressions. They come out stiff and cold. I ain't got the water."

He may not have had the water, but he almost finished the mural. Somehow, in the story of the Cross, he included lilacs, ailanthus trees, dusty roads, breezes blowing, the country of the South. There were meadows and distant hills. You could almost hear music—harmonicas, guitars. In the foreground was enacted the tragic tale, overwhelming the dreamy past in his soul with a set of fierce panels which covered three walls of the church. Within the intense circuit of his painting, Holy Rollers rolled and barkers barked and a falsetto bass-baritone bishop shrieked curses and warnings at his parishioners, promising doom three times a week, once each on Saturday and Sunday evenings, with a matinee Sunday afternoons. Soon the minister, Bishop Willy Bedford, brought darkness into Howard's life, and rage and misery, and trouble without end.

Someone told Bishop Willy that Howard was a lawyer and a mess-up, some kind of beatnik legal nut, and that he would surely demand payment for his year's work on the Stations of the Cross. Bishop Willy roared with indignation. An artist? For God? Money? "Mammon, oh Mammon!" he howled. He howled this word so often that the deacon answered to the name and began sweeping, but this time Bishop Willy's decision against sin had immediate practical consequences. By executive order Howard was barred from the St. Booth Church of God in Every Soul, Inc.

Howard came to work the next morning to find the door

locked and three strong men waiting. They explained. He asked to use the telephone to call Bishop Willy. They explained again, and added that he could not use the pay telephone in the lobby. Mammon, the deacon, stood there with his broom to give the devil a jab if necessary.

Howard went to the record shop two doors down and called Bishop Willy. The bishop screamed "Mammon" at him. Howard, worried about the last problems of his mural, went home to brood. There were two important issues in his mind at this moment. He wanted to finish the Stations. And he began to fear that the bishop would have the mural painted out—ruining his life's labor, the vision and hope which had finally brought him regular hours and a sense of meaning. Even his speech had slowed down in recent months. He knew he was growing well, less sick; he was a mere sinner; the bishop had no right to deny God's will, working through him to create a masterpiece of art and a control on the flow of words. He could smell green and dusty roads when he painted; he was finding his way to putting human expression on the faces of Jews, Romans, Pharisees, women, judges. Bishop Willy had no such right.

He returned to the church the next morning, having spent a sleepless night conversing with himself, and again demanded admittance. "No," said the guards. Their arms in short-sleeved shirts were folded over their chests. No unnecessary violence was their collective plan. "Go 'way, man," said Mammon, choosing up sides with himself on the broom. Right hand won.

Howard heard noises within. Was some nonunion painter smearing pink wall paint over his Saviour? He thought he could hear drop cloths being dragged. He thought he heard laughter. Howard flung himself upon the guards, and without much trouble—his strength was as the strength of ten—broke through the line of mercenaries and past the deacon's broom. Inside, he bolted the door while they consulted without, on the sidewalk.

There was no one in the church. He had imagined the sounds of destruction and profanation. So much the better.

He ran cold water on his bruised hands, stirred up the thickened paints, and went back to work. Pilate's eyes gave him trouble. They stared but were not tormented, or they were tormented but did not stare. He needed both the staring and the torment in order to say what he wanted to say.

When the police came to expel him, there was a fight. "You gonna wuk me ovah?" he shouted at them from the window of the church. "Come on in heah, you mothahs, an' wuk me ovah." The parody of Southern speech must have been some little joke working in him almost without his knowledge. He fought them; they beat him, and used sharp jabs of their sticks in his groin when they had him pinned, in order to take the last fight out of him. The jab in the groin is good for subtraction in this problem of police arithmetic. Three of the arresting officers were Irish; one was a black man—new policy. The deacon, who had always hated the mess Howard made with his paints and brushes and drop cloths, tried to hit him with his broom. The police halted this infringement on their right.

Howard had made friends among the newspaper reporters covering North Beach. He was a charmer. Perhaps for this reason, he was released on his own recognizance a few days later. There was no precedent for the crime of painting the Stations of the Cross and resisting expulsion from a church. BEATNIK COMMITS HOLY TRESPASS ON WALL, said the early edition of the *Chronicle*.

The night after he was released, Howard returned to the church. He broke in—the lock had been changed—and lit up the whole building and stood surrounded at midnight by Jesus, Pilate, Mary, the Romans, the Jews, his Prince Valiant horses and chariots. Outside, the chicken and pork smells of Fillmore, and the angry traffic, and the shambling, ambling,

lazy, desperate life of the Moh. Here—the permanence of a
quest for meaning. He found his paints and brushes in the
men's room and went back to his wall.

This time when they came for him he had barricaded the
door. Also he had an automatic pistol, which he pointed men-
acingly from the high windows.

Consultation outside. It seemed ridiculous to use tear gas on
a mural painter. At the same time, it was an insult to the social order to let a crazyman turn an automatic pistol on anyone
he chose. It could be loaded. The gathering of experts bore its
complex fruit—sirens, loudspeakers, firemen, and trucks. Also
Dr. Martin Bubkin from the Mount Zion psychiatric clinic
nearby. At that time Dr. Bubkin was occupied in the divorce
courts by a wife who spent her happiest hours contemplating
the California community-property laws and thanking God
that he had decided to do his residence in San Francisco. (He
liked sailing and the hay-fever-free climate.) For his own reasons, Dr. Bubkin decided to try to settle matters with Howard
without human or property damage. Howard was persuaded
to admit the doctor alone through a side window. He crawled
through, puffing, out of condition.

"I might run amuck, Doctor," Howard warned him.

"You couldn't make things any worse for me," Dr. Bubkin
morosely replied.

For the first twenty minutes, Howard and Dr. Bubkin gos-
siped warily, complaining, keeping their deeper secrets, with
no real meeting of spirit. The automatic pistol followed the
psychiatrist's every movement. Then they got onto artistic
matters, and the trouble with women, and the relation of the
Jews to the crucifixion, and almost every topic that might occur to two intelligent, cultured young San Franciscans, except
that they never bothered to discuss homosexuality, drugs, al-
coholism, or Oakland.

"You know, Howard," said Dr. Bubkin, "you're the first

178

person I've been able to talk to in months. I've been nervous."

"You jes' sayin' that so's I put down this here gun."

"That's true," admitted the doctor, "but I mean it, anyway. However, I'd be much obliged if you would stop waving it at me. Also—how come you slip in and out of dialect like that?"

Howard, nervous himself, didn't want the doctor to be nervous. It still hurt where he had been jabbed by a club between the legs, where he had been insulted by the Philistine bishop, where he had been disbarred and discommoded and bored and made anxious by his life on earth. He thought he might explain about his many dialects and talking so much. They sat in a pew and chatted while the firemen and policemen peeked in the windows. Many man-hours of public-servant time were expended; no one interfered, though a captain of detectives offered his commentary: "Serve that goddamn shrink right he get plugged by a mad rampaging colored gentleman."

His style was altered in midsentence, due to the neutral presence of a bunch of old envelopes in the hand of the jazz critic of the San Francisco *Bay Guardian*. The other hand was writing with a soft lead pencil.

The police captain watched the hands and tried to talk at a convenient speed. He liked giving interviews. It was one of the rewards of public service, in addition to the tax-free bags of cash from bookies.

In the meantime, inside, Howard and Dr. Bubkin, good friends by this time, were speaking of the doctor's unhappy marriage and Howard's troubles with the shouting preacher. Both of them had found their art forms. Howard's was painting and conversation; the doctor's had been sailing and interpersonal communication. Neither had known the greatest success. The doctor had been forced to sell his Spinniker. Now they sat in silence, grieving; at last Dr. Bubkin sighed and inquired if Howard would mind giving up the automatic pistol and going out and getting committed to a nice clean insane asylum.

It didn't seem like much of an idea. Dr. Bubkin had little faith in it himself. He wasn't going to try to sell it hard to Howard, an artist and a good talker. Dr. Bubkin shrugged and let the matter drop.

"I guess so," said Howard, fatigued after the long day. Everyone has to make sacrifices in this vale of tears. Sailboats, machine pistols. It's lonely to be in conflict with society without institutional or ideological support. Even the college beatniks banded together. But no union for painters of the Stations of the Cross.

The crowd was hushed as, first, the doctor emerged, and then Howard. Dr. Bubkin squeezed Howard's hand, man to man, promised to see him soon, and handed him over to the police. They waited until the doctor drove off in his blue Chevelle convertible. Then they jabbed Howard between the legs with their clubs as preventative action against resisting arrest. He groaned and cried out, but bore them no animus. That, he knew, was the way of the world, and the cops could no more keep themselves from using their clubs after a period of strain than he could help his being a light mahogany in color. Negritude and coppiness are all part of man's fate—stations on the way to eternity.

From being treated as crazy so much, Howard began to act insane. His friend Dr. Bubkin did come to visit him several times, sitting on the edge of his bed and discussing life and assuring him that the occasional beatings to his groin would possibly cause no permanent harm and that he might even recover his virility. Then they discussed Dr. Bubkin's virility vis-à-vis his wife, or former wife. Howard urged Dr. Bubkin to stop thinking so much about sex and take up a hobby, such as

painting or girls. After giving the doctor advice, Howard felt
much better. He remarked to the psychiatrist, "Nice profession you got here.

"Yes, Howard. We strive to cure ourselves, and thus we get
it both ways. Paid, too."

Perhaps Howard's situation tended to close his normally
open nature. "You're getting paid for talking to me?"

"No, never mind, don't worry," said Dr. Bubkin. "You're
my hobby, like you said. Painting, girls, or good conversation.
I'd like to learn to be more spontaneous. Call me Albert."

"Well, that makes me feel better, Albert," said Howard.

"In you," declared Dr. Bubkin, "I am searching the I-thou
relationship well described by the distinguished German philosopher of Mosaic extraction, Martin Buber."

"Hi there, Albert."

"A communication without reason, Howard, but telling of
man's love for all nature, not excluding you. I don't think it's a
joking matter, Howard."

Howard wished that he could blush. A little more Caucasian on his mother's side and he might have been able to manage it. Several of his children, especially the ones by Helga
Swenson, knew how to blush.

"Spontaneous, you're so spontaneous, Howard," said Dr.
Bubkin. "Even your kidding is like that. I truly admire your
ability to kid spontaneously, Howard."

"There are many things I can't do," said Howard. "I'm limited by pigmentation, for example. Limited by all those limits."

Dr. Bubkin waited.

"Albert," he added.

Dr. Bubkin beamed. "Thank you, Howard, thank you," he
said. "Now let's talk about you."

But it turned out that Albert's visits didn't do Howard
enough good. From brooding about his inability to blush or

paint, from the contrast between their easy conversations and the rest of Howard's life—shock treatment, camisoles, soilers, guards, therapists, pills, failure all about him—he began to grow weary and depressed. It took the form of objecting to being kept in a ward with Negroes. Howard insisted on a ward for the mulattoes. He explained that he had nothing against Negroes personally, as such, so long as they kept their place, but he wanted to associate with his own kind. "We mulattoes don't want our sisters to marry Negroes," he explained.

A kindly guard interrupted his breaking up the furniture with the promise of a dime and phone call to Dr. Bubkin.

"I'm desperate," said Howard, "Albert."

"Look, Howard," said Dr. Bubkin, "you haven't got a sister in there with you. Ergo, this is not a reality problem, don't you see?"

"I'm going to rip out this telephone. But first, Albert, did your wife get custody of the sailboat and the library?"

"She returned my textbooks, kept the *Horizons* and *American Heritages*. I have to pay her for the sailboat. Look, Howard, don't do anything till I get there. I'm coming down to interpersonally relate to you right now, okay? Now, you wait right there."

But by the time Dr. Bubkin arrived, his friend had gone into a rage, a brainstorm, a fury, a paranoid decline. Shock treatment. He turned against life, friendship, and painting. This was because painting, friendship, and life itself had let him down. But insulin and/or electricity remained faithful. More treatment. He received a series of twenty-four, plus a strained back from a leather thong left unsecured by an attendant who had been distracted by Howard's pleas for mercy. The presiding doctor interpreted the attendant's error as a covert act of hostility produced by a passive—dependent, but aggressive—character disorder. He recommended group therapy for the attendant. But Howard now had a slipped disc, which made him seem a little less loose and easy when he hobbled through the ward.

After a while the state and Howard grew weary of each other. He became tranquil; the state was appeased. The art critic of the San Francisco *Purveyor* wrote an article about the mural, and so many white visitors came to the St. Booth Church of God, etc., that Bishop Willy, sensitized as he was to the demands of Mammon, decided not to paint it out. When this good news was brought to Howard, he reacted with neither delight nor curiosity. He had lost interest in painting—another sign of cure. "We sometimes use the word 'cure,'" the head of the Service declared at the Monday morning conference, "when what we mean is 'remission.' That right, Howard? How do you feel, Howard?" Howard stood waiting before the amphitheater filled with doctors, residents, psychologists, technicians, and their friends. He didn't answer back. "I would call this a good remission," the doctor said.

He was let out on weekend passes. Friends in North Beach housed him. One friend was the mother of several of his children; others were colleagues from the Bagel Shop days. They had traded in their unemployment; they had jobs and shaving cream; some had good jobs, after-shave lotion, talcum powder. But they were nostalgic and happy to see Howard again. Parties, quiet strolls down Grant Avenue, wry reminiscences about the good old days when lentil soup at the Enigma was occasionally supplemented by steak tartar at Enrico's, courtesy of a television producer or a visiting reporter. Bishop Willy reported no sign of Howard in the vicinity of the Stations of the Cross.

After a few months of trial visits to the outside world, Howard was released. He found a job as receptionist in a car wash. What the job consisted of was this: standing in the street with a large white rag, grinning and waving and flagging down motorists with the promise of clean windows and trim. But Howard, gradually regaining his wits after the cleansing action of shock treatment, liked to describe himself as a receptionist, like the girls out of Mills College who couldn't type but wanted to work in fascinating jobs in advertising or finance.

The years sped by. A bit of gray appeared at Howard's temples. He seemed well-adjusted to being part white; he bore no ill will against Negroes, Caucasians, or mulattoes; he accepted himself. He sent Dr. Bubkin a wedding present when he married his new wife in Tucson—an anthology of *The Best from Show*. They corresponded. Howard opened his own car wash on money saved and money borrowed. Dr. Bubkin took a small share as an investment. The business prospered. Howard gave special rates on sports cars because of their size. This was his contribution to the smog and traffic problems. He encouraged the purchase of smaller cars. It was evident that a soupçon of his previous reformism survived, but not enough to cause serious trouble or indicate unbusinesslike attitudes. He was accepted. Only occasionally did people remind themselves that he was a disbarred lawyer, a retired chief of the beatniks, an expert on the Stations of the Cross. Now he was a Black Capitalist.

He gave money to the mothers of his children when he could. The children were mostly doing well in school. Several of the mothers had married—one to a bearded photographer who told everyone how proud it made him that Howard was the father of his children. "Howard comes from better stock than me," said the photographer. "He's creative, intelligent. Eugenically I'm inferior, and I consider it my ecological duty to have no children. But I'm a good stepfather."

"Aw," said his wife. "Howard has flaws, too."

"No, dear," said the blond, silky-bearded photographer. "Flaws is one thing, but talents is another. You read the article on the murals, didn't you, dear? Actually, the camera is a secondary art form. Howard has gifted our kids with primary talents and inner strength. You can't beat that for getting ahead in life, dear."

Howard, who occasionally took tea with this happy couple, listened to the discussion with embarrassment. Since he couldn't blush, he took the children out for ice cream cones. He brought back a quart of lemon ice from the Safeway to cool off the parents. Then he continued on his route up Telegraph Hill to Union, where he had a child by a young lady formerly active in SNCC, now getting involved in Women's Lib. She usually wanted to talk to him about the Problem; she wondered if passive resistance is more truly vital than rock throwing; he sighed and put up with it for the sake of the child. It was his youngest, a boy aged four, and the apple of his eye. He held the boy on his knees and told him stories. He liked to baby-sit while the mother went out passive-resisting. Lately she went out Gestetnering—a revolutionary duplicating process.

These strolls among his old friends in North Beach turned out to make more trouble. Perhaps life itself, plus the risks of having a personality and a soul, were the undoing of Howard. After the end of the beat movement, the new San Francisco Bohemia and the old Bohemia and the debris of the beatniks conspired to keep North Beach green. Hip was beginning to happen. Two bookstores, the Discovery and City Lights, still operated on Columbus Avenue near Broadway, separated by the Vesuvio Bar, which advertised its slogan, "We Are Itching to Get Away from Portland, Oregon," and kept booths for psychiatrists who wanted to study the clientele. The drug of choice became methedrine sulfate, a stimulant which constricts the blood vessels, causing rich fantasies and impotence, a confusing congeries of sensation. The methedrine addicts would steal books from the Discovery, sell them at City Lights for a few cents; then the owners of City Lights would return the books, or vice versa. This was a service the rival bookstores provided for each other. Otherwise they competed ferociously.

Howard, who had a keen eye for illegality, asked the owner of the Discovery, "Why don't you turn in those speed freaks?"

"Well, you know," he replied.

Watching a thief at City Lights, he remarked to Kellogg Kim, the bearded Korean poet and critic, who guarded the cash register, "Look, Kellogg, another booster."

"Yep," said Kellogg.

"So call the cops!"

"Aw, he's part of the family," said Kellogg, plucking at his package of Rice Krispies as the meth head strolled out toward the Discovery, his belt lined with paperbacks of James Baldwin, John Updike, Wolfgang Kohler, and a Sierra Club book about *Some Nice Walks under the Condemned Redwood Trees*.

Philosophy was not dead in Howard even though he was part owner of a car wash. He began to argue the relevance of this tolerance of criminality. He admitted that to steal for food and drink might be justified under certain circumstances, especially in an economy of abundance, but to steal for drugs . . . Kellogg answered that it was not his task to judge the needs of another . . . Howard said the moral man must make decisions . . . Kellogg said he had another code . . . Howard derogated this code . . . Kellogg gently insisted . . . Howard gently insisted . . . Kellogg reinsisted.

At this point in the discussion they both paused to watch another book thief leave the store in the direction of the Discovery. For Howard this was the last straw. He asked Kellogg for permission to stop him. Kellogg said no. Howard gave Kellogg one more chance. Kellogg turned away and opened a copy of Lawrence Ferlinghetti's *The Alligation*, a book about alligators. Howard hit Kellogg on the nose.

Bleeding, Kellogg said to Howard, "Look, I'm a Buddhist. I can't hit you back." A spot of blood dripped from his nose. It lengthened and hopped nimbly to his beard.

Howard danced about, saying, "You got to hit me back, Kellogg. I hit you. I ain't no Buddhist, I ain't no gentleman neither."

"I'm very strong," said Kellogg. "If I hit you, I'll kill you. That's why I'm a Buddhist."

"Hit me! Hit me!"—dancing about and jabbing the air, knocking over the racks of paperbacks, backing into a pile of *Ramparts* and *Partisan Reviews*.

"I can't," said Kellogg.

"Hit me, you yellow-skinned Jap!"

"I'm a Korean. Call me a gook. I'm a Buddhist." Somehow the discussants had been showered with Kellogg's Rice Krispies. They crunched underfoot; they were stuck in the Korean's beard. It looked like a Zen wedding in Battle Creek.

"You mutherfur!" screamed Howard.

Kellogg wiped some of the blood from his nose and beard. He looked at the blood on his shirt. "This stuff stains," he said softly. "But you're a part of the family."

Howard began to cry. He was not touched; he was frustrated. The long period of abstinence from sex, violence, drink, painting, and garrulity had left him fatigued in his soul. If only he and Kellogg could have enjoyed a good old family quarrel, exchanging a few family blows, Howard might have been spared another painful encounter with the police. If nonviolence doesn't work, give a man some violence. When Kellogg refused to strike back, Howard went out and stood on the corner of Columbus and Broadway to weep. He attracted a crowd tired of watching the topless dancers at the Condor. *Look, black tears, black man weeps!* was the general view of matters. He sobbed, he mewled, he showed all the signs of despair. When the police tried to lead him away—the crowd was blocking traffic—he refused to go. They shoved and pushed; he resisted. He held on to the door of the chili-teria.

Oh-oh, there it goes again, a small voice within warned him. Voice unheeded.

187

He refused to enter the paddy wagon. Voices unheeded. More sticks to the groin.

A few days in jail, and then removal to Napa for therapy. Friends operated the car wash, but it went to pieces fast. Plumbing and finances all came apart. Howard's charm had kept people churning through for clean cars. The car wash passed into other hands. Howard seemed to be a permanent resident of Napa.

Nevertheless, he has attained a certain status as a patient. He enjoys weekend privileges. The last time I saw Howard, he was limping along Broadway with his friend Dr. Bubkin, who visits him whenever he comes to San Francisco. Howard is now a tall, gaunt, gray-haired man who looks like a mild bourgeois with his briefcase, his meticulous but shabby clothes, his tranquil smile and nod—*rational*. He doesn't have the rheumatiz, but he has a slipped disc. He talks a great deal again; it sounds as if he is doing it on purpose.

"I'd like you to meet my friend Dr. Bubkin," he said, introducing me.

"We know each other, Howard."

"I forgot. It's not fair."

"Anybody can forget things, Howard."

"I forget too much."

"Well, it'll happen that way, Howard."

He paused and looked toward the fog-shrouded Broadway tunnel. "I had girls, children, business. I had a painting—no, it was murals I did. I had lots of things. I used to be a lawyer. It's not fair."

"Well, what can you do?"

"I used to have the water, all I needed was the bucket. Now—"

The crowd near The Committee swept about us, students, tourists, lovers, hippie strollers filled with the joy of evening. A lovely blond dropout, maybe sixteen years old, was selling the *Barb*. There was the smell of woodsmoke and the sound of an amplified guitar. The Peppermint Tree invited dancers; the Balkan restaurant offered shish kabob, and baklava dripping with honeyed chopped nuts. Howard wore a tuft of cotton in each ear. He was protecting himself against the ocean damp.

"Now," said Howard, "I'm a mentally disturbed senior citizen. I'm a socially deprived. I ain't got the water."

THE OLDER WOMAN

A STORY

JIM STANFORD had gone to Berkeley because his name was Stanford. If his name had been Jim Berkeley, he might have applied to Stanford. He wasn't related to either distinguished family in any case, and a lot of his life was pretty casual that way, and he dropped out, and now he had the dropout mustache and a place on upper Kearny in North Beach and a job by the hour at the post office. He could walk to work. At work, he walked and sorted. He started out as a third-class sorter, but worked his way up to zip-code plucker. The sorting machines were sort of inaccurate, so he helped them along, doing the good work of helping junk mail find Occupant, doctor's bill find surviving patient or heirs, and only occasionally losing someone's social-security check in the grinding gears of the noncomputer.

It was a friendly scene at the Rincon Annex of the U.S.P.O. in San Francisco. Together, the civil service and the Republican party had made a high-level decision not to hassle the new generation too much on the night shift. They could smoke in the midnight streets, embers glowing between fingers, and wear their hair on the job. Of course, the day shift was another matter—meet the public with *hair?*—but Jim worked the late late show. All he lacked was a sense of meaning, a connection to real life—and heck, what right had he to ask so much?

So when he met Sheila . . .

But first, one more revealing touch of background: what if Jim's name had been Harvard, and so he'd have had to go to Yale? Or Michigan, and so Ohio? That was the kind of yuck he put up with out on the mail-truck bays, where he ate his lunch at 1 A.M., cool rear on cold concrete. It explains why he was a little bored with the life of integrity, too. He was available to the Sheilas of this world. The dudes with nothing but integrity and dope on their minds were sometimes monotonous in their kidding, it seemed.

So then he met Sheila, feminine star from another half-generation. She had both shallows and depths, and her skin was still good, with just those little laugh lines at the corners of the eyes, a smudge of turbulent nights beneath them; and though she was twenty-eight, she needed to be taken care of. When he was with Sheila, Jim, aged twenty-two, felt like a tiger, an antiestablishmentarian tiger with so much healthy integrity it sometimes made him feel faint and blurry in the head.

A tiger who also purred and loped by her warm flanks (blue jeans, white jeans, a funny wet-silk Peter Max frock), but very little chance for tiger roaring, due to the fact that she was loyal to her obligations and her true love. Then she started looking with judgment-wrinkled rather than laughter-wrinkled eyes at their mutual friend Jerry Fichter, the printmaker, the obligation with whom she lived. Jerry had spent the last two years doing a self-portrait, but he could never get the wood block right. During these days, nights, weeks, and months of travail, Sheila sometimes stood by Jerry's arm and said, "Um, um, good, that's good," but much of the time she was left to sit in the Trieste, drinking coffee with Jim. "It will be a portrait of Man," she said.

"Yes," answered Jim.

"You believe that?" she asked.

"You said it," he said.

"A loyal friend is what this world needs," Sheila said. "Do you think another cappuccino would be bad for the hypoglycemia?"

"Do you have sugar in the blood?"

"I get depressed, up and down, but no. Jerry has it, though. He uses so much energy cutting away at that wood and it comes out with a Beethoven mouth—"

"You're even loyal to his diseases."

"—instead of Man. I'm a woman, not a women's-lib," she said. "But buy me a cappuccino, please, sweet. Sprinkle some sugar on top."

One day they all gathered in Jerry's studio to look at the final version of the wood block. Ah, beautiful, both Jim and Sheila declared. They looked at it by electric light and by daylight, and as the afternoon wore into evening, by candlelight. He inked it and made a proof. They loved it. They said they loved it and they really did like it a lot. It looked just like Jerry—pouty, morose, hypoglycemic Jerry. It was pretty good. They thought it was okay, passable, a B plus. Beethoven's mouth and ears. He signed the proof *"Epreuve hors de commerce pour mon amour Sheila,"* and dated it, including the hour—10:43 P.M.—and gave it to her.

Sheila said thanks and hung it over the bookcase to dry. "Duh-duh-duh-*dumm*," she said (Beethoven's Fifth). Though it was only a proof, he had done it on fine Japanese rice paper. "Say, you got any Squirt?" she asked him. "Funny thing, I'm so thirsty."

Later in the evening they were in the kitchen eating spaghetti which Sheila had made, and drinking wine which Jerry had provided, and smoking grass which Jim had brought, when it turned out that Jerry did not love his self-portrait as much as they said they did, either. He disappeared for a while (time has no meaning). He was back in the studio (grass brings peace to most people, but not to every troubled spirit with Beethoven's ears). Sheila and Jim suddenly smelled smoke (heightened sensibilities).

Run, run, hurry, run.

Sheila and Jim ran the short distance into the studio. They felt as if they were pounding on a treadmill. Their whole lives passed through their heads and it all had some kind of meaning. When they got there, three yards away, the wood block was burning in the fireplace, wood shavings piled around it, fine rice paper for the starter.

Jerry was weeping. He felt like a failure.

Sheila said, "Oh, shit."

Jim went home. He had switched to days at the P.O., but he decided Jerry needed to be alone with his soul and with Sheila.

He went to bed and an hour later there was a knock at the door. Sheila. After Jerry had finished burning his portrait, he wanted to burn Sheila. He tried to hit her. Though she was not a women's-lib, she knew a little karate, just enough to get along. She had made her getaway, thanks to a purely defensive first-strike capacity (side of hand on windpipe).

"Take me in," she sobbed; "I'll be no trouble. Poor Jerry. Poor Jerry," she wailed. "But he's a brute, isn't he?" ·

"Come in," said Jim.

"But you know what? It wasn't very much of a portrait of Man, was it, Jim?"

This woman was cutting her losses, Jim decided. She was sad, but not all that sad. She really liked Jerry. She was too kind to break his Adam's apple. However, when a thing is over, these older women know how to cut their losses. Over.

"Mind if I crash? So tired," she said.

Emotion tended to tucker out his own generation, but apparently it also fatigued these older women.

She tottered to bed, the only bed. She swayed gently. She toppled. She fell asleep. Tousled long reddish hair, almost clean; a dewy, slightly worn fret at the eyes; damp, warm, barely parted lips. Deep breathing at a delicate, sexy, delightful and tender presnore level. Jim stood gazing upon her—a full-blown flower in disarray—and wanted to do something for her. She needed help. He also wanted to do something for himself. He needed help. He lay down beside her.

In her sleep she gave him a tender, grateful, nonkarate shove onto the floor. There were splinters. It was for his own good. She wasn't going to put out, so what was the use of his tormenting himself in his own bed?

She slept. Probably if she had known about the splinters, she would have made some kind of arrangement.

He made himself a pallet on the floor. (Sleeping bag, blanket, pillow from the Goodwill couch.) Wasn't there a song about that in another generation?

He woke up later and tried to climb in again.

Ouch.

He passed the night and early morning somewhat stiffly on the floor. A sleeping bag is okay, but a sleeping bag at the foot of one's own bed causes grief and tension. In those bygone generations maybe they were used to this sort of thing. When he got up to go to the post office, she didn't quite rise to shine with him. "Eggs, raisins, blood sugar," she murmured. He scrambled her some eggs with a side of raisins, she sat up with eyes half shut, ate, staring at the Sunkist maid on the front of the box, said thanks, and fell back down asleep. Her lashes were tangled and lovely. Life with Jerry had really given her the fatigues.

He sorted a bunch of mail that afternoon. Sublimation got a few nonzipped letters to their destinees almost as fast as the zipped kind. He hurried home to see if Sheila would still be there.

Sheila was still there and Sheila was still sleeping. He sat by the bed and watched her. Occasionally she would thrash about a little, apparently in an erotic dream. Her dream stirred him, but he couldn't crawl unasked into someone else's dream.

Most of the time she just breathed gently, refreshing herself with blessed Lethe. He was lethargic, too, and in the moments when she opened her eyes ("Hi, Jim. Really great you let me crash here") she barely gave him time to reply before she dozed off again. "I'm tired," she said. "But I'd sure like a bite to keep my blood sugar going."

Eggs, bread and jam, apples, raisins, canned cling peaches (heavy syrup, slurp), and once a cheeseburger, though Sheila, *gourmet dormante*, hibernating honeyfox, wrinkled her pretty little nose at the hiss and bluster of fat on the stove. Then she began to snore. He moved her head and she stopped snoring. She ate the cheeseburger, remarked, "Sleep has always been my escape, it's so refreshing," and disappeared into her own soul again, Jim watching by her side.

She promised him it wasn't drugs. It was just tired, plus depression, plus an old way out that worked. The sleep cure has been tried by the Russians, and probably by some Swiss, too, so why not Sheila?

"I thought the Russians used the yogurt cure," he said.

She didn't answer. She couldn't answer. She was asleep.

The Sunkist box was crumpled, but the bent and squeezed Sunkist maiden still beamed at Jim from the heap of bed-clothes.

Three days later, three shifts at the P.O. later, Jim came home to find the apartment swept up, the dishes washed, the laundry done, the pillows plumped, the bed made, and Sheila's rump sticking out of the fridge as she finished a last cleaning of shelves. It was Better Pads & Gardens time at Jim's place on upper Kearny. "What the devil?" he asked.

"Where do I dump this stuff?" she replied. She had wrapped the trash and dust in newspapers and piled it in a corner. "Of course, ecologically speaking, I'd rather recycle it for some use. But it'll make you sneeze if you leave it around. Spores, fungus—*yecch*. Hi, Jim, I'm rested now."

"I'm glad you feel better."

Now she was answering speedily, almost snippily. "I feel great."

"That's wonderful."

"Ah . . . feel . . . *good!*" she sang in a passable feminine imitation of James Brown. She looked deep into Jim's eyes. "Thank you for the eggs and everything," she said. "I got Jerry out of my system. I recycled him while I slept. You were so good to me, Jim—Jim?"

"What?"

She looked even deeper into his eyes. "It's time, Jim," she said.

They did it like dogs and cats, they did it like furry and fuzzy animals, they did it all over the place, and afterward Sheila cleaned up. It had been time and Sheila was grateful. They did it every which way and in others Sheila had forgotten to mention earlier. They did it in ways previously thought extinct, like dodos and auks. Being twenty-eight, she had a lot to say to Jim about how it was. She said it with her body. Dodos and auks were extinct but not forgotten.

Afterward they rested and she cooked, and then it started once again. About three or four days of this. Between times, Jim went to the post office and missorted mail. "I'd move in with you now," Sheila said, "what we've done together and all, but I'm already here." Not only did she move in a suitcase or two with a few clothes and shoes and things, but also there was her healthy, sweet-smelling, opulent body circulating about Jim in mysterious ways, like a tropical wind. There was her presence, her aura. He breathed it in and was a tiger.

"Hey, where'd you get those splinters?" Sheila asked him.

He was too sleepy to reply. Sleepy tiger.

"Poor Jim." But with a squeeze of two fingernails which hardly hurt at all, out slipped the nasty little prickles of lonely floor. No scars, no itch, and that sudden ease of release when an old splinter makes a quiet getaway. She went over his body in great detail to make sure there were no more anyplace.

"Hey, hey, not there—ticklish!" he said.

"Got to make sure," she said. "Got to be very careful. Can't always feel them with the fingertips, got to find them with the tongue."

He tried to lie still. It was hard.

"It's ever so much more sensitive, you know," she informed him.

They settled in together for a season of pleasure which was so much like happiness that it deserved the name. Call it happy. Happy Jim working in the Rincon Annex of the post office, happy Sheila staying home and shopping and cooking, happy two having a good thing together. Sometimes, for example, they would go strolling in the North Beach evening, just taking the world off the top. Once, near a redevelopment project, Jim saw an old hot-water heater sitting on the sidewalk. "Excuse me, I got to make a call," he said, stepping toward the boiler. Sheila began to laugh. The sky spun; urban-development sky of bricks and charred wood and damp city holes digging through old bottles and bay fill, the salt sea or earthquake bubbling beneath. He panned away from himself, eye of Jim watching eyes of Jim, and saw how Jim was tickling Sheila. Oh, she was happy with him. "Left over from a kidney transplant, are you?" he asked the boiler. "Hi, Sir or Madame from Venus."

Sheila leaned, loose with laughter, against the boiler. It started to sway. She staggered and fell in development gypsum and mud. The boiler clanged in another direction. Jim fell on top of Sheila.

But because it wasn't a movie, it was real life, they didn't do anything more just there. They went home to bed and did it. Project terrain is picturesque, scenic, and a great location; booms, derricks, and dust; however, it's a bit gooey and grainy and hard on the skin if you get into serious real-life love-making.

"Oh," Jim thought, "this woman Sheila has taken me out

of the sad and lonely movie of my life and put me in a happy revival of another time."

"It's not a movie, is it?" he asked her.

"Does it seem real?" she asked him.

"Yes." A dream time which had never yet been.

"Then don't ask so many questions."

He was puzzled because he hardly ever asked questions. He just lived along with her, singing along with Sheila. He lived along her freckled arms, her plumpness, her narrowness, her half-closed eyes and open mouth, following the bouncing balls. Sheila asked few questions—and he wasn't inquisitive. Still, they had much to say to each other. Despite her greater age and experience, she deferred to Jim's intellect. "When Cleaver says that about the problem—if you're not part of the solution, you're part of the problem—you know what he means, don't you?" she asked. Maybe that was a question.

"Yes," said Jim.

"I knew you did," Sheila said proudly.

They just didn't need a lot of words, was all. They understood about commitment, and no man an island entire of itself, and the need to take a stand. They were taking their stand. They were on their voyage. Jim knew not where it would lead, but the great explorers always had high hopes, distant imaginations, and a willingness to face what comes. So did the auks and the dodos.

One afternoon she went to a button store and spent half a week's salary (his) on funny sex and peace buttons. They looked like Costa Rican generals when they adjourned to the Spaghetti Factory for dinner after a late-afternoon tussle in the sack. Sometimes they did it on the floor, as if they couldn't wait. They were developing bruises, scratches, smudges, and bites, as if the Costa Rican general staff had bravely fought off an invasion of maddened kitties across the Nicaraguan border. Lucky thing they had spaghetti for dinner; Jim was too tired to handle anything with bones. He could get into the meat-and-

bread balls okay with the soft side of his fork. No, forks don't
have soft sides. His head was nicely softening. This bemedaled
Costa Rican marshal wanted to retire for the rainy season to
his ripe banana plantation high above Puntarenas. He ate the
meatballs with gratitude and was asleep before Sheila, giggling, could steer him into bed. "I like it that you look so
happy tired," she said. "A happy tired man, and I made him
so."

"Thus," sighed Jim, and slept.

The next evening Jim and Sheila were just strolling up
Grant Avenue, in search of nothing. Jim was under the oedipal
weather; he had received a letter from his mother in La Jolla,
reminding him that he had forgotten her birthday again.
Funny how stubborn she was: he *never* remembered her birthday. It was a whole year in between and that was a lot of time
for forgetting. But now Jim had a little idea: to buy Sheila a
friendship (if that was the word) ring; it would be a surprise
and she didn't expect anything and that's how it was best.
Dawdle, amble, and tickle. He swung around her on a parking
meter. He stroked her hair in a familiar way, just as if she were
the chick and he the older man. She smiled delightedly at
him, her warm, healthy, freckled skin glowing. No warning,
just pleasure.

When out of The Camels, a rough leather-trade drinking
establishment (vinyl trade, suede trade), a man's body shot,
propelled by the strict diesel lady who guarded the door and
stomped those who were crass, rude, unattractive, or vomited
on the fine polished mahogany of the bar. He sprawled on a
fender of a pickup truck illegally parked near the fire hydrant.
THE CAMELS IS COMING, said whorls of paint on the
truck. HELL'S COMMUNE. The man groaned, stood up,
stared with eyes widening at Jim and Sheila, and it was Jerry.
Jerry had just known unhappiness—getting kicked out of The

Camels by Miss Kim—and now he saw happiness: Sheila and Jim. And somehow it was not his fault. And yet he had given Sheila up to Jim. Well, not exactly, was the way he must have felt about it. His lips were compressed. Beethoven. He had given her up, sent her out, packed her away, but that meant he wanted to send her into oblivion. She had no right to get healthy and happy and blushing so pink with his former friend Jim Berkeley or Stanford or whatever he said his name was. Jerry wanted Sheila out of his life completely, not neatly into his good friend's life. That was, Jerry seemed to feel, unfriendly of them both to get so cozy together.

"What you looking at me for like that?" Jerry yelled.

"I'm not looking," Jim said. Kim was also looking.

"For like that?" Sheila inquired, bemused that she could ever have cared for this preposition-crazed grammarian. Who took so long to make a wood block which he then destroyed. Because in his vanity, which he had plenty of, he cared too much for some ideal vision of himself, *yecch*.

"Just passing by, was all, Jerry," Jim said.

"You think I'm an idiot, don't you?"

"No, no," Jim protested. "Not at all, Jerry, I like you a lot and admire your talent."

"Yes, he does think you're an idiot, Jerry," Sheila interrupted. "You are, a little, you know. But I'm sure it's not your fault."

Jerry was an artist, and reality often troubled him. Jerry was an artist, and simple declarative sentences, like Sheila's, made him want to strike back. Jerry was drunk, but he didn't want to hit Sheila again—after all, it had turned out badly last time, it turned out she came to be happy with his friend Jim—so he struck out wildly (oh, *pow*) at Jim, and Jim fell toward the sidewalk.

"Ouch!" cried Sheila. She strained something catching Jim. She broke the fall, but she felt a sharp crick in her back. "Ouch, ouch, you crud!" she cried.

They both knew she meant Jerry. Jim was up in a rapid scramble, barely bruised, thanks to Sheila, and onto Jerry like a tiger. A tiger doesn't just make love; he also protects his territory and his mate.

P.O. tiger fights the Beethoven gorilla. Blood and blows and yells out there in front of The Camels—real name, The Camels Am Coming—a rockier bar for heavier street people. Diesel Kim cocked her head and gave the fight a B minus. "I've seen better in the ladies' room of the Atlantic Richfield," she said to Sheila. But it wasn't bad; that's an above-average ladies' room for fights. The drinkers inside The Camels went on absorbing their boilermakers. "A shot'nabeer," someone said.

"Shot'nabeer, right here," the bartender yelled through the tumult.

Dieselly Kim, the friendly girl bouncer, was holding the swinging doors open so everybody could enjoy the action out there on the sidewalk. This is the Wild West, isn't it? And, slugging and slugging and being slugged, Sheila dancing around and trying to get a hold on Jerry, Jim heard the word *shotnabeer* like a war cry above the Rolling Stones whine from inside the accoustical cave. Drunken and sad, Jerry groaned bitterly as Jim hit him about the liver, stomach, face (Kim said, "No, a B plus"); Jerry morosely punched at Jim's liver, stomach, and head, indicating with low grunts a complaint about the difficulties of felling a man with bare fists when they are evenly matched and old friends, the troubles of love and art. Once Jim toppled him back through the door of The Camels and Sheila cried out, "You're great!" and a voice from inside answered, "You're a good kid, whyn't you go play basketball someplace else?" as Jerry came revolving out, sped by a kick from the bouffant hair-spray diesel guarding the door.

"I threw her out, anyway!" Jerry bellowed. He meant Sheila.

"But now everybody's throwing you out," Sheila remarked. The two exhausted battlers swayed and rocked against each other. It's isometrically taxing to keep slugging when neither party goes down for the count. Jerry and Jim looked haggardly into each other's eyes while Sheila yelled to hit him, hit him, finish him off. Muscles in upper arms twitched which are seldom used in normal city life. *I can't,* they both were thinking.

"Say, it turned out surprisingly good, developed nicely by the end of round two," Kim said. "By the way, what you doing a little later on, Sheila?"

Swinging red Cyclops'-eye atop the squad car heading in slow motion through the traffic of upper Grant. "Let's split," said Sheila.

Jerry was discouraged, anyway. He rounded the corner, shirt in shreds.

Jim considered himself the victor, and so did Sheila. He leaned burping against the pickup truck while she said, "Oh God, now it's sour-stomach time. But you're beautiful, Jim, you did it for me. Now let's get out of here."

It was a fine alley-warm night in San Francisco. She salved his wounds, though he wouldn't let her put lettuce on the bruises. She said it was cooling—folk remedy. Spinach would be cooling, too, and maybe it was even mentioned in the *Whole Earth Catalogue,* but he preferred ice and the cool touch of a woman's hand. Whoops. He forgot his hurt. It was only physical, anyway. The emotional hurt of loneliness and twenty-three had been far worse. Nice Sheila. Sweet Sheila. Tenderly stroking Sheila. Oh, good.

In the morning she said, "It's time," and packed up to move to Phoenix.

Why did she want to leave him? He was twenty-three already; she was still only twenty-eight. But she felt like a woman, he felt like a kid to her. She knew that scene would make trouble later: keep him from growing up, or give her up when he came to a new stage. It wasn't exactly May-December, but it was June-July. She was a stage on life's way to young Jim Stanford.

"No, no, not like that at all!" he said.

There was gravity and calculation in this generous but sleepy lady, too. And she believed Phoenix would be her San Francisco anew, now that S.F. no longer was. She seemed to have plans which he didn't know about. Probably she didn't know, either. She explained further, "It's time."

"No," he said. He didn't like to tell her how much he wanted her. There was a space-shot confusion in his stomach at the thought of losing her, and a spacey sense of meaninglessness in his head—distant whirrings and hummings when he tried to say just one word: "Nnn—" and then, "—o."

She wept. "You know what I'll do when I get to Phoenix? I'll sleep, I'll just sleep, I'll miss you so."

She smothered her yawn already.

He thought: She'll find a man and then she'll sleep and then she'll get her strength back and then, in her grief, she will tell him, "Time, buster."

"Why Phoenix?" he asked.

"Dry climate," she said.

"Why leave me?" he asked one more time.

"No fungus, spores, or allergies."

"*Why leave me!*"

"It's time," she explained patiently.

It was odd how having been beaten up for her the night before, and then having made great love all night long, seemed to deplete a fellow's emotional responses. It committed him to her, but then, he was tired. He stood by while she packed. She hummed and smiled and said she needed no help. She said she liked him a lot, but it was time for a change. Maybe it was the half-generation gap. She would write to him, perhaps daily (he didn't believe that). She would never forget him (he absolutely believed that). She called a cab to take her to the bus station and advised him to go to work, to sort lots of mail, and to put her out of his mind; and above all, in case he had any doubts, to stay away from girls like Kim at The Camels. She kissed him. "Um, good," she said. "Jerry used to wipe his lips before, or maybe it was after. You kiss better. Bye-bye."

To tell the truth, the first days were calm and sunny ones. He felt uncrowded, free, and energetic. The spacey feeling was that of an acolyte in loneliness. His sexuality flowed back and made him very alert; early horniness was a vivid pang, like strong coffee. He must have been too young for so much re-sponsibility, especially the care and feeding of an older woman, because he valued his boyish, monkish isolation in an apartment on upper Kearny which suddenly seemed nicely roomy again. He might even remake his friendship with Jerry, an artist whom he admired, with those handy, trustworthy Beethoven ears.

When the itch became an ache he wrote a letter to her; and when the ache became a pain he found another girl, a kid, a nicely kiddish person his own age. "Oh, that's dirty," she said. "I like it, where'd you learn that?"

"From an older woman," he said, grinding his teeth.

"She must have been a great chick." Then suddenly Sharon sat up in bed. "She wasn't like *sixty*, was she? I mean older, but you're not a creep, are you? Fifty-five? Fifty?"

"Twenty-eight," he said, interrupting what he was doing.

She flopped back down. "Creep. I'm jealous. Ooh, go on, I'm so jealous, make it up to me, honey."

He missed Sheila terribly. In the mornings, when the Shar-ons left (then Karen, then Gail, never Kim), he missed Sheila; and in the afternoons and evenings, whatever shift at the P.O. he sorted on, he missed Sheila through erroneous zip codes, packages containing bits of things which worked their way out of the wrappings, postage due and incomplete cancel-lation. He started to make more mistakes than the civil-service inspectors could approve, so they put him with the stoned contingent on the baggie detail, rewrapping packages mailed from Mexico and the Middle East after they were examined for grass, coke, speed, mescalin, hash and hard stuff. His colleagues were a sleepy crew, mostly having nervous breakdowns, at the brokedown phase, and they didn't talk too much. While he put the approved debris into baggies to be forwarded faithfully to addressee, through storm and dog, strife and leg-weary route walkers, he would think of Sheila and miss her more. Which he did, more and more.

One day he got a letter from her. "You son of a bitch," it said, postmarked Phoenix with no other enclosures. "What am I going to do now?" She was pregnant. He had always thought she was using the pill, but maybe she had gotten scared or not used it enough or decided, at age twenty-eight, that maybe she shouldn't any more. Was it his fault? "You son of a bitch and bastard," she wrote. He guessed it was his fault.

He went around to his bank where he had a few dollars, the rent money, something for his mother's next birthday in case he remembered; and then around to a few friends where he had never borrowed money; and then he went around to Western Union and wired the money to Phoenix.

Then he got another letter from the hospital where she had had it taken care of. "You angel, you're an angel, I love you," she wrote. "Everything's fine. No hassle. Of course I'm hurt inside emotionally, but I don't feel it. I feel fine and happy and thank you so much darling you're a sweet darling love Sheila."

She was a winner. He thought of taking the bus to Phoenix to see her, but he had no money, no savings, and no prospects to borrow any for a while now. He intended to pay everyone back. He also looked up Dilation & Curettage in a medical textbook and felt much wiser with all the things he was learning about life, thanks to Sheila both present and absent.

Her sudden flow of mail (you bastard, you angel, you love, you son of a bitch) was keeping him a little off balance; but she had kept him kind of balanced when she was with him, and his finances were a bit off balance now, too, but perhaps he owed it to her. Though far away in spirit and flesh, she was nevertheless present in hurt. He could see why Jerry flipped out over her. Now that wounds had healed on all sides, except for one peculiar permanent black-and-blue mark on Jim's cheekbone, they occasionally had a beer together and talked about the woman they loved. They never got into the matter of whom *she* loved.

It was nice having Jerry around, someone to talk about Sheila with, someone who understood about her. In addition to the bruise on Jim's cheekbone (Jerry), there was a monkey bite on Jim's shoulder (Sheila). Once they decided to meet at The Camels and Kim said, "Say, whatever happened to that yummy old lady?" So afterward they usually met at the Minimum Daily Requirement.

One day after Jim had finished putting all his memories and souvenirs into one crate—snapshots of Sheila, letters from Sheila, a Zigzag cigarette-paper folder and a pair of panty hose and an empty box of Sunkist raisins, little things like that— not to mention the memories which were all permanently stored in his head—another message arrived by the magic of the U.S. hand-delivered (sometimes) postal service. Printed. An announcement. Sheila was getting married. No, look again at the date and study it sullenly. Sheila was already married. It *seemed* that he was being invited to the wedding, but in fact she had sent one of the extra announcements after it was over. It looked like an advanced flower ceremony in the desert, guitar music, hand-composed ceremony, tie-dyed minister hung with lovebeads and quoting from Bertrand Russell and the Doors . . . Oh, she's really gone now, it hurts.

Jim got drunk for the first time in his life. No sense in picking a fight with Jerry or anybody, but at last he really understood how Jerry felt. Hangover, despair, awful desire.

He had Excedrin Headache Number One Thousand Six Hundred and some. He would take a Compoz for it, and if that didn't work—off the Golden Gate Bridge.

A few days later another letter, this one handwritten, complicated, with that funny punctuation of Sheila's—triangles of dots, so: ∴ , and dashes and arrows, trying in Sheila's way to control his breathing and his heart's rhythms—making Jim read the letter over two or three times before he could sort it out. She really cared for him. She was married. She cared for him, but she loved her husband. She was pregnant again by her husband. But she cared for Jim. And she felt sad about the hard time and the money and the baby they didn't have. No matter what they felt about the ecology of it all, O tempera! O population control! Their upper-Kearny baby haunted her dreams. And since she was pregnant now and it was her husband's child, there was no problem. She would come to San Francisco for a weekend and stay with Jim. To make him happy. She only wanted to make him happy. And then he could kick her out first thing Monday morning. Well, she had to be home, anyway. P.S.: The reason she was coming that particular weekend—oh, you know, Stan's mother in Des Moines and it would be such a drag for her to go with him to see somebody's *mother*, even if the someone's mother happens to be your very own mother-in-law . . .

Arrows, dots, double equal signs ≡, and, for some reason, a Christmas tree full stop.

Eeek, Jim thought, like a boy goosed in the shower.

That wasn't very masculine of him, so he thought instead, Oh no, she can't pay me back that way. Enough! No! She says there's no harm in it because she's pregnant already, but no harm in it! No, no, no! No! Removing the heaped-up dot triangles and the funny curved arrows, and it still came out to Oh God, messy.

He reached her on the telephone. He neglected to think of the trouble if her husband answered, but it was okay. Stan had a daytime job. "Don't come! No! I miss you, but no! You can't! Don't! Please!"

She listened thoughtfully as he failed to make many complete sentences. She was humming to herself in Phoenix as he begged her with all the love in his heart to stay away from him in San Francisco. "I think I understand," she said at last.

"Thank you," he said, thinking it would be even better if she joined Women's Lib.

"You don't want me," she said.

"Thank God."

Pause. San Fran to Phoenix daytime person-to-person rate.

"But you're wrong," she said with finality.

"*What?*"

"You've got to face your feelings, which are facts, Jim. You can't avoid your risks like that. You can't miss out on your deep experiences."

He was getting physically aroused, just hearing her calm, sure, husky voice, and he was pleading with her to stay away. But he could imagine the spermy squiggle with which she would underline *deep*.

"You can't avoid what you really want, Jim . . ." Laughter, haha. "Especially when I want it too, so much, Jim . . . I'll just come to your place from the airport."

And she hung up.

Jim thought of moving out. He thought of going far far away. He thought of hiding under the bed. He had heard of pregnant women and their funny feelings. He knew no good could come of it.

He knew he would wait. He tried to figure out the meaning and moral of the experience he had had, Oh Lord, he was still having. Every older woman is younger than some other fellow. No, that's nearly it, but not quite.

She was knocking at the door.

He was answering.

Come in, complication.

LETTER FROM A FAR FRAT

1

WELL, the fraternity house still exists. I almost thought it went out of fashion with Dick Powell and Jack Oakie and the great homecoming games of early M-G-M musicals, but by golly, the old beer-spraying, girl-harvesting, ear-splitting article can still be found on, say, the campus of the University of North Carolina at Chapel Hill, which is an excellent school with high standards. Since I was a guest in the house, I'll invent a name for it, Kappa Lambda Pi.

Okay, on a Saturday night the fine old lovingly demolished mansion is surrounded by MGs, Sprites, American convertibles; the lawn is covered with heartbreakingly . . . beautiful? well, cute— It's covered with girls, and weaving about the girls are the boys, casting their spell, making time. The band is an amplified rock group, good strong sound, tough and nonpsychedelic, out of Carrboro or the country surrounding—black, of course, and no one else is. The hospitality is immense and genuine. They are lovingly demolishing the place by hand; it's a local craft. Echo says, and echo replies: "Have a beer, have a brew. Here, have a swig. Hey, sir, have a drink of mine. Aw, come on, have fun with us, sir."

The boys of KLP are celebrating losing a game. On other nights they celebrate winning the game, or rush week, or the water shortage, or exam week, or the visit of Spiro T. Agnew to Raleigh, or it doesn't make any difference. The faucet in the kitchen is never turned off. Since there has been a prolonged drought, and a crucial water shortage which threatens to shut down the school, it has seemed a fine joke to some good old boy to get out of various academic problems by doing his best to drain the lake. Some of the would-be adults in the house think this is childish behavior ("he hadn't ought to do like that") but it's a matter of esprit de corps. It would be finking on a good buddy to interfere. When one fellow twisted the faucet shut, his good brother got red-eyed and sore, silent, but that's the limit of it. Well, it really means something to him, that water-lover. Hurtie tough-titty feelings. Anyway, they might get the emergency pipeline from Chapel Hill to Durham in time to relieve the reservoir. And in a democracy, every man should be free—shouldn't he?—to decide whether or not the town has any water.

During the festivities which I attended, sex and politics were the prime subjects. So far, so good. I've heard of them. Water and studying were a distraction from real life. The future is a slightly disagreeable consequence of the present, following it by association as "liver" follows "cirrhosis of the." The smell of beer, which I thought had disappeared from campuses, is making its last stand in North Carolina. Beer was a stranger to me (I've spent a lot of time on California campuses, but anyway, according to the *New York Times*, October 26, 1968, "Beer consumption per capita has dropped 2 to 2½ per cent in the last two years"). A tall, sandy, snub-nosed brother called Boyce explained about things: "We can't be too cool, man. We can't operate like them Ivies, you know, smoke a joint and then zap her upstairs. We got to plan and work out a three-stage campaign, not like those Ivies up north, man. I prepped at Lawrenceville, I skied in Colorado, so I had that experience, those Ivies. We got to work a three-stage campaign—not cool, man, not like those Ivies, man, sir."

"I understand," I said, almost understanding.

"First stage, we got to dance a little, get 'em a little slushed up, you know, hot, not like those Ivies. That's first stage. Love 'em up a little. Then second stage: into the car. Sir, let me explain, that's trouble, getting 'em out of here and across the parking lot into the car. Now, they want it as much as we do, don't misunderstand me, sir, just like those Ivy girls, they want it, but they stumble, they make it tough crossing the parking—okay, into the car, man. Then we have these apartments in town—"

"You mean you can't take the girls upstairs?"

He looked at me, shocked at my presumption. He offered me a swig from his can. He defended Southern womanhood. "Here?" he asked. "In the house? In front of all everybody?"

"I'm sorry," I said.

"Well, we drag 'em out the door and through the parking lot. Course lots of times they yell and scream and laugh and throw up a lot, but we get 'em out, because they want to as much as we do, you know, that's human nature. So then we get 'em to our apartments in town—oh, maybe three-four of us share an apartment—and then . . ." A grin lit up his face. It was like the sun rising over Georgia. "Man, can I just tell you what I did to that little girl over there—see, that one? No, not that one, sir—you like her? Cindy?—no, the one next to Cindy."

He pointed to a little flower of Southern womanhood stubbing out her cigarette against the veneered wood atop the TV.

"You don't know her, do you? So it's all right if I tell you. But listen, sir, if you'd like to meet her . . ."

First, however, he described stage four in the three-stage plan.

I was also interested in his political views, but first we got involved about this girl.

Oh well, I have prurient interest, too.

"Come here, honey," Boyce called to the girl (not Cindy). She came over, mussed and sulky, with a great hair-collector's mane of yellow hair, and then shot me that marvelous, easeful, flirty Southern smile which nice girls down there give not only their men but also girl friends, pregnant ladies, small animals, and the short-answer questions on a nursing exam. She had liquid brown eyes, lovely, hysteric eyes, soft stalks with contact lenses perched atop the irises. "I just been telling him what we did t'other night, honey."

"Went to the movies," she said.

"No, not that night—"

"Saw *Disaster Angels* with a revival of camp classic *Suddenly Last Summer*—"

"No, the next night, night we had the party."

"Oh Boyce, you're a . . . you're a . . ."

He grinned while she suffered her failure of vocabulary. But she seemed about to cry—hysteric, remember?—so he apologized gently, saying, "Aw, honey, don't carry on like that. I didn't show him the Polaroids."

I realized that I was getting mired in interpersonal relations and it would be better all the way around, including my development as a thinking human being and a visiting writer, if I heard some of their views on wider topics. It took no time at all to find a group of men tired of dancing, resting from beer, without dates or with their dates passed out or having disappeared through the parking lot with their good buddies. As for many men, politics is sometimes a substitute for other work in the world.

2

FLOYD JONES is an activist. He has been to Europe on his summer vacation. He thinks about local option and states' rights (positive). Hair and hippies mash around in his emotions (negative). In Europe he noticed the happy faces in West Berlin, the unhappy ones in East Berlin, and that settled Communism for him. It was all clear now, Roger and over, and this led him straight back to American politics. "I met these German men in a bar," he told me, "good old boys, spoke good English, said why don't we kick the shit out of

those hippies and draft-card burners." He had discussed everything from Vietnam to race with those happy faces and they
compacted together that Communism must be stopped.

Our conversation took place during the heat of the last presidential campaign, just after a Northerner, Curtis LeMay,
native of my home state of Ohio, had been chosen to assist
George Wallace in his mission. "He's a good old boy," said
Floyd, as the dancers flailed about us. The cigarettes were
falling into the carpet, the fastidious were drinking out of
plastic-foam cups, the forthright were drinking out of their
cans, and the group had me backed against the color TV. The
sound was turned off, but the light show flickered and spat-
tered against the screen. I reached behind to turn it off so
that the radiation wouldn't catch me behind while the vocal
emanations and renditions took me afront.

Floyd is the only man I know who was overjoyed by the
three major candidates for the Presidency. Hubie was a good
old boy, loyal to Lyndon, a virtue all in itself, and of course
Wallace had the clearest and finest ideas, but personally Floyd
was voting for Mr. Nixon. It was a class thing, he felt; a duty
to live up to the word "responsible"; and Mr. Nixon's
speeches nearly brought tears to his eyes. They were that sincere. Also, he hoped he'd kick the shit out of those draft-card
burners and long-haired hippies.

"You really like all the candidates?"

"They're loyal Americans, aren't they? That's what I ask
of a man."

I offered some objections to Floyd and the others, but
mainly I tried to play Socratic Method. Questions: Is this a
happy country? Do you really think more weapons for the police are the "answers" to law and order? What is your conception of America's role? One very tall, horn-rimmed young
man, with a look of poetic angularity about him, hung on my
words and I thought I had an ally. He too seemed puzzled by

America circa 1968. He suddenly burst out, "Wha yò so gol-darned negative? What is this negative bit?" Astonished by his own anger, he added, "Sir?"

A few girls had joined us. One of them was Cindy—eyes afire, that old golf-club menace in them. There was some kick-ing and giggling going on below the level of the conversation. It was stage one and a half of the campaign, I decided, not like those Ivies.

I must have asked a question, because the sensitive-looking brother burst out, "Course I wouldn't kick the shit out of 'em! I just say that!" Then he smiled shyly. "Wouldn't want to get my shoes dirty"—and nudged me. "Aw, sir, I just say that. They got the right to free speech, too, so long as they don't go tearing down this country. You're not always so negative, are you, sir?"

It was time to be their buddy, I decided. I too had done my term at Fort Bragg and elsewhere, though this was before their birth. I reminisced about Fayetteville, North Carolina, which we called "Fagleberg."

"You mean Fayettenam?" Floyd asked. "When they call me there, I'm going. If they cancel my deferment, sir, I'm go-ing. But I'm going to try to finish my education first and get into a good position, and if the Lord is good to me I won't have to fight. I can tell what you're thinking, sir. I got strong feelings. But like I already explained, killing's just not in the American line."

He was wearing tight maroon pants and a white button-down short-sleeved shirt with notched vents at the sleeve. One of his Hush-Puppies was unlaced. He leaned on me a little, partly out of friendship and desire to be understood, saying, "Now, don't get me wrong, hear? They call me, I go. I got this deferment, no gol-darned evasion."

"I'm not a pacifist either," I said.

"But I never did meet any Marine from Veetnam commit-

213

ted an atrocity who enjoyed it, hear? Hear me, sir? We just got
to defend the American perimeter, it's as simple as that. So I'll
go, I'll go, sir, soon as they call me."

When it came time to part, two of the brothers insisted on
walking me home to the Carolina Inn. It had rained gleaming
flip-top Burgie friendship rings on the Carolina earth. The
brothers scuffed along, bumping and uneasy about the discussion. The men of the KLP House have a complex feeling
about life—a minority on this campus, a majority in their own
hometowns, but are they a majority in America and the
world? It is no longer easy to find the tides of right, and float
back and forth on them. Kappa Lambda Pi is in trouble as a
way of life.

There was a shy moment in the fragrant Indian-summer
evening, hot rods and flowering trees and sweet echo of amplified rock from the Carrboro Rhythm Ramblers. Something
had been left unsaid. Some generation gap had been left ajar,
some culture gap unclosed, some stony silence in the meta-
physics. We all wanted to be close and warm, and yet we were
not close and warm. We had kidded around, but what else? In
a world of making out okay, and getting bugged by it, we had
made out all right, and gotten bugged by one another, just like
the Ivies; and yet there must be something more than paltry
victories in love and politics. There might be, for example, real
victories. Stage five. Stage six. Stage seven.

On another part of the campus the 1 A.M. showing of underground art flicks was just beginning, and the Dandelion, a
head shop, was just closing, and the Racial Confrontation
group was continuing out under the famous Davie poplar. As
we walked by, a tall black man in a denim suit, a refugee from
Resurrection City, a pioneer of Freedom City, was smiling and
saying softly, "We're sick of trickeration; we won't stand still
for extermination, so we got to have communication"; and an
earnest young white student said, "But we got to talk it all out

first so's not to frighten the other people"; and the man from Resurrection City said, "Son, that's trickeration . . ."

One of my escorts shook his head, grinning. "Man oh man," he said to me. Some of these jerks were beyond his comprehension.

All over the campus the gritty Indian-summer smell of autumn leaves was helping lovers and celebrants and reformers and late-night scholars fix the memory in their hearts, whether they knew it or not: *This is it, this is it, this was college in my time.*

As we walked along, beer fizzing in the jiggled cans, a member of my honor guard said, "It's just, sir, we didn't want you to get the one-sided impression about this school."

"I appreciate your hospitality," I said.

We were standing near the rocking chairs on the porch of the Carolina Inn (widows, conferences, and faculty visitors). "Don't get us wrong," he said. "We have strict rules at the House. We don't always live up to them, but we try not to be litterbugs. We might be tarheels and we got a lousy team, but we have fun, too, sir." He gazed wearily back across campus to the traditional Davie poplar famed in song and story. Chapel Hill's little Berkeley was still strolling and consulting near that spot. "—Just didn't want you to go away thinking we're all a bunch of stupid intellectuals."

Often I have felt out of touch with great, true-hearted, straight-arrow America for being a weirdo artist with irregular habits. And then, with hardly any transition, I have felt out of touch for having wife, station wagon, baby, when everyone else is warlike and weird, taking peculiar chemicals and living a fantasy of youth. But at the time this story took place, middle-aged and set in my ways as I must have seemed—reliable, paternal, with credit cards—I still had that beard.

The potential for random violence in America, a weight of chagrin and loneliness which leads to cruel excess, is not hidden even from families which travel in station wagons, with the newest Procter & Gamble paper diapers. There is the radio news, and the normal chance everyone takes by either going outdoors or staying inside. Who cannot tell many tales of how he almost died, almost killed someone? Random violence, like brain damage and storms in the metabolism, may seem like an act of God. This is a name we give our ignorance. How to name the nameless, make a model for the random? First of all, we must meet the trouble without flinching. There are the crazies, right there—and in the mirror.

AN EVENING WITH A BEARD IN JOPLIN, MISSOURI
1

WE STOPPED for the night in a motel on Route 66—station wagon, baggage, man, wife, infant child. Hypnosis of highway, anxiety of a day at the wheel, queasiness of too much coffee, and the decelerating relief of finally arriving at—what?—a mark on the map. A shower eased the shuddering fatigue of five hundred and twenty miles since morning. And then my wife and I went for a walk with our three-month-old in her collapsible stroller.

Joplin is, itself, a place on a road, a place in the history of the mid-south, the mid-west, mid-elsewhere (Mark Twain in books I've read, memories of the war in troop trains I rode, shuttled, sidetracked, stared at by farm girls in skirts down to their shins); and also it was a land out of all time, warm and humid, cut free from routines, a new life for one night only as we floated unequally between home in California and a destination up ahead and eastward.

The ceaseless cars and trucks sped past on Route 66. My wife spotted the muddied THIS TRUCK PAYS OVER $3,257 IN TAXES, which we had first overtaken, heaving and snorting, near the Arizona border. It was a fat and sickly taxpayer, rocking on its shocks, belching exhaust. Well, it had the jump on us now, and would disappear into St. Louis or Chicago before we were awake in the morning.

A few blocks down the road we found a restaurant—hot, nearly empty, furnished in franchise pub style, cast iron and red leather and black leather and a painted wooden coat of arms centered neatly in the front window. It had once been a truckers' diner; now the city had grown, and it was the place where the discriminating of Joplin could meet the top gourmets of Route 66. It was Chez Vico's now. Eggs-over-easy eating was replaced by a décor for Maine lobster, flown in from South Africa, and Chicago cuts, guaranteed from Chicago. Our host, Vico himself, greeted us at the door. Pencil mustache, red cheeks, ample waist, white cotton turtleneck shirt with a wine steward's medallion on a chain. The place was nearly empty and he greeted us from a step or two on the sidewalk as we paused, not quite decided. He assured us that chicken-fried steak had been banished from his entire realm and domain. This was gourmet city, folks, and our tiny one was welcome.

217

He kitchy-cooed her twice and then ducked behind the water cooler for clean menus. He extended them with pride and said, "*Carte de vins* on the other side, folks. Also we serve a cocktail-and-a-half in this place."

While we decided, he stood near our table and pointed out the sights. There was a viola on an antique barrel nearby marked "For Sale." He said, "Girl came in the other night, she played that thing like a charm. Tuned it and everything." He was sweating; the door was propped open; it was too early in the year for air conditioning. "Bach, Beethoven, Brahms," he said, "she could play anything on that fiddle. I took it on consignment from someone who owes me. Never again does that bastard—excuse it, ma'am—get on the cuff."

"It's a beautiful instrument."

"Will you excuse what I said, ma'am? I just get carried away and feel at home with folks like you—where you from?"

"San Francisco."

In celebration of that good news, he brought us two glasses of wine. "Free of any charge," he said, "you want a whole bottle?"

He rejoiced at his own generosity and savoir-vivre, and to tell the truth, so did we. We were touched and grateful to have friends in Joplin, Mo., too; friends all over our America. Even the interstate highway, our tax dollars working for us, was a pal. "We broil with nothing but charcoal here, folks," Mr. Vico said. He took a glass and a sip himself, looking deep into my wife's eyes, and raised a toast to us before hurrying off to other business, his medallion swinging. He was our friend. He was bound for the kitchen to make sure the cook knew how to broil meat rare for folks from California.

The waitress loved our child. She too brought us something free of any extra charge—blue cheese for the salad. She showed us a snapshot of herself and a larger one of her family. I had the impression that business was slow here in gourmet city. She was blond, very thin, pretty, nervous, with little girl-

ish flights of elbow, chin, eyes as she explained herself. She
peeked good-bye at the snapshot and said, "I want you to keep
it." She was only eighteen. She wore a shiny white nylon uniform, partly transparent, shadowed beneath, the top button
unbuttoned. While Mr. Vico was still in the kitchen she told
us in a great rush that her loved one, her only loved one, had a
beard and long hair just like me, only much younger, of
course, and therefore couldn't get a job and had dropped out
of SMS, that's Southern Missouri State, and her family
wouldn't let her see him any more. She was just desolate
about it, she said with a cheerful smile. She rubbed her hands
on her uniform, sliding them across the narrow hipbones, and
hung over us as if we were a gift from the gods.

"If only more people like you had beards," she said happily,
nervously, "it would just change everything."

What was I like? I had a wife and a baby and we were eating
out and ordering steak and roast prime ribs. The baby was
drowsy in her stroller—content.

As we ate, she kept returning to our booth to refill our ice
water, check on the baby, admire my wife's sweater hung on a
cast-iron fleur-de-lis, and tell us her story. She was an orphan,
she confessed in another great burst over our coffee, and her
family, her so-called family, Mr. Vico and his wife, Hazel, and
her so-called brothers, were only her adoption family. They
wouldn't let her see Buddy. Actually, her real family were alcoholics or maybe dead someplace on the gulf coast of Florida.
This family, her adoption family, had been okay enough all
along, when she had been just a kid, but now they wouldn't
let her see Buddy, just because he had long hair and a beard
like mine and no job.

It wasn't his fault. He was willing to work. They wouldn't
hire him in Joplin because of his hair, and he wanted a job and
he loved her as much as she loved him, but he was making a
stand and she respected and admired him for it.

She respected and admired us, too. Whatever we did in San

Francisco, it must be terribly interesting. She wasn't going to pry and ask, but she could tell. One thing you learn in a restaurant, even one that's not very busy, is how to judge people, how to tell who is really neat and who is—oh, draggy. She wanted our address. She would write and let us know how it all came out. She didn't often see people like us in Joplin. Actually, despite appearances, they didn't get many tourists in the place. There was something that didn't work; maybe it was the location.

"The food is very good," my wife said.

"Don't tip me," she said. "I'm the daughter of . . ." And she indicated our host with a nod and narrowed eyes.

That was a surprise.

"I bet he has fifty suits," she whispered, rustling ice water into our glasses.

"Are you sure you want us to keep your picture?" I asked.

"Vico," she whispered, "he calls himself Chez Vico, but his real name is Floyd. He gave. you a free small bottle of wine, but he can't stand long hair." We were joined by an interloper. Her voice rose as if continuing another line of discourse: ". . . and the Age of Aquarius brings many surprises."

She stood by while our host shook my hand. "Good-bye, folks," he said. "Thanks for everything."

"Thank *you*," I said. After all, the wine was a gesture of great purity, since we probably wouldn't be passing this way very often and wouldn't have the opportunity to recommend his restaurant to our friends.

The girl, Debra, came to the sidewalk as we were easing the carriage down the step. "Good-bye, thanks for everything," she said, probably not realizing that she was using the same words as her adopted father. She stood waving and looking after us until someone called her inside.

Perhaps we were touched, too, by Chez Floyd's California burgundy. I took out the Polaroid and looked at it under a street lamp. It had been taken near a tinseled tree, probably last winter, and there were unopened presents and a fireplace and a sweet girl nestled in the arms of Floyd-Vico. In the photograph she looked very young, though already, a few months later, in the hot frazzling of late spring, she had the quick eyes, shiny nose, eager smile, and wiry body of a good-looking town girl. The nylon uniform had done her justice—mussed, frantic, charming. The attractiveness of pathetic clothes on a young girl requires no further study.

2

HAVING walked before dinner, we also needed to walk after dinner. I told my wife about passing through Missouri in sealed cars during the war, pressed with my buddies against the window as we switched back and forth in a town like this one, a crowd of girls staring at us in the station. We picked which girls we would take with us to our secret destination, which we knew to be in Texas (it turned out to be Camp Beale, a port of embarkation near Marysville, California). We couldn't have those girls, either; our officers kept the doors locked.

Our child asleep, my wife and I rested our hands on the bar of the stroller and allowed ourselves to be tempted by the denser lights of the town a few blocks away. Early-summer bugs were beating against the street lamps; the bugfree stars shimmered in the Missouri sky. We walked by a huge, hulking, irregular building, glazed- and unglazed-brick heaps of stone— ungainly among the other buildings on the block as the tax-proud truck was ungainly—and my wife looked through the wide door and said, "Look, a wedding," just as I was saying, "Look, an elephant."

We were both right. An elephant in acres of bridal gown was being married to a clown in a bulbous pink nose and scooter-sized shoes with gaping pink tongues. It was a circus in the Shriners' temple. Mendelssohn's "Wedding March" drifted out onto the street, oom-papa-bride, oom-papa-white, and roustabouts gathered about the couple with bowed heads, and one—the father of the bride?—wept with great heaving boo-hoos, and roars of laughter arose from the conjugal crowd, family funning together. We bought our tickets. We stood watching the end of the ceremony at the entrance to the hall. The elephant ducked its head and swayed its trunk, pawing the ground, not unlike the shy ladies of history. She looked nice, but she was a tease. The crowd screamed with joy as the clown reached up to touch a pendulous cheek and then brushed it off with three fingers of his white cotton glove and then hopped up to kiss the place. Then, suddenly, nimbly, he jumped aboard and seized her ears and rode her off down a ramp into the recesses of the Shriners' garage. When the roustabout in-laws opened a door to let them through to their honeymoon, I felt a hot celebrational gust of elephant, hay, popcorn, sawdust, caged animals, and unbuttoned crowd.

A fezzed official helped us all the way down the aisle to ring-side seats. "Thank you very much," my wife said.

"Boy or girl?"

"Girl."

"She's real cute. I'm a dentist in real life," he said. "The rest of the time I'm an usher at the circus. Have a real good time in our city."

We were seated in time to say *ooh* and *ah* for a set of death-defying acts by muscular, aging acrobats, performed without nets but with false eyelashes. They ran off like kids, rumps twitching. Then with no respite, there was a burst of South Seas music and a famous Hawaiian princess on the high rope, direct from Tahiti and Madison Square Garden, twirling on her charmed cord with the aid of a powerful midget in a satin-lined Dracula cloak. She hung by the teeth from a small metal loop while Dracula ran about in little circles in the sawdust, snorting with effort. His cloak flew in dramatic folds, and I thought I could make out part of her name in white spangles on red satin—Princess Kulaku . . . But not the rest of it, and not very accurately. She twirled midair with a fixed, business-like smile. Our usher stood in the aisle with his fez tilted back, studying her mouth with great respect.

In the meantime, roustabouts were setting up the cage in the center ring for the leopard act. Captain Schultz, the distinguished leopard tamer, sole and only righteous heir to the great leopard tamers of the past, governed them without a whip, but an assistant stood outside the cage with awful forked prongs in case a leopard got loose to devour us. Captain Schultz didn't need him, but it was a state and federal law. The great tamer had a troublesome flaxen pompadour toupee which he kept adjusting, heedless of his beasts, as they rolled beach balls and stood on platforms and built stealthily, cat-like, to a climax of jumping through hoops lined with flaming rags. One leopard refused to jump ("Yay! Yay!" from a couple of nonconformist kids behind us) and the tamer stamped his foot, but the leopard was stubborn and the expression on Captain Schultz's face never changed. He gave up, saluting grace-fully. With one hand he lightly held his long beautiful yellow hair as he clicked his heels to the four Shriner directions. Despite his name, I'm sure he was Hungarian. Poseidon with his fork stood impassively near the cage, rising out of sawdust from the ankles, also Hungarian. Captain Schultz, risking his hair, nodded to him as he trotted off in the same direction the bride and groom had taken. The door opened and shut; we were alone with the leopard, but Poseidon had them neatly in hand with modular cages.

The heads of families whooped and twirled their tassels; a few kids scrambled up and down the aisles to scream at their friends; two high school beauties wobbled past us on their high heels, being escorted toward pop by stately, bored crew-cut athletes in short-sleeved shirts with vents to release their muscles. The band played Magyar romances for the dancing bears and the bike-riding chimps. A baby chimp enacted a bondage drama, leather straps wound round and round, arms and legs working desperately, without bones, it seemed, trying to climb out of a white nylon uniform which made the chimp look terribly naked and vulnerable. Though it was a baby, it had long tufts of hair on its wrists.

The foursome of beauties and athletes returned refreshed in time for the joys of intermission.

Entertainment was ceaseless, rising over us in waves, as if the crowd could never have enough, and in its gaiety and eagerness, could generate its own, along with body heat and friendly straw and hard-fry smells. But self-reliant as we seemed, we were not to be put to the test. "Now, with each and every Hershey chocolate candy bar for only fifteen cents coin American," said the deep and booming amplified voice of the midget assistant of Princess Aloahkalukami (ah, that was her name)—he strode back and forth in his cape with a traveling microphone—"we of the Famous-Regis Circus, with the aid and encouragement of the Hershey chocolate people of Hershey, Pennsylvania, as an advertising and publicity campaign only, to celebrate their many years of candy-making for the Famous-Regis people, plus their gratitude for the loyalty of their many friends throughout Missouri, are privileged to offer with each and every Hershey chocolate candy bar a guaranteed chance and opportunity on a gold watch, a platinum hair clip, and a genuine furry, fuzzy, friendly, nonflammable baby lion, plus many other American-made prizes too numerous to mention. Now, the vendors passing among you will offer one chance and one chance only—"

"I'll take one," I called to a vendor passing among me.

"Yours is the choice and decision, friends. We don't have but ten minutes to give away all these prizes, because the rest of our show is ready and raring to finish in time to get you folks home in time to show off your gold watch, your platinum hair clip, your genuine—"

We didn't win the bead necklace; we didn't even win one of

the prizes too numerous to mention. When I asked the clown handling the prizes—volcanic pearls of sweat bubbling through his painted smile; he must have been terribly clogged inside—if I could have the friendly lion anyway, he answered, "I only work here."

Deluded by his smile, I continued the conversation. "But it's for my wife. She likes lions."

"I'll call a cop, beatnik," he said.

I had forgotten. The Aquarian Age brings many surprises. Paranoia means you think there are more people judging you than really are, but if you're not paranoid, there are still usually more than you suspect. (Is there a name for the trouble which is the opposite of paranoia? Delusions of nonpersecution?) I have a beard. It got me free wine, but also a bit of angry lip in response to my kidding lip.

It was time to feed the baby; she had awakened. We left the circus a little early. The elephant was waiting in the lobby for her final curtsy. For a recent bride she had a rather mottled and warty hide. Her husband was the mean clown. I was happy for her that the marriage was only in jest, since the elephant seemed to have a sweet temper despite her complexion.

I held up our daughter to see her first elephant, but at her age it must have seemed just an out-of-reach, nongraspable expanse of gray. She would rather take milk.

On the street outside, we found someone waiting for us. It was Debra, the waitress from Chez Vico. "Oh take me with you," she said, "oh please, I'll do everything for you, take me with you, take me, take me."

"LET'S KILL THE FIRST RED-HAIRED MAN WE SEE ..."

1

A GROUP of amiable artists and rock musicians came together a summer ago to plan a grand free outdoor festival of
their joyful crafts in San Francisco, but a man who called himself Mother John appeared at their meetings and said he'd tear
them apart, he'd burn them down: "I ain't rational and I'll
wipe you out."

"What's your last name, sir?"

"Motherfucker John from Out-of-Town."

The insurance went up and the folks got scared. There were
ten or twenty or thirty of these mothers, or maybe the same
one with ten, twenty, or thirty faces, but they were all talking
about burning, ripping, exploding, and such. The festival in
the park was canceled.

Why did the mothers threaten? They wanted to hurt.
Why? Well, maybe they were fascist right-wing third-world
meth-freak Maoist hippie deviationist paranoids, or maybe
they were just out-people wanting in, fearing that someone
might find fun and profit in the festival. They really don't
know or can't say. They are rebels without a pause.

The man who commits random violence always thinks his
attack is justified, of course. "He gave me a lotta lip"—the
true-life explanation, folks, for shooting a fellow shopper. Or:
"I just don't like guys who smile to themselves." But we know
that the gesture is in excess of the provocation. Maybe logi-

cally we can't explain it, but a lotta lip isn't reason enough to kill in a busy department store during the January White Sale.

In my novel *The Great American Jackpot*, a young man named Al Dooley robs a bank because he's lonely and seeks meaning. Well, there are other reasons, even good ones. But *he* doesn't really know them, and to the world, too, his action seems eccentric, unpredictable, irrational. He is strung out and strange to himself, and a menace to others. He wants to greet reality with an answering blow. I think him a frequent American.

Traditional violence usually had a clear aim. The man with the stick hit the other man to grab his goods, land, or woman. Contemporary random violence has murky origins—killing without hatred, rape without lust, war against phantom enemies. It hits first because otherwise someone might hit back. Causeless violence? No, but action far in excess of cause, similar to methedrine speed in excess of organic velocity.

On the Lower East Side of New York, for example, a fertile plantation area for the Mother Johns of this world, speed freaks, motorcyclists, disaffected workers, chafing neighborhood nationality groups, blacks, cops and mimeograph Maoists, all are battling each other in some weird parody of the troubadour games of murder. "Okay, world," they seem to be saying, toeing the earth shyly, "here we go with a free outdoor X-rated movie. And bring the kiddies to the slaughter."

This is a violent country.

Everyone who walks the streets of America knows it. If you can't walk, you read the newspapers. If you can't read, you see it on television. The subtle mining of violence under the surface control of America goes beyond anything a law-and-order manipulation of police authority can resolve.

For a time I accepted a wry, half-paranoid suspicion that my own person (horn-rimmed novelist, nosy face) invited attack. I've gradually come to realize that I'm no worse than others, but just being alive invites attack. For example:

227

I was walking in a heavy rain. The street was deserted. A man came toward me in black-militant drag, boots, leather, beret, and his lips moving, discussing with invisible enemies. But I was visible. Our eyes met. I stopped for a moment to let him by and he glared at me. "Hi," I said weakly.

"Man, I don't see it like that," he said. "I'm gonna *kill* you."

But there was no action. There was only the wish to murder.

And there is also, oddly enough—this is often ignored—the reciprocal wish to have violence done. I know a girl, a very pretty actress, who has been raped twice. Does she invite it? Well, she undresses at night, with shades up, and when she hears a sound at the window, she goes to open the door to see what's happening. And I was standing on the street near the San Francisco Art Museum when I saw an old acquaintance, the girl friend of a friend, and I jokingly went up to her and said, "Hey, chick, you want to do something really filthy?"

She paused and looked up into my face with a welcoming smile: "What?" Then her face darkened with disappointment. "Oh," she said, "it's Herb. I didn't recognize you at first." She later explained that she was kind of upset that day and bored and—oh, you know, looking for something to do. I realized an odd fact about rapists and molesters. They are offering a product which not many women want to buy—*but some do.*

There is no lack, of course, of the traditional kinds of violence—between colors, races, generations, classes.

My wife and I were strolling in Berkeley after a party. A group of cops was hassling a couple in an old station wagon decorated with hippie, love and peace insignia. The five policemen were teasing the kids, looking for drugs, it seemed, or maybe just *looking.* A boy of high school age, long hair, blue jeans, called out, "They don't have a search warrant! You don't have to let them!"

It was careless of him to incite the police.

One huge cop went lazily moving toward the kid. The kid started to run, very fast—ahah, he'll get away. The cop thumped after him. We kept walking in response to the other cops' jerking thumbs: *Keep moving.* But in the direction of the kid. He slipped and fell, bounced to his feet and kept running, but the cop was close now. Suddenly, to our amazement, we heard a thud of feet. *All* the five cops had abandoned the car and were chasing this boy who had yelled at them. They passed us, grinning, clutching clubs, some with hands on their pistols. They rounded the corner and I heard the boy scream, "I surrender!" He stood with hands up, trembling. The first cop to reach him cracked him on the head with his club and sent him staggering and bleeding. The others gathered around as a small Saturday-night crowd appeared. He gave them his papers. He was okay. He was even white. A couple of Berkeley ladies, spinsters or schoolteachers or grandmothers, were standing nearby. The cop who had hit him said, "Okay, kid, go home now."

They didn't arrest him. They had made their investigation, administered justice, and dismissed the case, all in one swift comment of billy club on skull. He was bleeding from the nose. He was vomiting. He needed to see a doctor. The ladies soothed him and led him away.

The cops were pleased that they had made another request for polite attention to one's elders. But they had also created another cop-hating radical, ready to kill. And not just the boy, of course, but the ladies and me, too.

2

WHILE trying to work out an explanation for the upsurge in violence in contemporary American, random violence beyond the traditional violences, I happened to be in my bank in New York City, formerly Fun City, during the months when it is supposed to be a Summer Festival. New York offers a natural environment for thinking about random violence. I was waiting to have a check certified (speeding ticket, speedometer defective, H. Gold the Mild-Mannered Novelist feeling morose). A mousy young man came up to the desk, wrote his name and account number on a slip of paper, and said to the bank bureaucrat, "Excuse me, sir, I'd like to know how much money I have."

"How should I know?"

"I mean, in my account."

"What do you mean, don't you get a statement?"

"Yes, but there's a discrepancy—"

"Can't you add?"

"I think so, but it doesn't come out the same—"

"It'll cost you a dollar. There'll be a charge of a dollar."

Timidly the supplicant said, "Won't you tell me what I have in my account?"

It was like the tide rushing through a weak place in the wall. The put-upon, underpaid, not overbright bank clerk saw weakness and found pleasure in crushing it. "We can't just stand here all day and answer stupid questions from stupid people who can't add. I said it'll cost you a dollar. You want me to call downstairs?"

The dejected supplicant took his slip of paper with his name and number on it and walked away, gray and defeated. No matter that the bank probably wouldn't and couldn't legally charge him for the service. No matter: he believed in the authority of the Man Behind the Desk, a man exasperated and rubbed raw in the great city, a loser himself. The teller turned to me and said, "Stupid idiots, asking stupid questions, they think all I got to do here is answer them?"

I said that the supplicant walked away gray and defeated, but I'm sure there was also murder in his heart. Not against the bank or the teller, not a cop, not some authority. But against someone weaker than himself—a black man, a hippie, a kid. Isolation from power makes men look for a mob in which they can be strong.

Random violence is not really random or accidental, of course, and the man or mob, kid or gang, deciding to kill the first red-haired man in sight, is not unconnected with the rest of the fate of America and the world. There are fifty or sixty million more people in America than there were when I was a child. The rat-sink theory holds that animals go crazy—perverse, violent, self-destructive—when the density of population increases beyond a certain needed living space. No reason to think that the anxiety of rats is sharper than that of overcrowded human beings. Every study of ambulatory psychosis and neurosis comes up with a large store of ticking time bombs walking the streets—and driving, waiting on people, directing traffic. They are damaged, we are told, by broken families and crippled families, by historical examples of cruelty, by rage and resentment, by boredom and anxiety, by jealousy and frustration. Now we also hear of chromosome damage and genetic defects leading men toward senseless attack. Prison systems all have isolation chambers for enraged men who snarl like beasts and want only to destroy, who must be kept apart, unreachable by therapy; and some of these seem to burn out and are released, and some have not yet committed acts which get them in prison. Repressed, suppressed, tormented, unconscious, the desire to kill is a part of the risk of city life, like postnasal drip. High school basketball games turn into rampages. A community in Washington protects itself from the world with fences, towers, electric eyes, dogs, guards, patrols—an armed concentration camp for suburban luxury living. The statistics about senseless crime, child beating, sniping at strangers, arson and assault, and gang sadism should make Jean-Jacques Rousseau spin in his quiet Swiss grave. If man is naturally good, he is sure going against his nature more and more of the time. It sounds like a bad joke: the paranoids are after us.

Violence pours out of city men like water out of broken fire hydrants. And it's not just the city, of course. The small-town jukebox roars out Johnny Cash songs or "Happiness Is a Warm Gun," and the bouncers hit and the cops flail and the shards of plate glass decorate the pavements.

Nietzsche said: "It is only the powerful who know how to honor, it is their art, their domain for invention." In other words, power is the opposite of violence. The powerful man can respect the stranger, not fear him. The sense of being cut off makes men want to find reality through the ancient pride in bloodletting. Powerlessness corrupts; absolute powerlessness corrupts absolutely. Stabbing strange women or setting drunks on fire does not seem to be the moral equivalent of war, which William James said America needed. But if the tax man and your parents and your employer give you trouble, and you can't strike at them openly, why not declare war on their surrogates, on the weak or the strange, on humanity itself?

3

THE psychiatrist Bruno Bettelheim argues that a misunderstood Freudianism has led to a hypocritical pseudo-permissiveness on the part of frightened parents, and this in turn leads to guilt and weak control in children. The kids know their parents want them to be decent human beings, but also that the parents are afraid to assert authority. The child needs authority to provide examples for learning. The childish temper tantrum is a common means of testing. It needs to be mastered, but often isn't by the time the child has an adult's body. The character-disordered or psychopathic personality may seem to be intelligent, controlled and in touch; but, in fact, all it knows is one lesson: I want, I want at once, I want only what I want—and I'll take it.

When a man respects no one, and not himself either, but wants wants *wants*, there is no reason to defer his hatreds and revenges; and when he doesn't really know why he hates and needs revenge, he may express his childish storm of temper with a high-powered rifle from a rooftop or a knife in a crowd. How quickly the "love generation" turns to hating yippies under pressure about Vietnam and cynicism about American virtue. The kids can throw flowers, turn on, and make lovely rock music, but if they are goal-less amid affluence, they grow impatient with a doctrinaire forever springtime designed like a record jacket. The tender communal living arrangements seem to work out fine, as they did for a sweet flower child I knew a few years ago: "We love each other, we live at peace, we share everything."

"How long has this been going on?"

"Five days," she said.

But the grooviness ended with thievery, fights, jealous rage, and a contagion of breakdowns. A Panglossian reaction might be: Okay, let's work out the violence, it's the price we pay for superorganization. The trouble with this is that violence *expresses* other feelings, but only *communicates* itself—the desire to hurt. It does no good to the victim, unlike the victim of a poem or a song, who may benefit from the composer's expressed rage. And it does no good to the perpetrator, who comes to understand nothing, but may develop a taste for blood.

A businessman in Detroit hopes that holdup men are rational and want his money; he can offer money—it's the ones who just want to kill him that are a bother. A childhood friend, a funny red-haired man from Cleveland, carries a tear-gas gun in his pocket. "Why?" I asked him.

"Some people don't like red hair," he said.

Mace, karate, judo, personal weapons—HELP! Stop! The police say that the worst criminals are the amateurs, out for kicks, not purses; pleasure, not gain. A presidential report on violence, released on the first anniversary of the assassination of Robert Kennedy, says that Americans are a "rather bloody-minded people." In the past, it notes, violence was generally initiated by white Anglo-Saxons against Catholics, black men, labor organizers, and pacifists. Now black violence, campus violence, antiwar violence, political assassinations, and spooky random violence are added to our turbulent past. Eric Hoffer, who hollered on television that we are not a violent people, wrote in his column in the San Francisco *Examiner* (June 9, 1969): "A day of wrath is waiting around the corner, when the saturated resentment of the long-suffering majority crystallizes in retaliation." He bemoaned an "incredible submissiveness in an age of violence," and seemed to be urging the public to rush the "foul-mouthed, bushy-faced punks." People shouldn't put limitation on the police; do-gooders are the enemy. His solution to the problem is on a similar level to the one reported in the *New York Times*, where Associate Justice Paul C. Reardon of the Massachusetts Supreme Court urged that a campaign should be mounted in the nation's schools to search "for a brief synonym for police officer and policeman to supplant that unfortunate word all Americans currently employ." The headline reads: NEW WORD FOR "COP" SOUGHT. Obviously the word "pig" won't do, but if we call the cops "angels," it won't be long until the word "angel" means what "cop" means. If there is violence and hatred in America, new words won't make them sweeter.

How can we live with random violence? Well, one way which is seldom mentioned is just to go on going on, as we do with automobiles, smog, cigarettes, airplane failures, brush-fire wars—making irritated little gestures toward improving our chances but essentially enduring what malfunction or destiny bring. In the rat-sink city we may have to think of berserk paranoids as another health hazard, like leaking stoves. Recently I visited a prisoner in California who was convicted of kidnapping and tormenting a child. He is intelligent, gentle, thoughtful, and says he doesn't mind prison so much because it gives him a chance to catch up on his reading. (It has also dried out the drugs in his blood.) But when he is caught up on his reading and ready for the world once again, and maybe ready to try speeding through his mind with the help of methedrine sulfate, are we to think of him as just another hazard, like the defective automobile or the mysterious disturbances in our lungs which come from breathing city air?

Suppose we're not content with this new hazard of sudden death by twitch and impulse?

The police, either kindly or repressive, must always be fallible solutions. Either they are not there when you need them or they are too much there. Massed police tend to riot; police power means police brutality. What about personal armament, going about with little private jets of mace, which can be bought in grocery stores and "at fine cosmetic counters everywhere." There are too many quick tempers abroad. When everyone is armed to protect himself, who will protect us from the protectors? What about that walled suburb of Washington? This sort of panic is a reversion to the life envisaged during the great fallout-shelter craze, a retreat to something fetal and subhuman in human nature. Then what?

Other styles of child rearing, deeper and truer education, meaningful work, creative interchanges among people—everyone talks about the ways that might make it possible for masses of men to live together on a limited planet. Improved medicine calms the distraught, tranquilizes the defective. The reform of cities, and a public life which is less hypocritical about suffering, war and injustice, can influence people to meet each other without rage. Drugs, cops, institutions and karate—well, these stopgap controls may be with us forever and we will use them when we must. Humankind requires deep solutions to the demand for animal and spiritual joy. Rage, violence, ulcers, twitches, crying jags, and melancholia reflect an imbalance of personal expression and opportunity in the world. A song of a few years ago claimed morosely, "I ain't got no sat-is-fac-tion," and I've heard that song danced and sung in Los Angeles, New York, Paris, and Biafra. It's a universal anthem. The dream of love and joy seems further away than ever. Doctrinaire injunctions to love one another—love! love goddammit!—clearly don't work. Nor does anarchic self-expression when *my* freedom binds *you* to pay the price. The others out there will find their pleasure in revenge.

The billions are here, and billions more coming fast, and we must learn to live with them. There will be more of everything, including red-haired men. Is the red-haired man coming toward you your brother? No, in fact, he's not. He may be your friend or your enemy. He takes up your space, he eats your food, he jostles you. He covets what you covet.

A few days ago, waiting at the post office, a sallow, irritable, self-absorbed young man tried to slip in line between a couple of women ahead of me. I reached out to put my hand on his shoulder. I smiled sweetly. I said, "Okay, fella, tell you what. You take that place in line and I'll take you, okay? agreed? fine?"

He looked at me and saw a menace to society. I wanted to kill. The ladies in line shrank away from me. I was Mother Herb from Out-of-Town. I was not rational. And worst of all, I was proud of it.

More messages from the exiles of art. These three stories tell about Bohemians—artists, near-artists, would-bees, should-bees, might-have-beens, never-wases, hope-to-be-agains—of the three responsible ages, young, middle and old. Bohemia has been a persistent American community in almost every college, in all big cities, in the exiles of Europe, Africa, and the Caribbean. It's a questionable society, which makes it necessary to ask questions about it. The answers are always partial ones.

Despite ridicule and the shakiness of his position, the outsider, displaying his colors as an artist, is in possession of something permanent and touching, no matter how foolish or selfish he may be. He seeks a rhythm which can give meaning to his life. His work and his play are one. He aims to keep the child alive in the man's body, and runs the risk of bearing into old age the soul of a baby which only knows how to bang on his high chair and cry, I want. What he really wants is the deep thing, truth and beauty, a shape to his time on earth, a mark on the future. Often he gets much less —delusion and paltriness.

Is he like other men? He is never content. Then other men are like him.

WAITING FOR THE FORTY-ONE UNION

A STORY

THERE was this girl, Peggy, he could call any time. They had an agreement, Karol and Peggy did, they were old friends. "You get the night frights, you telephone, we'll talk," she said. "Any hour, I don't care. I can talk you up, I'm really good,

Karol. Up and out of it. And if talk doesn't do, we'll cuddle together, okay? I won't even ask you for taxi fare, okay? I'll just throw on a raincoat over my nightie—"

"Thanks, Peggy." Good old Peggy Something.

"Um."

"Yes, Peggy."

"I get the night frights too sometimes, Karol. Oh, bad. That means, um—"

"I throw on the raincoat over the nightie and—"

"Yes, Karol."

So Karol never took Peggy up on her offer. Down as he sometimes slid, he knew enough to know her downs were oftener than his, and pretty soon he wouldn't have a night to call his own. Good Peggy, nice and pretty Peggy; but Karol valued his privacy, his sleep, and even his sadness too much to shuffle through them with cuddly sex from a sweet and friendly North Beach chick whom he didn't want to carry around with him through a difficult life.

Nevertheless, when the bad nights came, they were very lonely and bad indeed. Who and what and why am I? he asked the Alcatraz foghorn, the maroon fog glowing with city lights, the outcries from the Broadway strip and Chinatown which drifted up Russian Hill to his whitewashed little studio. And the answer to the question was lacking. Perhaps the question itself was not clear. He had lived with it so long that it was almost an esthetic question now. Just as he couldn't paint dream and horror by smearing ink or a little wash over his vision, so he couldn't answer the basic question by asking it in this outrageously vain manner. Me, myself and I look out at the glowing dark? I don't want to paint, I don't want to pain, I can't sleep or think and why?

Selfish questions.

Worse: unclear questions all rolled up into one bad question.

Noisy head!

Not finding the answer in bed, not wanting to find it in Peggy—in fact, certain it was not to be found either in bed or in Peggy—Karol arose swiftly and put on the clothes not meant to be worn until morning. Modestly, as he dressed at midnight, he turned his back on the table, a flush door on horses, on which he was carving a wood block of his friend Lew the Poet. He didn't want half-born deadwood to see his misery and look chips of sawdust and curly filings at him.

He snapped the light and felt wide awake. He need never sleep again; perhaps it was only that. He heard his shoes on the concrete stairway and hoped he didn't wake any neighbors, or if he did, that they thought he was a serious person with serious business at this hour. Well, in San Francisco, they don't worry; this was no longer Evanston. Rioters, burglars, cops, kids, transvestites, even artists and nobodies and semi-somebodies wander the night, and only when the stockbrokers come stalking down the hills at dawn in time for the opening of the market, three hours earlier by Pacific Coast time, do the sleepless wander home to bed and leave the night world to a few vendors of the Berkeley *Barb*, skipping on speed as if still alive. Down the hill toward Broadway. Past the haunted house: this time he wouldn't do it, wouldn't, wouldn't.

But he did.

He saw the girls dancing in the window, as he had seen them three years before on New Year's Eve when, reconciled with his own lady, with loins exhausted by reconciliation, they headed this way to a party and he glanced into the window and saw the girls jerking like marionettes—no strings, no music—jerking and swimming and smiling and silent, flying to a rhythm he could not hear, with men he did not see, early celebrants with the joy of girlishness frantic on faces, hair, lips, teeth, shadow of neck. Now it was like a slide inserted between his eyes and his brain each time he passed that window, an image of hope and desire, youth leaping to unheard sounds, girls deafening themselves with dance.

He moved on by and it flicked off. Thank God; relief; the panic subsided. They were so lovely, and he feared them so.

If the real girls of three years ago still lived there—stewardesses, were they? secretaries? students?—he could have charmed them and known them and finished with them. But there was a parade of tenants in that building and he was caught with a memory that could never be tampered with by reality, silently dancing on a New Year's Eve which never ended in a new year. He never saw them afterward.

The night air made him feel fresh, lively, almost grateful for insomnia. Down Broadway he strolled, to the corner of Columbus where the barker for the Condor stood hoarsely importuning sailors, salesmen, and conventioneers: "One drink sees the entire show! One drink, come on in, only one drink and see the famous San Francisco bottomless!" A police car, two lounging cops grinning, was parked in the bus stop. One officer had a clipboard in his lap, but he wasn't looking at it. A voice cried out: "Karol!"

It was Harry Cameron, a day stroller whom Karol knew from the street. He had been a doorman, manager of a defunct rock band, poster-maker. Lately he said, when asked what he did for a living, "I'm getting healthy." But now he was standing at the bus stop, jiggling up and down, and shouting at Karol though Karol was standing right next to him.

"What's the matter?" Karol asked him.

"Wait! Ing!"

"Waiting for what?"

"Wait! Ing! for the Forty-one Union!"

But the bus had just pulled up, lying clumsily out in the street to avoid the police car, and Harry didn't move for it. It smoked and rumbled and the gears shrieked.

"There's your bus, Harry."

"Still wait-ing for the Forty-one Union!" Harry sang, letting the bus by. He hopped and jiggled, and his beefy face was purple in the reflection of lights from the Condor.

Karol hadn't known that Harry used speed. Now he also guessed what he was doing out on the streets all day. He was dealing in the product.

"I thought you were getting healthy," Karol said.

"Getting healthy on the Forty-one Union! Getting healthy tomorrow! Getting healthy is a state of mind! Getting healthy—"

He was still discussing his coming good physical and spiritual organization as Karol moved off. Karol was sure he didn't notice that his friend was gone. Future health on the bus out of North Beach was of primary concern, and Harry was still making points in the agitated neon air as the cop ate his sandwich on a clipboard tray.

Karol decided he would get hunger taken care of as his own way to a good night's sleep, even if it turned out to be a morning sleep. He turned down Grant toward the Hui Chao, an all-night basement mirror-and-steel restaurant. Beef and tomatoes and noodles were cheap and provided everything a man needed to live healthy, though none of the late-night diners confirmed this theory by their appearance. Well, maybe they were young Red Guards eating raw fish, old toothless and used-up refugees from Hong Kong and Taiwan eating only noodles or soup. No one stared in the mirrors, which reflected Hui Chao basement within Hui Chao basement within Hui Chao steel, chrome and mirrors and scrunched-over-eating basement. It was a mistake. He felt healthy now, but depressed, lonely, and artfully horny. It had been harmless to be a jittery insomniac; there was trouble in being a sleepless night wanderer. If he could have used electric light to paint by, he'd have been better off to try working. That's all right; he didn't want to be better off.

He paid his $1.75, which included the rice and tea, and moved past the splintered crates at which an old man, stoned by age, not opium, sold scraps of Chinese newspapers which looked as if a new one hadn't been published since he came to

town. Back out of Chinatown to North Beach, through the
alley past City Lights and Vesuvio's and onto Columbus,
where he saw a girl he knew. She was the friend of Stan
Wong, she was blond, she had a baby, she was crazy, she had
traveled with the first acid freaks; she didn't remember his
name but she knew she knew him; she came up and said, putting out her open hand, "I want to lay this on you because I
love you."

There was a pill in his hand. And then again, it might be
only a Rexall aspirin.

"What is it?"

"Because I love you," she said, chattering something else to
an invisible companion as she hurried down the street, pulling
her two-year-old by the arm. The kid needed to have his nose
wiped. And it probably wasn't an aspirin. Karol only took aspirin when he needed to deaden a cold, when his nose was
blocked and he was dead already and needed some additional
deadening to forget his sinus and brain; and what it was she
had given him, whatever it was, he was pretty sure he had
never taken it before. And wouldn't now. And the nighttime
North Beach street smells were alive and whirling in his network of sinus which was merely an extension of the fingerprint
whorls and swirls of his brain.

What was her name again?

Maria Something—yes, that's it. Maria. Maria Velveeta,
they called her.

She and the kid, sleeping on his feet, disappeared up Columbus. The kid just hung like dead fruit from a tree, waiting
for a breeze for its excuse to fall. Well, he could always call
Peggy.

The speed freaks were rushing in and out of the Dante, the
Swiss-American, the El Dorado hotels, slamming doors, stum-
bling against one another, in a hurry, heads busy. Constricted
blood vessels made their nerves squeak. It must have been
about three now, because the gogo dancers, the topless and

bottomless artistes with stars in their eyes and spangles in their orifices, miraculously transformed by closing time into sallow and spine-sprung dropouts, were being met at the sidewalk by their old men and guardians, sharpies hoping to leave pimping behind them on the golden road into show business. They would have coffee and eggs at the Ferris Wheel, or omelets and potatoes at the U. S. Restaurant (spinach omelet the specialty), and the fellow would have to listen to his client's tales of a hard night on a hard beat. The Filipino guardian at Enrico's was watching over the sidewalk, saying, "No, closed, too late, no." A pair of cops were frisking a girl in a cape at the Kearny steps. They looked in her hair and pulled it off. It makes a ripping noise. Well, they had known in advance, with the deep intuition of cops, that it was a boy in a girl's wig, not a girl in a girl's wig. The city had recently declared war on transvestites who didn't pay off (confused so many sailors recently home from Vietnam).

Karol had the taste of noodles and tomato sauce in his mouth. He could see the sailors waiting up the hill for the cable car. That was something to do: walk up the hill and let them know the cable car had stopped running for the night; a little patriotic deed for which no one would thank him, only the sailors, not the government, the President, the Congress, or Peggy, unless he telephoned her. But he was not willing to incur this debt. He stood in despair, but he thought ahead. "Hey, fellas! Doesn't run any more!"

"Don't mess around with us," a sailor said, strolling toward him with hat tilted over one eye.

"No, I just wanted to tell you the cable car stops for a couple hours," Karol said.

"You want to mess with me?" the sailor asked.

Karol retraced his steps down the hill. The sailors, waiting for the car, yelled and dared him to come on back up.

The sailor reminded Karol of Peggy again. When you get the night frights, that's what you should do: think of messing

around with Peggy and get happy. But he didn't want easy
oblivions. Like the man waiting for the Forty-one Union, he
preferred to work it out his own way, looking for the magic
lady, the dream lover who would be looking for her magic
man, her dream lover, himself.

The sugar was diminishing in his blood. The spurt of energy, three o'clock closing time in North Beach, was closing
down. A few drunks rambled; a few freaks stood in doorways,
looking for sales or buys. A dusky orange glow was reflected in
the fog, the early false dawn of cities. A truck dropped a bun-
dle of newspapers at the corner, twisted about with wire so
that only a kid with wire cutters could mess in them.

Karol knew what he needed to do now. Just keep walking
until there was nothing for it but sleep. Tire himself down
into sleep, like a good boy, breathing easy after his tantrum.
Down Broadway toward the Embarcadero, down the slope toward the warehouses and showrooms. As he paused for the
light at Sansome, he heard someone giggle. "What?" he said.

A giggle, but he saw no one.

"Who is it?" he asked.

Morning commuters were already heading onto the ramp,
sleepy chaps locked into their cars with the weather-news-
music breakfast to keep them steering straight. Later there
would be coffee carts in the halls.

"I been following you," Maria Velveeta said, stepping out
of a used-car-emporium doorway. She didn't explain how she
could have followed ahead of him, but perhaps he hadn't noticed or perhaps she hadn't really been following him.

"Where's the boy?"

"You're the boy."

"The *boy*."

"Oh, him. Beddy-bye time. I dropped him off at . . ." She
shrugged. "Left him home," she said. "Hi, King Karol of Ru-
mania."

"How did you know?"

"Just guessed it. Take that pill yet, which will make you a king?"

"How'd you know?"

"Oh, I know, I'm a friend of mine, I'm not as crazy as I let on."

Karol extended the linty bit of stuff. He had rolled it in his fingers, stuck it in his pocket, and now he offered it to Maria. "I don't know what it is," he said. "I don't want it. Here, have it back."

"I don't know what it is either," she said. "I want it."

He watched while she rolled her tongue around to moisten her mouth. She grinned and made a jerky lifting gesture of her chin, and her throat rippled. Down, like a chicken eating corn.

"It'll take at least twenty minutes for whatever it is," she said. "Maybe it's an aspirin."

"We got twenty minutes to be straight in."

"You got a whole life to be straight in. Me, I got twenty minutes."

"I'll bet it's an aspirin."

Maria looked hurt. "But I said I loved you when I gave it to you. I wouldn't lie like that."

"You can love someone and give him an aspirin."

Maria looked at him as if to say, "You're deep, you're heavy, what a trip." Who could tell what she was thinking?

They stood at the chilly corner. Maria sighed.

"Listen," she said, "before my straight twenty minutes is up, let's."

"Let's what?" he asked.

"*Let's,*" she said. "Right now. I want to."

He stood waiting in the dark as the headlights swung over them, then up the ramp.

"Okay," she said, "just let me." She pushed him into the doorway. It was still dark. It would be dark for a while, then it would be tomorrow. The headlights up the ramp just flicked across, climbing their bodies, nothing more. She grabbed him

245

and held him to her coat. He smelled leather, suede, grass, patchouli. "Oh, that's good," she said, "good." She undid him. Rapid handwork. "Oh, good, good." He was saying nothing. He was pressing his mouth against her hair. "Now let me," she said.

They were leaning against each other in the before-dawn glow of fog. A cop car passed slowly but didn't stop.

Karol was slipping and sliding. He was standing up and leaning. He remembered Peggy. He remembered someone else. Her hair. He remembered nothing. She was guiding him. Strain in his thighs. Yes, he was allowed to help a little. Leaning back and riding, lifting, riding. "Oh do it, do it, do it, let me," she whispered ferociously into his ear.

Oh, good.

She patted him, stroked him, shook him.

They leaned against each other. Karol tried to think tenderly of her, but thought only of needing to walk back up the long slope of hill.

A flashlight beam caught them. Two cops crossed the street. They had been watching them from another doorway. "Hey, you two kids—"

"Naw, they're over twenty-one," said the other cop.

"We were just talking," Karol said.

"Oh, boy. We didn't hear you talking." He shined the light up and down their bodies. "Christ, and you're not even kids," he said. "Go on, just don't pee in the doorway."

And the cop switched off his light and the two of them moved on heavily, back into their car, laughing and breathing and off to their breakfast breaks.

Karol stood there out of breath and frightened.

"It's okay," Maria said. "Are you nervous again? Want to do it again?" And her hand finding him.

"No! I mean, no thanks."

She patted him sweetly. "That's all right. Excuse me, will

you? I got to go look after my baby. Sometimes he wakes up early and I left him without a sitter."

"You'd better," he said.

She didn't move. There was more on her mind. She said, "Oh, by the way, there was something I meant to ask you."

Now she'd put the ask on him—rent, food, the kid. Okay, he had it coming. First crumbling pill and she loved him, then crumbling against her in a doorway. If she weren't a good girl, he'd have said she was setting him up. Sure, he could help her out, five, ten, probably no more than that. "What?" he said.

"Anything?" she said. He wasn't sure if she was coquettish or anxious. "Okay? You will? Promise?"

"Depends. Yes. Go on."

She sighed. She said, "How old are you?" and then turned away without waiting for the answer.

And he was standing alone in the doorway, shivering. Call Peggy? No, he wouldn't call Peggy. He looked across the street at the empty warehouse, a dusty window and a LEASE OR SALE TERMS in red, white and blue; and behind the sign he suddenly saw two girls silently dancing, fingers raised, hair flying, smiles of ecstasy on their faces. He hurried out of the doorway.

By the time he got to the corner of Columbus and Broadway, the sun had already begun to glint over the bay. There were diamonds of light on the windows ahead. Harry Cameron was still waiting for the Forty-one Union. Up the hill, past the retina confusion of girls doing the insane jiggle forever, grinning and lovely, ghosts leaping behind diamonds of sunrise; and to bed now, this time to sleep.

FROM PROUST TO DADA

A STORY

ONCE in Florence I came to know a man who was reputed, by himself and also by certain practitioners of minor literary history, to have been a beautiful boy whose long slender fingers and lively eyes were much admired by Marcel Proust. When I met him, his most startling characteristic was his great accumulation of years, but he was healthy, that mummified health of extreme tenacity, and he was still quick as a boy across the dust and debris of Tuscany in the summer of 1950. He also claimed to have enjoyed the particular friendship of a great English poet, dead in World War I, and to have inspired some of the poet's most memorable (now forgotten) lines.

Two generations ago Roland Mardi had been renowned for his beauty, his accessibility, and his wealth; he still had the last two qualities. You can imagine what an odd survivor he seemed to American students, GI Bill tourists, pre-beat beatniks in our twenties. It was a time of selling GI clothes to Arabs for travel money, of dodging the committees of experts who came over to judge our Fulbright seriousness and reliability while we, veterans by vocation, strove for a heroic Bohemian freedom. We had had enough of roll calls.

I met him at a concert of medieval music in a monastery courtyard in Fiesole. "You are—am I correct?—an American student, an artist, perhaps a poet?" he asked me at intermission, pointing his parchment fingers like a maestro.

Golly, he was so right.

"You are interested in Proust, in dada, in futurism?"

Yes, oh yes again.

"You would honor me with your company—?"

248

Well, I would be happy to honor us both by taking coffee and ices with him at the sort of plush café which would have been a black-market hangout in Paris and which here was simply out of my reach. He had many interesting facts to impart on many interesting subjects. Draw a subject, he suggested, in English or in French—which did I prefer? Ah, he should have been able to see by looking at me how well I spoke French, but there is so much deceit abroad in the world today . . .

He smiled, he had won his conquest, he had pale, washed-out, feverish eyes; we returned to our folding chairs in the little monastery garden. I had left my wife at our *pensione* that evening (headache, as I recall).

The music was sweet and tinny Italian baroque, played slowly, as if it were aspirant Rossini. The girls wore white gloves and were mostly accompanied by ladies in black veils. I was down from Paris for a few weeks to love Italy and the Italians.

After the last encore Roland Mardi settled us into the café and studied his nails and told me to order anything my little heart desired—chocolate, cookies, anything. With my famous perceptiveness in both English and French, I understood at once that he hated the smell of beer and wanted to do the talking for both of us. "*Un café*," I said, and he translated proudly into Italian for the waiter. He then asked why I had been staring at him in the monastery garden.

Hard to say. Maybe gazing intently, with deep interest—but no impolite staring. Why? His mummified body. His lacquered nails. The touch of rouge on his lips. There were so many choices, but I said something on the order of: "You look as if you knew Proust personally, the origins of dada and futurism, all the—complexities and mysteries of several generations of literary genius, up to and . . . and . . . and including today."

What intelligent perceptiveness in a young man! What ability to follow clues!

And what the devil, I asked myself, was on my mind? Well,
I was just idling. Back in Paris I knew hardly anyone but other
students, French, Scandinavian, Dutch, and American jetsam.
My wife and I were expecting a child. I was busy asking myself
what I had gotten myself into, and resolving to be serious
about life, and not entirely certain this was the best way to be.
We had taken this trip to Florence, and fallen in with a nest
of late-risers, and it was Paris all over again, in a splendid setting of umber stone, summer heat, sun-reddened dust. This
was the time of the first fine flowering of the Vespa. The
Ponte Santa Trinità was still an Army engineer's improvisation, black steel over the dynamited ruins, and the racket of
reconstruction was just beginning to distract Italy in its stunned and goofy rage of peace. We visited new Fascist-atrocity
trials and revived summer culture programs. The dark-eyed
Florentine women were learning to parade once more in their
white gloves, and they paraded in these white gloves near the
American Express. We stayed at the Pensione Berchieli,
where, it was said, E. M. Forster and D. H. Lawrence had
slept. No doubt that was before the invention of the riveting
hammer.

Well, I wasn't bored. But I felt there must be many things
more in Europe than what I knew, and Roland Mardi, grand-
son of the founder of a great bank, author of twenty-two pri-
vately printed books given to libraries and his friends—he did
not deprive the world of his daily journals—and two published
by publishers for the wider public, a Frenchman pared to the
bone, with electric, exposed nerves, the insulating meat worn
off by time and friction, provided a bit of variety to the spice
which was our lives. Generously he offered to the judgment of
history his recollections of Dreyfus, Jarry, Daudet, Proust, and
surrealism. Generously he offered my wife a bottle of his own
clear nail polish, bottled to his specifications in Lyons.
"Otherwise they crack," he advised her. "When you're not a

child any more, and you won't be a child forever, you must be careful to look pleasing for your friend."

And his face of an ancient child cracked with a burst of laughter, a short high-pitched squeal—so pleased! so pleased!

And so we hung out together in Florence. He took my wife and me to museums and lectured us, mostly me, about the traditions of Italian painting and his part in them, the beauties of the Boboli gardens and his previous views of them, Florence and how it had changed during the sadness. He had kept track of it.

"What did you do during the war?" I asked. This rude question was one of my hobbies. You were supposed to wait until the explanations came pattering out of their own accord.

"Ah, ah, that is a long story. You see, I was very old then, you see, and I . . ." And that delighted shrill squeal of laughter. "I'm much younger now, today, my friend! It was a dream; I think I was ill. Now I have found my youth again in this new world, and you wish the confessions of my old age. Shame, shame on you, nasty boy."

He did not have a definite or clear story. The lack of story pleased me after all the I-was-an-anti-Fascists I had met. Despite his old man's babble about the past, he disdained working this one out. Obviously, though, the money didn't stop. And there had been faithful retainers in Antibes while he wrote in his journals and organized his notes and waited for Ike's famous small-boy grin to debark after D-Day.

"The nasty war set me back," he said, pouting. "I could get my journals printed, of course, but it was impossible to mail the cahiers to my friends in all the cultural centers—London, Roma, New York, Berlin, Petersburg, Calcutta—I had subscribers in all the cultural centers—oh, by the by, do you know Mrs. Cornfeld in Charleston?"

"No, I've never been there."

"Oh, my dear boy, she's of the Mosaic creed—are you sure?

251

She sponsored chamber music at the college there, you know, the girls lycée in Carolina?"

He looked expectant. I shrugged. No light in my eyes. At first I thought he meant she was made of little tiles.

He looked sad. "My memory is going. She was one of my dearest ladies in the period of 1915 to 1917, Volume Seven. She married an American friend, lovely boy, he drove an ambulance for the Red Cross. I do remember, do I not, my friend?"

We strolled back and forth across the temporary bridge where the Ponte Santa Trinità had been. We pushed our way through the tourist crowds on the Ponte Vecchio, pricing leather items with the Florentine crest on them, bargaining for items to express love or friendship or a happy trip, and he offered to buy me . . . "Please, no rings or bracelets," I insisted.

My wife had a headache—fumes, crowd, a Vespa leaping a curb onto an old woman selling a hatful of black-market Chesterfields—and we walked her back to the hotel. Roland said, "God bless you, sleep well and soundly," and wanted to set out again on a wander through town. He was tireless and determined. He showed me Settignano, where "your sublime buffoon, Marco Twain, lived in the Villa Viviano. I remember him very well. Of course, I was too young to appreciate the full value of his vernacular. I was here with my uncle. I cared for nothing but the Goncourt brothers, but Twain was a sublime artist, just entering, I believe, the time of his despair. He wore a white suit and carried a white cane. He had curls like a boy. There were children exactly like that in the Tuileries, and I remember . . ."

His vitality was real. He crept back for a long nap before dinner, and to have his nails done by his man, and perhaps his long thin blue hair washed and rinsed, but he appeared in public again for the evening as fresh, in fresh starch, as the boys he remembered in the Tuileries gardens. I admired his brave and stubborn curiosity. "What," he would ask, "what-what—" and sneeze from the dust and use his inhaler and pat his nostrils with his frail and blue-veined hand and proceed with his question: "What do you do with your time, you Fulbright students and your colleagues, artists, *bohèmes?*"

"Well, we walk a lot, we hike," I said.

"I too, sir," he said, raising a finger, "I walk a lot, I hike."

And sure enough, he joined us in our touring of Fiesole and Florence, up hill and down *trattoria*, from the hallowed walls along which Dante may have idled (*pourquoi pas?*) to the Ristorante da Bing-Crosby, a popular spaghettying spot of that period when the U. S. of A. was still a novel delight to this part of the world. He would disappear for his nap, but then he would reappear, as agile as a spider. I already said fresh as starch. He climbed without sweating. He tramped, albeit lightly, pared down by time, care, and traditional routines. He offered me a bath in his suite at the best hotel on the Arno. He uttered a happy little aria about the nozzles on the tub— I would adore them if I could only find it in my heart to give them a chance.

My wife and I had this tiny room in a boarding house. She hid beneath an umbrella while I sponged myself in the sink, but still I never took advantage of his invitations to bathe in his bathtub in the hotel blessed by many Michelin stars. One afternoon he pressed his suit a little more closely. I was enjoying a lecture on futurism and the exaggeration of the buttock in the time of Mussolini, Numero Uno, when he suddenly said, "Come to Corsica with me, I have a beautiful house."

"Oh, I really couldn't do that."

"Do, do. You could read and study. I could show you my notebooks. They are judged to be of great interest."

"I really can't. We have to go back to Paris soon. My grant —the commission. And my wife should be near her doctor."

"She could go back to be near her doctor," he said happily.

"No, really, I must be with her. She is pregnant."

"Well," he said, "well, well." He grasped at straws. He cried out as if he had suddenly discovered the perfect compromise, "Well then, she could go with us!"

His way of saying *us*, making *she* another, a stranger to whom I felt obligations, seemed to get through my thick skull the message that something peculiar was going on. Until that moment I had been amused, entertained, and flattered by M. Mardi's attentions. Nothing was really real; this was Europe, wasn't it? Now conscience began to appear, and even a bit of panic. It was as if I were suddenly on the Public Square back in Cleveland. "No, we're heading for Paris this weekend," I said, having just decided.

"So soon," he said.

"We have to go home."

"Ah. Ah. Oh dear, it's four o'clock. I must go back to my hotel—a friend, a close friend . . ."

But sadness was bad for him and he determined to recover. He straightened his body, he stretched his fingers—a little easing trick of pulling one hand in the other—and he said, "Then I must offer a farewell party for you and all your colleagues. I insist!"

There was no necessity for him to insist. I accepted at once.

By this time, having been in Florence for nearly a month, I knew the great places, the gardens, statues, museums, and walks, and I also knew a dozen or so other would-bees—writers, painters, students, retired veterans and their ladies. I carried the happy word from café to furnished room: *Free meal!* The old boy was buying.

We met at the Ristorante da Bing-Crosby. Roland adored America, and the place reminded him of the America he loved —a private back room with antipasto, spaghetti, rogatini, scallopini, Broglio wine, and "apple pie"—little diced pieces of apple, sweetened and spilled on a spongy cake. It also reminded us of the America we had left behind—plenty of food provided by someone else. He grinned and tittered and toyed with his meal, overjoyed by our appetites. Our ladies, in pony-tails or bobbed hair and the cotton dresses which they had made themselves, occasionally chattered politely with him; most of the men drank and laughed and spoke English, which he understood, but not at him so that he could hear. He smiled, trying to have fun, and waved his hands in front of his face to ward off the smoke.

At the end of the meal he ordered the table cleared—at least the waiters listened to him—and new cups of coffee were brought, together with plates of cookies which were put at ei-ther end of the table. Roland tapped on a glass with a small silver spoon. He tapped lightly, but now he was not asking for our attention; he demanded it. Gradually the flushed faces gave a moment to this distraction; the jokes fell away; a little calmed by food and wine, a little startled by second or third cups of coffee, we turned to him.

He said, "And now I will read from my journal, sight-translating from the original French into English. I have noted and discussed Marcel Proust, Henri Bergson, and Jean Cocteau in my cahiers, and tonight I have the delightful op-portunity to include among these immortals the young people of the English and the American languages. And now I shall read."

He coughed and patted his lips. He must have memorized this speech. Eyes rolled. Knees were nudged, legs kicked under the table; no interruption. I suppose he had spent nearly eighty years developing his vision of the dandy, living a bird-like aloofness, singing in the wilderness for himself and for a few other birds; I suppose there was the melancholia of the ancient dandy. But then his head was bent and he was trans-lating the foolish words—old man's words: "I met some very nice young Americans. We talked about the *belle epoque*. One particularly seemed interested and nice to me . . ."

There must have been great sadness in his heart, but we in

that steamy room were impatient with his arteries. Someone whispered, "Gaga, completely gaga."

I sent a shut-up look to the whisperer across the table.

The high-pitched voice trickled on: "One of them, the one who was particularly nice, has informed me of much of interest to me about the new generation . . ."

The room was filled with smoke. Having finished our meal, we were impatient with sitting. This old-timey article with clear polish on his nails was a total drag. Someone else whispered; someone answered; many of us were talking. For a few moments Monsieur Mardi went on reading from his recent *Memoires Literaires*. He really did know Proust, Cocteau, Ezra Pound, Ford Madox Ford, and now us. "I got a stomach ache," Sam Moon, the painter, said very loudly. "*Yecch*, I ate too much. Why doesn't he pay the check so we can get out of here?"

Roland suddenly sat down at the head of the table and his fingers were twisting about the tiny silver coffee spoon in his fist. Tears ran down his face. "Oh dear, what's the matter with him?" one of the girls asked.

"Did he hear me?" the painter asked. He hated to hurt someone's feelings.

"I don't think so," his girl friend said. "No, of course he didn't, stupe."

The tears were running off his face and onto the open notebook.

"Then what's the matter with him?"

I heard myself answering as if he were alone in the room with me and I was taking notice of him at last: "*Il est ému.*" And then again, stiffly translating for the others, my friends, as if this stranger had disappeared from our sight: "He was moved."

YOUNG MAN, OLD DAYS

A STORY

For many springtimes it was Frank Curtis' custom to pay a visit to a man we'll call Justin in the Left Bank hotel Le Grand-Sèvres, where he has lived for twenty years. Justin and Frank were among the great buzzing hive suspended in Paris after the war by Fulbright Act, by GI Bill, by veterans pension, by remittance, by other mysterious conveyances and supports, intending to transform themselves from fretful would-bees, living by their nerves, to fretful celebrities, living by the adulation of others. Oh yes, and some of them wanted to do good work, had projects, had visions. They were painters, writers, musicians; a few film makers came later to the askew *chambres tout confort* of the Grand-Sèvres.

Justin wrote movie criticism, poems, stories; he became a great friend of Alice B. Toklas, who thought him pretty and one of the few geniuses of the season 1949–1950; he took tea with André Gide a few months before Gide died (Gide liked him, he reported), and received advances from publishers and charmed everyone by being a friendly puppy and by providing an energetic transit system for gossip. He scrambled for money, but he made out. He seemed to like everyone in the life of art. He knew his way around Pigalle and sometimes found special White Russian clubs and dawn exhibitions for friends or friends of friends. He was small, curly, compact, and fast. There were new geniuses for the season 1950–1951, but Justin kept his spirits up. He bore no grudge against Alice B. Toklas. He was sweet and traveled unarmed, like a medic—he had just missed the war and the GI Bill—amid the rivalries, boredoms, and battles to the death in the life of Art.

Their friendship was attenuated by diverging paths, as friendships usually are. At first they were near neighbors down the hall. He showed Frank the Buci market and Shakespeare & Company and told him to be welcome in Lutetia. He took him to the Café Sportif to cash his first check. Then, expecting a child, Frank and his wife moved out of the Grand-Sèvres. The child was born. They decided to return to Cleveland. Before they left, after a second year in Paris, his wife wept as they strolled the *quais* of the Seine—bicycles, Vespas, fishermen, lovers, it was not yet a roaring mini-superhighway —and she said, "We'll never come back, it's all over," and he said, "Of course we'll come back," and of course she was right, it really was all over, Cleveland was a way station to separate elsewheres; and when they came back to Paris, they came back separately and very much changed.

Frank lost track of Justin. He was briefly a professor of French, then (alimony and child support) an international advertising expert for American corporations. He spoke the language of Racine and Camus to consumers of Otis, Allis-Chalmers and Massey-Ferguson in France, Lebanon, and Senegal. When he began returning to Paris each year on various tasks and meetings, he knew nothing of Justin and scarcely thought of him. That was another time. He had not been a close friend. Nice Justin, sure he remembered, he had been around the scene.

But then, when the child conceived in Room 5 was ten years old, he heard that Justin was still holding the fort in the Grand-Sèvres—without telephone, without job, still piecing himself out in the city of light, a young man writing. He felt a heavy flush of nostalgia. What persistence and bravery, what stubbornness. If Justin was alive and well in the Grand-Sèvres, then Mouludji and the Tabou, the Rose Rouge and Juliette Greco in her *bloo-djeans* were still alive, fresh, true, beautiful,

and existential. Frank went to see him with a bad case of the
sentimental dizzies.

The old hotel was unaltered. A slightly larger bulb serviced
the *minuterie*, but there were still only eight seconds to get to
the next landing before the light went out. He used six seconds per landing, round and round to the top. He knocked
without warning at about one in the afternoon. Long silence,
and then a sleepy whispering and a voice crying out: *"Qui est-
ce?"*

He gave his name.

"Uh, uh, say, could you come back in about an hour?"

Clockwise downward to wait with *Le Monde* and a *café
crème* at the little bar on the rue des Saints-Pères. When
Frank returned, Justin was washed, dressed, and alone. The
room under the eaves was pretty much as he knew it, crazily
slanting, sinking into history; many somebodies had slept
there. Justin's hair was slicked down by water and Frank's congratulations were sincere: "You haven't changed!" This
pleased him, and Frank doubled his pleasure, doubled his fun
by inviting him to lunch.

"I haven't changed?"

"Not at all," Frank insisted, "honest," and it seemed true,
though the angle of slant had steepened and it was uphill from
the bed to the alcohol stove and he knew by faith and theory
as he hung on, getting his sea legs on the streets of Bohemia,
that other, invisible matters must have altered and rearranged
themselves in these ten years. The crumbling plaster was over-
laid with ancient horror-movie posters—Karloff, Lugosi, Fay
Wray, Kong—and they tunneled him beneath the late forties
and early fifties, when he had known Justin, to his childhood
in Cleveland, fright and magic time at Loew's Granada on a
Saturday afternoon. Between two features, while he bought
candy for the next ordeal, ghouls and zombies strolled the
aisles with fleas and bits of popcorn leaping in their fur. The
discontinuity with his time in Paris was odder than the whips,

screams, hypodermics, and monochrome werewolves stretched
and glued to the walls.

"It's an interest I have," Justin said.

"I didn't know."

"Oh, I didn't tell anyone."

They went to lunch and Justin gave him the little news of
the people who stayed on and on in Paris. "Karen gave up
journalism and opened a dress shop on the rue de Beaune
. . . Ferd works in surplus-export or the CIA or something
kinky like that . . . Archie can't get divorced—his Italian
waif got so fat, you wouldn't believe it—"

(Which Italian waif? What Archie? Ferd who? But Karen,
he remembered her—youngest girl ever to almost get a review
in the *New Statesman*—and wait a sec, Archie, begins to come
back, met the Princess Marguerite Caetani di Bassiano—now
there's a name that sticks—and she was going to publish him
in—)

"*Botteghe Oscure*," said Justin. "She took a story of Archie's, same issue as the first draft of *Under Milkwood*. He
does mutual funds for the Army—that waif really laid it into
him and got disgusting."

Frank never did place the waif. He vaguely recalled that Archie liked thin girls who read Kafka.

In return he tried to give Justin word of the States, but Justin got back every two years without fail, no matter how busy
he was, to see his mother, and so he kept caught up. He wasn't
interested in Frank's daughter born in Paris, conceived in the
Grand-Sèvres one floor below him, and only mildly in what
had happened to him since, but the lunch was affable and easy
and they strolled about during the afternoon (a bottle of La
Slavia at the Old Navy) and it was good to see each other
(teatime coffee at the Tournon).

Justin did a little reviewing—music, opera, dance. He did
some dubbing of films and once, thanks to a friend, had been
commissioned to write a treatment for a *nouvelle vague*

movie. No credit to him on the final product, but they came across with the down payment. He did irregular duty as the voice of a very thin secondary star in Godard–Truffaut–Robbe Grillet off-Boulogne movies, who was, however, seldom dubbed for the Anglo-American market. He wiggled on through.

"Say," he said, as if to prove how well he made out, "someone gave me a couple of tickets to the Ukrainian Folk Ballet at the Théâtre des Nations—they've been sold out for weeks . . ."

But Frank was busy. A dinner meeting with a disc jockey from the Luxembourg station, and then a couple of ladies, one for each.

"Every time Sartre makes up with the Party again, you can't buy a ticket to an Iron Curtain attraction for love or money. However, pal, if you happen to have both love and money *plus* friends in high places—"

It was a generous gesture. Surely he had many friends who would jump at the chance to watch the Ukrainians jump. Though he meant to, Frank didn't get around to the Grand-Sèvres again that trip. They exchanged New Year's cards six months later.

As it happened, he could usually work Paris onto his route to talk to the sheik or set up a meeting with the Rumanians (they always conferred real good but had to check with the Soviets and it was therefore zero time in Auld Bucharest). Each year when he visited Justin he bought the lunch, Justin bought the coffee, they moved the news around. His changelessness made Frank Curtis feel young. Justin was still doing what a very young man does; Justin and Frank were the same age; therefore . . . The syllogism stroked some atavism in Frank; well, vanity is the truer word, despite how ridiculous he knew it was and how he tried teasing himself while he also took the gain. He aimed to keep the truth in mind, anyway. Another friend in the hotel when he lived there had had five

children by a Sarah Lawrence girl he met on the stairway
when the *minuterie* caught them both in the dark. They lived
in Rockland County; he produced for educational television.
The lesbian of the second floor was married to a famous Nor-
wegian diplomat, superbusy with UN rescue missions in
emerging and submerging African states. A season of glory had
visited one of the writers in the hotel. He was now suffering a
reaction of public and critics—the most famous failure of our
generation, ready to be done up as an example in *Life*—but his
accountant had tucked away some of the money from the
good years in safe and tax-free places so he could stop to gather
himself together. He wasn't dead yet.

And Frank himself? Well, having fun and getting ready for
his move. Keeping a good grip on the past was part of it. A bit
of it was seeking and prying, rooting about as a rest from consolidating advertising accounts, but as long as he was young,
he could still be allowed to make ready.

Justin didn't change, but sometimes he looked tired,
plucked early and preserved in brine. Under the fluorescent
tubes of the revised café on the corner Frank could read some
of the cost of his perpetual youthifying in smudges and veins
around the eyes. His mother died, he got the money, but he
tarried on in the hotel. The only difference was that he didn't
have to return to New Haven every two years for those boring
visits when she would ask him, *Aren't you ever going to settle
down?* and he would answer, *Yes, Mother, I've settled down.*

It was she who eventually settled down. The inheritance
meant that he could have bought a small apartment on the
rue de Fleurus, say, but he saw no reason to move. People
knew where he was and how to find him. The crazily slanted,
winding stairway, the wood now white from being scrubbed
with strong soap in times of prosperity, time of the Malraux
cleanup of national monuments, made a comforting space between the Left Bank streets and his room. He had worn his
paths through the days and nights of Paris. The gypsy boy had

pitched his tent in one place longer than anyone. He liked being a young man, making out okay in the city of light, paradise of hope, capital of desire, home of the first *cinemathèque*.

In the original line from Valéry, that's the capital of hope and paradise of misery.

The last time Frank saw him, he was again just getting up, just about to get up—"What time is it, pal?" It was three in the afternoon, it was early spring and raining outside, and there was a heavy wintry chill in the room. He was getting over the usual winter bronchitis, he said. As usual, Frank invited him to lunch, but this time he said he couldn't manage it; he was waiting for someone. The cough was a habit (Gauloises bleu, bronchial inflammation); it tuckered him out. There was rain dripping down the eaves and the broken pipe. Someone was bringing him some soup. Rain, gray rain outside, and rain in the air inside. A corner of Bela Lugosi was peeling off the wall; the sword dipped in the river Jordan was coming unstuck. "There's this friend—he's terribly shy—he never goes out except in the middle of the afternoon, when he won't meet anybody . . . I suppose it's pathological, but how we treat it, we humor it . . ."

Okay. Frank supposed they had come to the end of these visits anyway. They had never been close friends; even the yearly renewals among the horror posters were crowding it a bit.

"But wait a sec, he won't be here for twenty minutes or so. It's part of the pathology—he's usually late."

Wearing a flannel bathrobe over his underwear, he made coffee on the alcohol stove. He had acquired a cat. The concierge must have changed the rules. Frank said, "When I see a bottle of Nescafé in Paris, I still think it's a black-market item—"

"Unh," he said.

Frank told him that his elder daughter was about to enter

college. He didn't argue the point. Frank told him he couldn't believe it. Justin neither confirmed nor denied this analysis of the situation. Frank told him once more that he looked unchanged.

That always got his attention. He looked up from the Nescafé. "I'll dye my hair if I have to," he said. He took a level spoonful from the jar of Lait Guigoz. "I'll go to Switzerland for a face-lift."

Frank started to laugh, but he meant it, and knowing this was their farewell, Justin pointed to his head. "Look," he said. It was as if he had spilled ink on his scalp. "Experimenting. Actually, though, it darkens the scalp, ick, I'll have to do a hair-knitting on it. They call it 'virile' baldness when it starts receding in front. That's not necessarily a good word for it. This is a temporary measure."

"Oh, a small matter," Frank said soothingly. "Actually, you know, you really look the same—amazing. I jog a little when I'm home, but I'm never home. You do calisthenics, Justin?"

True, he hadn't changed at all, and he looked worn out.

"It's partly your physical type," Frank went on. "And your life. Even now, when you're tired, you haven't been well, it's more like a tired kid . . ."

"Actually," Justin said in a cold rage—it was as if he had heard another judgment, "actually, wake up, will you? Do you know how long it's been since you cooked your supper on one of these alcohol stoves?"

"A long time," Frank said, smiling. But he drew his Burberry close around him.

"I face the truth my own way—do you, pal? Do you know how I pass my time, Monsieur Rip Van Winkle? I pass my time making out with boys who weren't even born when you lived in this terrible place."

The Life of Art seems impossible for a grownup. And yet the childish building of dream castles is how I have wanted to spend my days. While indulging the fantasies of my stories and novels, I've needed to rest in history—some moral validation of my own life through doing what I can in the world. Therefore I have reported and argued from various wars and troubles—the John Birch Society, Moscow, divorce and gambling, California politics and Israel, a young man dying in a hospital and old men paying twenty-five dollars for their haircuts.

Biafra is different. The case of Biafra is a crucial disaster in the life of the time. The horror is nearly pure, and the cruelty of the rest of the world nearly total. Our only chance now is to learn from it; even that profit seems obscene. We didn't require this lesson to know what we are. Too late for the nation of Biafra.

MY SUMMER
VACATION IN BIAFRA

A JOURNAL

In the spring of 1969 I was invited by telephone by a Committee for Biafran Writers and Artists and I accepted at once. The lady at the other end of the wire in New York told me about shots and preparations and then began to giggle. "You mean you're really going? You're not going to think about it and call back and say you can't? Do you know there isn't any place to sleep and you may not eat for a week?" It was odd to hear her laughter across the continent.

I telephoned a Biafran relief organization in San Francisco;

the reverend in charge was in conference, but I spoke to an assistant. "I'm going to Biafra on Monday," I said.

"You're going to be off on Monday?" he asked.

"Biafra!" I said.

"Oh, *Biafra*," he said. "Yeah, man. Cool. Why?"

Next I called an editor to whom I suggested writing about this trip. "Oh Jesus, we're up to our ass in Biafran babies." I agreed; I skip those articles, too. I have an image of the swollen belly and the mournful eyes, and it's classified, like the Vietnam war: a horror with which I continue to live, like everyone else.

Getting There

Biafra makes bad dreams for people who refuse to dream.

While the moon rocket splashes down, and all over the front pages, the red-haired babies are buried in the News of the Week in Review. I'd heard about kwashiorkor, "the redman's disease." But the hair looks more like a crispy grayish-red, and it doesn't look like hair—something weakly extruded by a disoriented body, and it looks as if it would break if you bent it.

"Hunger is a legitimate weapon of war," says one of the Nigerian generals. The Nigerians use it to destroy the Biafrans. The Biafrans use it to try to arouse the atrocity-drugged conscience of the world. The children die to these purposes.

These abstractions are not the truth of it. The truth here is suffering and the sufferers cannot tell it and I am trying to write my way out of shock. Floating through the suffering, immune and shaken, sleepless and immune, full of rage and immune.

Our party: Leslie Fiedler, literary critic. Miriam Reik, professor of English ("Just call me Dr. Reik"). Diana Davies, who calls herself "The Packhorse," photographer and black-belt judoka. H. Gold, who wonders what the devil he is doing here.

Jews and Ibos. "The Ibos should go home to their region." —Alhaji Usman Liman. "These people know how to make money."—Mallam Muhammadu Mustapha Mande Gyari. "There are too many of them in the north. They were just like sardines ["spawned in some estaminet?" as T. S. Eliot said] and just too dangerous."—Mallam Mukhter Bello. (These quotations are from an address by Colonel Odumegwu Ojukwu to the African Unity Consultative Committee meeting, Addis Ababa, August 5, 1968.)

Fourteen million people in Biafra! Hardly a tribe. We don't call the Irish or the Jews a tribe, not without some malice in there someplace.

I wouldn't have chosen this trip, but neither could I refuse it. I can only bear witness, and it's all I can do. Who is the meddler who was described as having lost some fine opportunities to remain silent?

"Captain Genocide" is the bomber pilot who boasts on the radio of killing children. He flies an Ilyushin, but they think he's a Belgian. About forty percent of the children are dead from starvation, so Captain G. is not a major producer and packager of child mortality. He relieves the protein shortage by reducing the demand. "Never to be born would be best for mortal man, but this happens only to a very few." The melancholy joke has another meaning in Biafra. Babies are born who are not born. Babies are born with death as their only and immediate future.

Biafra was an ancient African kingdom of which little memory but the name endures. However, the name is magic and its history is becoming real again at the command of modern war.

From the *Guardian*, May 28, an editorial urging freedom for Wole Soyinka, the Nigerian playwright held in prison because of his sympathy for the Biafrans: "In order to improve

Nigeria's public relations, General Gowon has lately made commendable efforts to scale down the bombing of Biafran civilians. He could win more sympathy by releasing an artist who is regarded abroad," etc.

San Francisco–New York–Lisbon–Luanda–São Tomé–Biafra. The crashing through time zones, confusion of nerves in day and night, is an appropriate prelude to mass murder and desperate hope in an African rain forest.

May 29: The Portuguese Island of São Tomé

The Biafran official has a habit I recognize—the Haitian one of grabbing his balls at odd moments when he needs reassurance. I don't think it's merely the heat and tight underwear. "I went to law school at Tufts," he beams.

We wait at the Geronimo Hotel for permission to fly in one of the relief planes, Caritas or World Council of Churches, Catholic or Protestant. We get drunk with the fliers. The pilots are (a) Steve McQueen, (b) Steve McQueen's Best Friend, the Crazy Kid, (c) the Old Boy Who Drinks Too Much But Give Me One More Chance, Steve. There are also the British flying officer who got into some unmentionable trouble with a guardsman; a smiling Japanese; a deformed Texan whom I think of as the Forceps Baby; and subsidiary do-gooders, ironic intellectuals, machined Canadians on leave from their airlines—the full cast of an outmoded flick. They are idealists in it for the ideal of money: they can make up to $3,000 a week. I especially like one whose real name is Johnny Cash (he showed me his driver's license to prove it), and another called "Jack Frost from South of the Equator"—"Jack" for short. When Jack heard that Leslie and I are writers, he began to tell us about the Biafran children, to whom he transports Formula 2, rice, and beans through the blacked-out, MiG-haunted sky.

A crowd of us hangs around the airport, trying to catch a flight. "The Princess" flirts with a Biafran official: she looks like Princess Radziwill, but she's a real princess. Like stop-action photography of growing vegetables, first you see her in Pucci pajamas, and then one frame later she's in starched combat suit and then in a sweet limpid little frock. We drink Cokes with the pilots and nervously visit toilets overflowing *à la portugaise*. The weepy American who wanted to rejoin his Ibo wife, the Italian reporter who has been turned away day after day, the Swedish team, the Swiss boy journalist, and the four of us with our letters, invitations, passes, and Dr. Reik to speak for us. Three of the six planes which went out returned without landing in Biafra. "Intruder" was back.

The ground crews in shorts, stained T-shirts, with the frazzled faces of old softball coaches. "Jello and a Coke!" one mechanic was yelling at the waiter. "No ice for the Coke on this goddamn job."

Jack Frost: "Now, you just stick close to me if you want to know all about the war—what paper you say you write for?"

Johnny Cash: "Now, here's my wife and four kids in Glendale . . ."

Jack Frost (as we climbed on a Super-Constellation): "So you're playing Bet Your Life today, are you?" We signed the No Harm agreement. He told us the Joint Church Aid flights are called "Jesus Christ Airlines." He has a whole repertory like that.

We lumbered off the runway on a Super-Connie called Snoopy with nineteen tons of rice and dried milk. We stretched out on the sacks. "You'll get rice mites if you sit on the rice," the pilot said amiably, "or milk worms if you sit on the milk."

The radioman said, "Shit, the Bomber used to fly with one of our pilots. He'd radio in and say, 'Man, I'll get you tonight.' " He was a South African.

"What about the MiGs? Don't you have any trouble with them?"

He grinned. "Egyptians. Six-Day War," he said.

I fell asleep, rice mites and milk worms, as we droned through the sky over tropical sea, and Nigeria into Biafra and Uli Airport. He waked me with a grin to see the flak below—pretty tangerine flashes following the sound of the aircraft.

Uli Airport Coming

We arrived in a pandemonium of blacked-out airfield. Planes unloading food, pilots screaming (they have to get out before dawn; they don't want to be bombed down here, either), trucks grinding and backing, officials greeting us and smiling: "Welcome to Biafra. Welcome to Enugu." Though Enugu has long been in the possession of the federals, they still carry on the fiction that the Uli airstrips are really Enugu Airport. Nearby, in a blacked-out building, I heard, no kidding, a band playing "I Ain't Got No Satisfaction"—celebrating two years of freedom.

We wandered about helplessly, looking for our contacts, nameless officials, in the faceless dark. Diana asked to take a flash photograph and immediately an eager-beaver soldier boy arrested us. While he went to get an officer, I wandered off toward the music: "I ain't got no sat-is-fac-tion, unh, unh, UNH!" Vaguely I understood we were under arrest, but at four in the morning in the tropics, in a strange land fighting a strange war, the music seemed more real to me than a red-tape misunderstanding.

The soldier caught me at the door to the dance. "You move very fast," he said, and in his voice was hatred, suspicion, stupidity, and bucking for stripes.

We were passed from bureaucrat to bureaucrat. Finally we reached the commander of the base. The sly, foolish soldier said, "She took a picture."

"She did not. She asked if she could take a picture," I said.

"Goddammit, the Committee for Biafran Writers and Artists is hereby dissolved!" Miriam Reik cried.

"In my opinion, sah," said the soldier, "she was ready to take a picture."

The commander said "Tut-tut." He was a former school principal. He explained to us that they were fighting a war for survival, to the soldier that we were friends of Biafra, and wrote out an official piece of paper declaring everyone innocent—us, soldier, officers, himself. We need this man in Berkeley.

Somehow in the mess of being arrested, soaked in the rain, shuttled about, we lost our contact. We slept on chairs in the customs house. Someone brought us cold corn and coconut for breakfast, and then coffee. A man from the Ministry of Information came to get us, carrying his copy of *Le Grand Sommeil, par* Raymond Chandler.

He drove like a madman down roads blocked with stumps so the Nigerians couldn't use them as landing strips. At the checkpoints the guards said "Welcome" as they pointed their antique weapons at us. *Le Grand Sommeil?* Is he putting us on?

A Day or Two Later

A blood vessel in my right eye has broken. Days without sleep, much heat, much strain. Our clothes haven't dried since the soaking of a few nights ago. Every official says, "This war, these conditions . . . things are rather difficult, really. We are decentralized, you know."

"Decentralization" is the euphemism for the capture of the capital, Umuahia, and all other cities. Though the Biafrans have recaptured Owerri and are moving services back into it, it is burned out, wrecked, nearly deserted, with occasional stunned and starving people squatting beneath the riddled Pepsi billboard.

Stopped by the side of the road, waiting for a pass which we needed in order to get to the place where we could get a pass

271

which would, in turn, enable us to get a pass, I handed out protein tablets that I carried with me. They are compressed lumps of fishy dust which had turned my stomach when I sampled them in the States. They were delicious. Diana had water in her canteen, a mouthful for each of us. The driver looked as if he were eating birthday cake and I gave him another handful. He was very thin and I asked him if he had lost weight since the war. "No, no, oh no, I was always like this."

Ibo pride, ebullience and optimism. Plus a bit of fibbing.

We got gas at a military camp. The Biafrans have created backyard refineries, sometimes even using wood as fuel for Rube Goldberg distilling contraptions.

Can they be defeated by the combination of English, Soviet, Arab, and Nigerian energy directed against them? And this would be a great loss—a gay, energetic, inventive people.

Is there a possibility of reconciliation with Nigeria? Father Doheny estimates over a million Biafrans dead already, a generation of men and children. He sighed and his Irish Cary Grant face crinkled: "Polygamy is unavoidable. There are so few men left."

But can Nigeria be defeated? Not with its overwhelming advantage in population, material, and allies. However, it can fall apart.

Is there something besides murderous stalemate in store? The Biafrans grin. "Nigeria will dissolve, it's unnatural." The separate states will follow natural (linguistic, racial, geographical) rather than colonial boundaries. And then perhaps there will be alliances and trade, as between the U.S. and Canada, which were enemies in 1812, or as among the nations in the Common Market, where wars were fought rather recently, rather than the Nigerian exploitation of tribe by tribe and struggle for power and corruption.

I asked a Biafran why American blacks, if they are interested at all, seem to support Nigeria. "Because they think we are like Katanga, the creature of someone else. Because they don't know how the Arab hates the African, and they fancy themselves Muslim and we're Christian. Because they don't know the truth, the world doesn't know, either."

Kwashiorkor in the Hospital at Ihiala

An Irish nun shows us a heap of about a dozen children on a mat. "Of these," she says briskly, "three may live—this one, this one, this girl."

When one whimpers, another dying child strokes it with a withered hand.

"Agu, agu, agu," a child is crying. This means "hungry." But he's a healthy one; the lost ones can no longer assimilate food.

"If they live, are they retarded?"

"They were so keen before," she says, "it takes a lot to put them down. But it's the first time for kwashiorkor. How can you know?"

One of the priests teases and chucks the chins of the soon-to-be-dead, calling to them in Ibo, trying to make them answer. These are the Fathers of the Holy Ghost, the Holy Rosary Sisters, the Hospital of Our Lady of Lourdes at Ihiala. They have given up missionary work for the duration.

Sister: "We're slack at the moment. If you think we're busy, we're not. We're slack. When the fighting was here, we worked twenty-four hours a day."

Wounded soldiers outside were playing checkers, joking, laughing, and studying mathematics and engineering textbooks. The priest got a group of children to sing a Biafran song for us. Leslie and I, escaped from the kwashiorkor ward, were happy to be among the legless, the armless, the eyeless. "Mending bones. Ah, that's nice," the sister said.

No dogs, no birds. They've all been eaten. I saw a woman with a target painted on her dress. She is the target. A priest is telling us how they have cultivated every place; how chicks are growing, but they need corn; how salt costs as much as $30 a cup. Along the roads there are signs such as THE UNIVERSAL INSURANCE COMPANY (INC. IN BIAFRA), advertisements asking for clerks, typists, offering barristers, herb doctors (diplomate in London).

The King of Ihiala

That's the translation of *oluha*: king. His name is J. M. Udorji. He gave me an audience, even though he was not well; he looked as if he was dying, burning with some fever, exhausted, emaciated, and tottering in his robes.

Poem dedicated to King Udorji on painted scroll in the antechamber:

> What the joint growth of arms and arts foreshow:
> The world's a monarch, and that monarch YOU.

He offered me the ritual kola nut, a bitter mild narcotic which relieves hunger. He offered me some food, but his hot hand and burning eyes made me think of germs everywhere. Women in the courtyard were singing and chanting for his recovery. Sometimes his voice gave out and he seemed to lose his thought in the middle of a sentence. I would guess he is about forty years old.

"There will never be a proper peace and understanding with Nigeria. Someone will always remember the horrors, the happenings, so many happenings. We will not fight a war of survival and then lose. Gowon will find it difficult to say, 'I am tired.' Britain, who supplies ammunition, is not tired. When Britain is tired, Gowon will be tired."

I excused myself early, wanting to save his strength.

I walked back to the mission, past the gun emplacement with its battery of homemade antiaircraft—greased pipes. The trench and dugout had been flooded by the rains last night.

The soldier guarding the antiaircraft symbol said, "Yes, sah! We are here all the time, sah! My brother and me, sah!"

"The word redeemeth, and food and weapons give life," said one of the priests.

I walked through a ward of children with kwashiorkor. These were babies well enough to be moved by plane to Gabon; they are expected to recover. But there was one child who suddenly toppled over and seemed to be dying. "Flora! Flora!" cried her little brother. And in the Ibo language: "Wake up! Wake up, Flora!" A black priest bent over her and spoke to her brother: "This is a scandal. You must wake her up."

The Leaders of Thought

Somewhere in Owerri province, in the middle of the night, we were driven to hear General Ojukwu address the Leaders of Thought on the subject of two years of Biafran independence. It was in a wrecked church. We were searched as politely as possible by a soldier who murmured, "Welcome, welcome." Black-beret honor guard, pride and seriousness, a Händel hymn played by a scratchy record. "Blockaded, starved, and massacred, let us give thanks to Almighty God for preserving Biafra as a sovereign and independent nation," said General Ojukwu.

Wearing clean fatigues, a shining-eyed, black-bearded, handsome young man with an Oxford accent and a solemn manner, he invoked "the Nigerian crime of genocide." While he read the speech, an aide took the pages one by one as he finished. "For the dead on the other side of the conflict, may their souls rest in peace."

"Amen," came the response from the crowd—officials, officers, priests, nuns, wives, and friends. The red, black, and green Biafran flag was draped about him; also a banner with lions rampant, eagle, knives, palm tree split by lightning, and

275

the legend: TO THINE OWN SELF BE TRUE. He denounced English imperialism, Soviet bolshevism, Arab expansionism, white colonialism, African servitude and feudalism. And with all these enemies, he was optimistic about the future.

"Some people are frightened by the word 'revolution'— good gracious! It is simply a quick change for the better." Once again he made the crucial distinction for Biafra; they did not secede from Nigeria, they were expelled in a series of pogroms.

Leslie and I collaborated on a name for his style: Monseigneur J. Pierpont Guevera X.

The speech took too long. It seemed to be an educational program—history plus consecration of history plus a program for the future. Several disparate speeches by separate hands seemed to have been yoked together and read with enthusiasm by a healthy young man who lacks a natural orator's rhythm. But the Oxford accent and slightly pedantic manner encourages hope that he is not a tyrant or rabble-rouser. Everything came in threes—"corruption, malfeasance, and inefficiency," "arrogant, insolent, and overbearing." Or in twos: "Love and friendship," "distrust and hardship," "proud and courageous." "Responsible, trusting, and loving," "industrious, resourceful, and inventive," "proud and courageous."

"Colonialism and genocide."

"Honor, pride, and glory."

But it's a relief to find a noncharismatic leader. We've seen the others lately.

Afterward we were taken to a buffet supper with General Ojukwu and other dignitaries. It was a silent and weary and somewhat stiff occasion. Fiedler and I circled warily about the other Americans present, Dr. Ferguson, Nixon's fact-finder, a light-mulatto gentleman with two aides, one from the Red Cross, one from Washington; they circled warily about us. Impression: that they thought us Biafran propagandists. We thought them pro-Nigerian. The Biafrans, unskilled politicians, seemed to enjoy us powerless writers, who could do them little good, and they mostly ignored the official mission from Washington, which was in a position to do them much good.

Few guards, few cops and soldiers: for a nation under siege, their confidence is astonishing and hair-raising.

About Meeting Leslie Fiedler in Strange Places

Attacked by MiGs at Ihiala. Two MiGs made two passes at us—that is, at the hospital and the mission house.

Leslie (to me): "We seem to meet in strange places." At a Princeton psychiatrist's house, at Hugh Hefner's mansion in Chicago, at Harvard summer school, in a men's room in New York—and now at the mission of the Irish Fathers of the Holy Ghost in Ihiala, Biafra, being rocketed by Soviet aircraft piloted by East Germans or Egyptians.

We looked at the crater a few yards from the mission. Then we went to see the wounded, dying, and dead in the hospital. No panic; much hatred. I see why the bombing of civilians doesn't end wars. The passion to resist is very powerful. *Don't Touch Me!*—I remember the American Revolution.

The Rehabilitation Center in Orlu

Dr. Imoke: "Once I was a doctor. Now events have made me a politician."

We drank palm wine, a sweet fermented cider, and ate African pears and rice with bits of what I took to be chicken gristle: it was stockfish—smoked, dried, salted cod. The house was painted with the letters ROCK OF AGES. Dr. Imoke told us about the Land Army; we see the plantings everywhere, yams, maize, okra, groundnuts, cassava, plantains, bananas, sweet potatoes. "The Land Army fights the Hunger." (One of the Nigerian generals said, "Starvation is a weapon of war.")

277

Dr. Imoke: "It is not possible to lose a war for survival. That has not happened in history, has it?"

We visited some refugee camps. At Umuhu we met a girl— homeless, emaciated, without family—studying a French grammar. Walter, the young Swiss journalist, gave her his two-week-old copy of *Le Monde*. She was a lovely willowy Ibo. I wiggled my ears for the children and made coins disappear, and was told by a spokesman for the crowd that I am a trickster.

Nobody begged. We saw lines of children at feeding stations, carrying their bowls every which way, on heads, in hands, juggled. The laughing optimism of this suffering people makes you believe in something congenital, hormonal, inbred about good nature. The building painted with the letters LITTLE HOUSE OF SMALL REGRETS.

We visited a backyard oil refinery: gas being produced by Rube Goldberg contraptions amid hellish heat and a constant hiss and roar and penetrating smell. An Ibo tribesman (trained at Purdue) directed the operation. Nearby, a crowd of mechanics was cannibalizing automobiles. Two years without spare parts, and still, the transport moves. Batteries are the great problem, but wherever a car needs a push, the nearest bystanders lend their shoulders. (My back aches.)

Uli Airport Going

Jack Frost of South of the Equator will get us home, maybe.

The State House customs routines, a parody of British habit which they cannot shake off, continue in blackout, under air attack, with war and starvation all about. In a smoky, lamp-lit cubicle, an emaciated clerk with glasses sliding down his nose asks, "State of birth?" "Ohio," I answer, and he nods sagely as if I have told him something, and he writes *O-h-i-o*.

On the form which asks for Port of Entry, he says, "Write

Enugu." But the Nigerians have bloodily captured Enugu months ago and we were not at Enugu.

"If you're going to be a correct official," I say, "why tell me to write Enugu?"

He smiles in the flickering yellow light. "Let me see your medical certificate," he says. He checks it and says, "Now follow Carol."

Carol is the girl studying a five-year-old copy of *Modern Screen*. She stands up, smiles, and disappears into the dark. Single file we shuffle through the crowd behind her. I'm afraid of losing her and put out my hand to touch her shoulder and a girl looks up at me and says, "Pardon, sah?" It's not Carol Modernscreen. We've lost her. I start to giggle at the lady whom I have grabbed in error. Carol finds us.

Despite all the pretense of customs and exit formalities, this is a parody, a society being bombed and starved into chaos but persisting in keeping the forms and ledgers filled. They ask us to open our baggage but can't see inside because there is no light. And what is there to smuggle out?

Now we have to find a relief plane heading for São Tomé. The pandemonium of the blacked-out airport. We drive about, bumping trucks, men, planes, crowds of workers. When a flight comes in, the runway lights flash on for about thirty seconds, to get the plane down, and then off at once. If you're on a runway when the lights go on, you get the hell off before you have a Super-Constellation in your hat. It's hot, jungle-wet, dusty, noisy, and dangerous. All the flights seem to be Red Cross flights for Gabon or Fernando Po. We wonder if we can get out at all. The props spread filth on us. All we need is a plague of frogs. Six hours pass, rushing in the dark from plane to plane.

Father McGlade, three times injured at this airport, says, "Don't worry, you'll get on." I'm ready to believe. We chat and I express admiration for his—well, I say stamina but mean bravery. "I'll take a vacation in 1970 or '72, when this is over." He is a wizened, energetic priest who reminds me of Barry Fitzgerald, with a cheerful hard face and a hand twisted into a claw by the Nigerians.

The airmen land their tons of food and stand screaming at the hatches as they open, "Get it off! Get if off! We got to get out of here!" They are making thousands of dollars a week, but they still don't want to be shot up on the ground. Their life in São Tomé: too much drink, not enough women. They are saving the money for trips to Lisbon or to buy a car in Glendale, California.

The pilot I called the Forceps Baby (smashed short from both ends, bulging and deformed fat, Bermudas, white socks, black shoes, an alligator sports shirt) stands looking at the mad blacked-out, moonlit scene of trucks and shouts at the work gangs. "Those bastards, they don't wanna work. They're animals, they'll grab that Formula Two right off the runway—yecch, filth—and stuff it in their mouths. Christ, the pigs, I wanna get out of here in five minutes." And shouts, "Get me outta here! I'm leaving in five minutes, fuck it!"

Father Finukin (sp.?), three hundred pounds of first-sergeant beef, is shrieking at the men sliding the bags down and hoisting them into trucks, "Quick now! Get it off! Hurry up, quick, you lazy boys!"

And to me he says, "They work hard, poor devils. They're tired . . . Back up the lorry, you, back it up! Quick, quick, quick!"

Forceps Baby: "Niggers'll eat anything."

Jack Frost winces: "Hell, if he saw those little tykes—you know, the kwashi-kwashi kids, those cute little geezers—he wouldn't say that."

The men looked like gray ghosts, exhausted, bone-tired. They work all night. I remember their cheerful song of greeting to us: "Wel-come to Bi-afra, welcome!"

The kwashiorkor children were being loaded from trucks in

the dark onto planes bound for Libreville. These were kids I had seen earlier, about seventy of them, for whom there was hope of survival. I met a sister from the hospital. "So you're here now!" she sang in her Irish lilt. And the Princesse de Bourbon-Parma: *"Bonsoir, monsieur."* She was nervous as a doll in her crisp fatigues, fatigue hat, crucifix gleaming as she leaned to talk with Father McGlade. Having met her repeatedly during the past ten days, we are old friends and she tells me how good my French is, and I, somewhat maliciously, tell her that her French is also very good.

A line of bloodied soldiers passes by: are they too being shipped to recover in Gabon? Bandages, casts, crutches; and they help one another.

The seminarians are helping load the children. I see the one who said, *"En-emy plane,"* the day of the air raid, who has given me a pin which says HAIL BIAFRA. I show him that I'm wearing it. "How are the children?" I ask. He grins. "Fair," he says. I promise to send him books through Caritas.

Father McGlade promises us again: "I'll get you on."

"Thank you, Father, I'll see you're redeemed."

Paul Emeku, our friend from State House, keeps repeating, as the night passes, his favorite refrain: "There are some difficulties really in these times . . ." There are pearls of sweat on his nose, unmoving, it seems, all the week long; the orange dust of Biafra in his hair; a look of gray exhaustion beneath his smiling, obliging, attentive face. "There are really some difficulties in these times."

At last we find a plane, a Joint Church Aid ("Jesus Christ Airlines") Strato-Cruiser, bound for São Tomé. Leslie and I say good-bye, kiss Miriam and Diana, and scramble aboard. The huge tube smells of fish, grain; there are a few mites and bugs which shuttle back and forth with the food. A hilarious crewman looks at us disgustedly (we must be filthy, we are bearded, we are probably journalist or do-good creeps): "Welcome aboard the Flying Formula Two. If you will proceed

into our Starlight Lounge, the stewardess will be serving cock-
tails and stockfish . . . Hurry up, we got to get out of here
before 'Intruder' comes back."

The doors clang shut and there's nothing for Leslie and me
to do. Good-byes are over; good-bye, Biafra. Engine roar and
flash: MAX POWER! Lights blink. In the dark, we lumber-
ingly move and rise, hoping again to be too slow and low for
the MiGs to track us. Only two planes flew from São Tomé
that night. One other had been shot up on the ground, and
the Canaire plane has suffered an engine failure. It was the
one we came in on; I remember those blinking warning lights,
telling of an overheated something-or-other. (We later
learned that one of the Red Cross planes we had chased across
the field was shot down that night by the Nigerians; no survivors.)

In the past few weeks, in their hurry to get at the cargoes,
get the aircraft off the ground, several men had walked through
propellers. One machine had been bombed on the ground and
the pilot had broken his foot jumping out. Another plane had
lost its landing gear and crash-landed.

Blacked out, we were droning over Nigeria now. The airmen
were passing a jug of lemonade back and forth. One of them
was telling me about San Francisco. "What I do in San Francisco," he said, "I go to Johnny Han's for Chinese and the
Domino Club for steak. That way I never do get disappointed . . ."

I was covered with a sticky paste—flour, sweat, dirt. Down
below, there were orange bursts like rotten tangerines in the
air—antiaircraft fire searching irritably for us, but of course all
they had to go on was the sound of the engines.

I was thinking that the good Catholics of Biafra have the joy
of believing in God, which means that they can curse Him.
Now I return to San Francisco and all I can curse is mankind
—but first, of course, I'd like to join my pilot at the Domino
Club. I have left the starving behind and am thinking of food.

They, despite their hunger and suffering, are thinking mostly of victory. Hail Biafra!

THE DEATH OF BIAFRA AS SEEN FROM SAN FRANCISCO

Saturday, January 10, 1970
 "Let's buy our plane."
 "Okay, let's see him."
 I want to meet the pilot who has volunteered to fly food into Uli Airport if we buy him one of the three DC-6 work-horses in good repair at the Oakland-Alameda used-airship market. We have been hearing reports daily of the accelerating starvation and defenselessness of the Biafran population. Frank (Dr. John Francis Catchpool, nutrition expert, head of Aid to Biafran Children medical services, two years in Biafra) has been invalided home with hepatitis. He has shown me his snapshots of the food piled up in São Tomé, covered with rats and cockroaches, no way to get it in. The Red Cross has stopped flying, since one of its planes was shot down in June, the night I left Uli. The Soviet MiGs and Ilyushins, flown by Egyptians and East Germans and British and Belgian mercenaries, have harassed Uli so that the Joint Church Aid airlift has been increasingly ineffective. Starvation is now at least five thousand per week, probably much more. Ben Burlap (I'll call him) flew supplies for the Biafrans. He knows the airport. He is willing to go in.
 The deal is this: we can buy a million-dollar aircraft for

twenty thousand dollars; the market in used propeller craft is weak. Ben will pick up food at São Tomé and head through the antiaircraft fire into Uli. He'll charge much less than the charter companies which do this. We will not insure the airplane; the cost is prohibitive and we'll take the chance ourselves. Ben will agree not to do other charter free-lance work. We are buying it for him for one purpose only. The charter companies and pilots are getting rich. Ben will prosper, too, but more modestly. Of course, he deserves his gain. He knows the risks. They are enlarging the graveyard for airmen who try to fly into Uli.

We have arranged with Dierdre Silverman, the pert, cute, and fanatical Australian revue dancer-singer who is head of the Bay Area Committee to Save Biafran Children, to buy a load of food to fly from San Francisco. Her organization will pay the five to seven thousand dollars needed for gas on the flight San Francisco–Shannon–Portugal–São Tomé. We can raise the twenty thousand dollars and will lay out the down payment ourselves.

Now the only question is to talk with Ben Burlap and see if we think him a good risk for a noninsured City of San Francisco airlift.

I've never been in Alameda before. It's a taco-and-burger, 88-cent-store and hot-rod suburb between Oakland and the bay. In mucky winter weather, with that perversely fickle San Francisco sky occasionally letting sunlight through, we drive around bay-fill and motel developments, trying to find the spit of sand where Ben lives. Frank talks about trying to get back to Biafra. I wonder if I can go back. We find Ben's address—a number and a letter behind a flaking green pool in a sloping construction in California Motel Write-off style. He lives on the third floor. We ascend in a throbbing plastic elevator which feels like the john of a DC-6.

Unemployed pilots, overage airmen, mothers without partners, California indefinites live here. Lots of little flag stickers.

Ben is happy to see us. There is a plate of French pastry and coffee and bourbon. The little woman is nervous, wears lipstick, carries a dish of hairpins into the bedroom. Ben has too large a rump for chinos, but wears them anyway. He sends the kid out with his girl friend so we can talk. The kid can take the car, he says. The kid is his wife's son by another marriage. They turn off the stereo playing The Turtles. Ben has a belly, a boyish smile curving all around his chin, thin reddish hair, a gimpy foot (little accident); the apartment carries out the motel motif. "Overage, unemployed pilot" is the message. He is anxious to please us. We drink coffee and crunch cookies, but all we want to do is get to the business.

It turns out that Ben was the co-pilot on a famous flight into Uli, carrying nineteen Biafrans from a mission abroad, including the finance minister, and a cargo wrapped in lead foil. Over the ocean the plane lost power in two motors. It was flying so low they could see the white tops of the waves in the moonlight. Depressurize and open the doors! Heading into Nigeria and the antiaircraft, their only hope was to dump weight. The plane was lurching and losing altitude. Ben started to unhook the cargo. They smelled oil and salt. The nineteen Biafrans had a rapid conference and then their leader spoke to the crew: "If we jump instead, will you try to get this freight to Uli?"

The captain ordered them back and they proceeded to slide the load to the door and shove it out. The plane made it through. The lead-foil packages dumped into the ocean off Nigeria contained a million pounds—about three million dollars —from the Biafran treasury.

Ben shrugs. He could use some of that now. He is willing to go back and earn some money because he likes those crazy Biafrans.

He will carry repair equipment and do his own work. He

knows a crew. He is ready to leave at once. He agrees to all our conditions. He knows Biafrans. He knows the code. He knows the way. He will take off as soon as soonest.

We shake hands. We'll call him in a few hours.

There's a thin winter drizzle when we leave. Saturday evening traffic. We agree that Ben could easily steal the plane and do his own business with it. He has a history as a smuggler and arms-runner. There's plenty of work in Africa for free-lance pilots with planes on the spot. But we think he really wants to fly into Biafra, will underbid the Joint Church Aid charters; and we both have visions of the tons of extra food shuttled in by Ben Burlap. The official airlifts don't do nearly enough. Now is the time for individual initiative. (I recall the Biafran ground crews at Uli, rushing up to the planes before the propellers stop whirling, sometimes walking through propellers in the blackout. I remember seeing them licking with their fingers at the spilled milk powder on the oily red dust of the airstrip.) We'll take the chance on Ben.

Okay. Frank switches on the radio as we cross the Bay Bridge. The news is that Uli Airport is under bombardment by the Nigerians with their new Soviet cannons. It's all over.

"They've said that before," Frank says.

In thirty months of war the Nigerians have often announced victory. The Biafrans have stubbornly hung on. We both feel this time is different.

"They've said that before," I say.

We drive the rest of the way in silence. I think about my friend Vance Bourjaily, now in Biafra with Miriam Reik, who took me there. I suggested him for the trip. When his New Left friends told him Biafra was another Katanga, I urged him to have a look for himself. He has a wife and children in Iowa City. If Uli is overrun, millions may die, including the white foreigners, missionaries, relief workers, and the couple of writers who have gone because the journalists don't cover this war except from elsewhere.

Sunday

There's no doubt now. It's over. The MiGs and Ilyushins have finished Uli Airport. I keep flashing on the people I knew —the seminarians at Ihiala; the writers Cyprian Ekwensi, Chinua Achebe, Gabe Okara; the soldiers in their camouflaged makeshift barracks; the nuns in the hospitals; the robed dignitaries at the second-anniversary celebration; the exhausted, sleepy commander of Uli, formerly a school principal, pushing his steel-rimmed glasses back up his nose and commenting, "Things are rather difficult these days, really . . ."

President Nixon says there is enough food for thirty days. This is one of those maddening TV truths. There is food—in São Tomé, in Lagos—but it's not *there*, in Biafra, where the people are starving.

I hear from Tina Bourjaily that Vance got out on one of the last relief planes. He and Kurt Vonnegut say there are many thousands of people dying of starvation at the airport—right where the food landed when it could come in. There are hundreds of thousands on the roads and trails and in the bush and dying in the refugee camps. I remember the camp I saw in June: emaciation and a French class conducted by a black girl who looked like a Vogue model until I realized she was starving, not chic. Miriam Reik came out, but then was trying to get back to do her best, by her presence, to prevent massacre. Vance isn't sure if any planes were able to unload at Uli, though some flew in.

Right now hundreds of thousands of people can be saved if food gets through by air. There should also be neutral observers to prevent slaughter. The Nigerians are not permitting any reporters with their troops.

Dierdre, Frank Catchpool, and I go to the *Chronicle* for an interview, along with a couple of local Biafran students. When the story is published, the reporter doesn't even mention the two young Biafrans. (They spoke only to appeal for help to save the women and children.) In the city room I have that uncanny sense of business as usual, pinups, clipboards, telephones, familiar faces, friendliness and ease and the steady flow of disaster which nourishes a daily newspaper. My friend Charlie Howe's face falls when I am too distraught to gossip with him.

All the media reports are obviously leading toward a combination of sentimentality and solace. Situation bad, really sad, a downer; but we're doing all we can. War is hell, but we are kind-hearted.

PRESIDENT RICHARD M NIXON

WE URGE IMMEDIATE INTERNATIONALIZATION OF ULI AIRPORT IN BIAFRA TO PERMIT UNHINDERED ACCESS BY RELIEF AGENCIES WITH FOOD, MEDICAL SUPPLIES AND PERSONNEL, AND NEUTRAL OBSERVERS. FOOD IS ESSENTIAL FOR STARVING REFUGEES, MEDICAL AID FOR VICTIMS OF WARFARE. OBSERVERS ARE ESSENTIAL TO INHIBIT HAUSA MASSACRES OF CIVILIANS. FOOD AND MEDICINE RUSHED TO ULI CAN SAVE THOSE IN ENCLAVE. AID SENT THROUGH NIGERIA CANNOT ARRIVE IN TIME TO HELP THOSE CRITICAL NOW.

Dierdre Silverman, Committee to Save Biafran Children

Dr. John Francis Catchpool, Medical Director in Africa for Aid to Biafran Children

Herbert Gold, Committee for Biafran Artists and Writers

I worry about Miriam Reik. Frank worries about the doctors he left behind at his post. Pretty little Dierdre is a dynamo of ideas and proposals. When I talk to my Biafran friends, they are gray, in shock. "How are you?" I ask.

"Fine." The generous smile.

There are reports of the last troops going into battle singing, but with no ammunition. Military experts say they were finally defeated less by Soviet and British armor and planes than by hunger. At the last, even the soldiers, relatively well-fed when I was there in June, had one meal of a thin root soup—no protein—every two days. Soviet cannon and planes, British technicians and equipment, East German and Egyptian and Algerian fliers, with a few Belgian and British mercenaries, also help to solve Nigeria's problem with the troublesome Ibos.

Monday

The whole world is rushing food, medicine, and sympathy *toward* Biafra, but not *into* the enclave. The American position is clear: Do nothing to anger the Nigerians. I talk with congressmen, senators, officials, press people—or, more often, their assistants. Gradually, by persistence, I climb toward contact with authority, but authority makes no decision in this matter. The President does.

From Washington I hear a matter-of-fact summary by a friend there: "The highest-level decision is to follow political rather than humanitarian motives." In other words, oil and spheres of influence rather than Biafran lives. No offense to Nigeria.

This is comparable to the slaughter of the Armenians by the Turks, of the Jews by the Nazis, but now there is no communication gap. It is happening right now, today, and they know; and nothing is being done except to exploit it for pathos. The President speaks in his flat resonant voice about his discovery of the trouble, and in speaking, reassures people that our government is behaving decently. We are letting them die.

The Reverend Norbert Semperfrantz (I'll call him), a Protestant missionary from the Nigerian side, telephones to

289

talk with me about my "public statements." He wants to meet and discuss. He says he has a tendency to see things from the Nigerian angle and perhaps we can learn from each other. He comes to my studio.

He is a gray-haired, stocky, worried man who has spent ten years in Nigeria. He knows the colonels and reports they weep when they think of the starving Biafrans. Of course, he grants that the Hausa warriors believe they go to heaven if they kill a Christian, and the weeping colonels are not in the front line or with the occupation troops.

When I ask why the Nigerians don't permit—or even urge —a temporary international airlift of food and medicine into Uli, the Rev. Semperfrantz says, "They're jealous of their sovereignty. They want to do it themselves."

"Who flew their planes?"

"I see what you mean," he says. There is a pause, and then he adds, "Well, they don't like the Ibos. There's a saying, you know: 'All the Ibo wants is power and money.' "

I think of the nineteen Ibos wanting to leap out over the ocean to save their cargo. I think of the sacrifice, generosity, and good-humored devotion of the Biafrans I had met. Of course, they are intelligent and well organized, which means they sometimes find money and power and can even hold off the hordes against them for two and a half years.

We talk inconclusively and I feel he is a reasonably sympathetic man. But he accepts the inevitability of the slaughter. "Mercenary-missionary," he says with a smile. It's a problem. With their shaky grasp of English, the Nigerians will not spare missionaries. The words sound too much alike.

Tina Bourjaily tells me by telephone that she has reached her senator by telling his assistant: "This is too much for an Iowa housewife to bear alone." People say to me, "Oh my God, what can I do?"

And all I can answer is: "Send telegrams to the President."

But the policy is fixed now, and the moment when perhaps it could have been changed is passed.

Tuesday

Vance is back in Iowa, stunned. Before he went he was dubious about the Biafran revolt. Tribalization of Africa and the so-called Third World line about One Nigeria. Now he knows about the hatred of Moslems for Christians, and of the immense spaces and separations of history. And about the Biafrans? "They're some of the best people I've ever met," he says, and I can hear him gulping and swallowing.

Hepatitic Frank wants to go back but doubts that he can, even when it's over. We are now thinking of friends we might save, not about masses of population. It's too much for the imagination. We go for some lunch at Enrico's Coffeehouse and he says, "I envy you with roots in San Francisco. I'd like to stay here. But it isn't the place for work in malnutrition . . ." Dierdre keeps suggesting: "Let's . . ." Someone gives me the telephone number of the wife of the British ambassador. I don't call her. But Senator Cranston's assistant calls me and I tell him what I know. "Oh my God, we've got to do something. The senator will make a statement."

A psychiatrist from Berkeley comes to our house with his wife. He is itching for a groupy encounter and senses my irritation with him. He is a Jungian. He changes the subject from Biafra to Jung and makes his profound judgment for the day: "A shadow lies over all mankind." But he decided not to look up the evidence of Jung's collaboration with the Nazis because he didn't want this particular shadow to interfere with his own analysis. He enjoys myths and racial memories; they please him a lot, and seem profound. I tell him that therefore there is no point in discussing the matter with him, since he doesn't want to know history or facts when they disturb his comfort.

291

"You're kind of moralistic about things, aren't you?" he asks me. "I mean you take things so moralistically. First Dr. Jung and now Biafra."

Thanks to deep insight and many years of analysis and searching, he comes to realize that he is not wanted, and leaves. I am part of the shadow over mankind.

Wednesday

General Effiong, not an Ibo, the Effik officer I recall as a quiet, serious, intense bureaucrat, makes the surrender to a grinning Gowon. Gowon has read all about Lincoln, Grant, and Lee, and does a little Appomattox act—embraces for the cameras. Earlier General Effiong appealed to General Gowon to slow down the advance of the federal troops in order to control the panic. Gowon announces that all who participated in aiding Biafra are *persona non grata* in Nigeria. Neither Frank Catchpool nor I can go back. Nigeria wants no aid in relieving Biafran starvation, Gowon says. We can do it ourselves, he says.

All Biafran officers are being shipped to Enugu. The Biafran fear is extermination of the élite. The three hundred journalists in Lagos are still not allowed into Biafra. What's happening to those officers?

A group of six foreigners, guided by the Nigerians, have spent a few hours in Owerri and report no starvation in Biafra! May they burn for their lies. I see the Colonel Blimp Britisher, the sleepy international commission-servers . . . (The Pole knows the Soviet line, the Canadian knows the British line, and they are escorted up to Owerri and then back for the press conference which is the point of the whole thing.)

A friend telephones to say that his wife has left him after thirteen years. I receive some exceptionally hostile advance reviews of my novel *The Great American Jackpot*. At the moment I'm not interested.

I sit with Frank over lunch. We try to see what else we can do. Nothing. He sings softly the chant we heard soldiers singing as they trotted down the roads, children singing in the hospitals:

"Bi! ah! fra! will win de waw!
Bi! ah! fra! will win de waw!
Bi! ah! fra! will win de waw!"

I write a letter to the *New York Times* protesting the libel about the "white Mercedes" which General Ojukwu is said (dateline: Lagos) to have taken into exile. I return some telephone calls about telegrams and petitions. Frank is frightened for the German doctor left behind at his clinic.

At last I hear from Miriam Reik. She couldn't get back in; the relief plane couldn't land. I ask if it's true that the Nigerians are feeding the Biafrans. Her eerie laughter over the telephone. I ask her what I can do. Silence.

A pro-Nigerian article by a doctoral candidate from Berkeley is published in the San Francisco *Chronicle*. The Reverend Semperfrantz calls to make sure I read it ("a balanced presentation," he says). It admits the massacres which began the war, "perhaps triggered by Ibo unwillingness to accede to decentralization." The doctoral candidate goes on to promise that Gowon intends to "leave living space in the new Nigeria for the Ibo people. It is perhaps not as expansive as the Ibos would like, but it is probably their fair share, since they can no longer pre-empt others' jobs or land."

Like the Jews in Germany?

"War is hell," writes the doctoral candidate, but: "All the world's leading nations have gone through the experience of civil war and probably emerged the stronger for it."

Which makes Nigeria now definitely one of the world's leading nations.

The Biafran radio—my friend Cyprian Ekwensi was organizing a cultural "Third Program"—played Beethoven's Fifth

293

Symphony, the World War II symbol of victory, before General Effiong's surrender speech. "May God help us all," he said. And then the Tchaikovsky "Pathétique" afterward. I recall the Biafran anthem, which ends:

> But if the price is death for all we hold dear
> Then let us die . . .

Friday

Not yet a week has gone by and already the soul-deadening takes over. When there is nothing to do, you do nothing. And when you do nothing, you gradually sink from hysteria to anesthesia. Futile excitement puts others to sleep. And so eventually you fall asleep yourself.

How the world loves a winner and learns not to meet the eyes of losers! We make do with Franco, and dislike the dispersed and defeated gray old men of Loyalist Spain. Nigeria becomes a victorious modern state, and the Biafran underdogs, once sentimentally appealing (smart, pragmatic Ibos!) now appear in the news magazines as losers who made a lot of trouble for everybody. Peace to the souls of the departed. The Israelis know history and know it's better not to lose wars. Even the Pope's pity takes about a week to dissipate.

Another historical implication to be drawn is that the world is willing to let Roman Catholics die as grumblingly but uncaringly as it let the Armenians and the Jews die. So long as they are black Catholics, at least.

The package I sent the boys at Ihiala, the seminarians who wanted souvenirs of San Francisco, was returned by Caritas in Gabon. Not deliverable.

I haven't spoken with Dierdre or Frank in two days.

But a telephone call from Ben Burlap in Alameda. "Say, now that Biafra's finished, how'd you fellas like to buy me a plane for Sudan? I hear there's lots of starving folks over there."

STORIES I GUESS
I WON'T WRITE
1

HAROLD HILL, warrant officer helicopter pilot, was back from Vietnam with ribbons, medals, wounds, and heavy tales of jungle descents and whirring, roaring rescues: flash of fire from the Cong, gasping and grateful GIs, Marines hooked miraculously aloft to safety. He told his friends in a modest monotone, not boasting at all, depressed and astonished by this new manifestation of Harold Hill as a hero.

It had been an unusual war.

His friends listened politely for half an evening, sometimes less, and then said, "Aw, knock it off."

There was nothing in the American tradition to match it. Out of the eye of death he plucked this mote.

"Aw, knock it off, will you?"

Every writer has a lot of stories in him, more than enough for his lifetime, though never enough, either; and there are some that nag at him, but he doesn't write them for one reason or another—they hurt, they cut too many ways, they are more conception than story, they are personal and involve his friends, he's lazy. The story about Harold Hill has bothered me a long while. I think it's true, true to our lives, in that it tells the awful fact about the American connection with the undeclared war in Vietnam. We feel it as an annoyance, alas;

not a tragedy. But it is also very distracting to write this moral history as an insult to suffering. Am I sure of my own moral purity? Then better stay clear of judging others so harshly till I purify myself.

There are times, of course, when unjustified rage makes a kind of art. I've given way myself to rage in writing: to the desire to destroy my enemies. But if I start to think about it first, then all is lost; I can't be unjust by calculation, though I can out of my own pain. Harold Hill and his friends, this America and that war, are ideas in my head. I mustn't persecute ideas as if they were people; assault them, yes; nag at them, no.

2

A CHILDLESS couple in Detroit sleeps with a fluorescent cross over their bed. The bed is heart-shaped. They are both credentialed schoolteachers, graduates of Bob Jones University in Greenville, South Carolina. They very much want a child, a little angel to complete their happy household, but it's impossible, despite all their prayers, because they have taken a vow to abstain from sexual contact, in addition to tobacco and alcoholic drink. Being educated people, they recognize the problem of reconciling their desire for a child with the happy gift of their bodies to the Lord. Mobilizing their intelligence, they come up with a logical solution: adoption.

The social worker, sent by the agency, listens to their pleas. She realizes that they are gentle, loving, kind, and tender people, eager to take a little creature of sin into their happy household. She makes inquiry into the reason for their barren state. She herself has been through a traditional Freudian psychotherapy, and also she has participated in group encounters, psychodrama, T-groups, and, once, this funny orgy in Coral Gables, Florida, on her way to Miami Beach. Well, it was an experience.

The fundamentalist couple explains that they want to raise a child with their own principles, generosity, givingness, tithing ten percent of earnings to Bob Jones University, no drink, no tobacco and, um, no carnal acts. In addition to being gentle, loving, kind, and tender, the social worker decides, they are also paranoid.

And yet they function smoothly as teachers—no traffic warrants outstanding, no blemish on their job records, no financial problems. And all over the dreary town of Detroit . . . Flint . . . Lyndale, there are those little tykes, offspring of waitresses and hippies and troubled adolescents, languishing in institutions.

And so she asks them . . . She tells them . . . She decides . . . She remembers how she opened up this poor repressed postoffice clerk . . .

Well, that story doesn't work through; it's unyielding. I may lack a little sympathy for the lonely couple, and as targets for irony or wit or attack, they are too foreign and easy. Now, the social worker might be an interesting tack to take. Suppose I see the conflict of a traditional fundamentalist aberration with the contemporary normal aberration of the passionate do-gooding analysand. I might bring in the social worker's boyfriend—a slouching Brooks Brothers hippie with a dropout mustache, an antiwar marcher—in fact, maybe one of the people who doesn't listen to Harold Hill. Hm. A linked series of stories about the failure to make contact in contemporary America; its real passions and needs are—aw, nuts, that book is published every day.

If you're interested in the questions which agitate folks today, you run the risk of being banal. If you take the classical topics, you may simply be out of touch. So find the classical in today, and make it relevant, true, moving, and yet mysterious.

297

3

BIG feel sex story. Young professor goes off to play tennis
with graduate student at Utah State University. But her rac-
quet is being restrung, so instead she takes him up the Wasatch Mountains to look at the view. She tells him she feels
lonely today. He tells her he is *always* lonely, including today.
They get out of the car in a secluded spot and start to climb in
the June sun. Dry heat, isolation, sweat, smells of body and
sagebrush (look up Utah-Wasatch vegetation in atlas). They
joke about her husband. They joke about his wife. Conclu-
sion: both after a little. They touch, they talk, they grope,
they stoop and glance around. They are, man, like isolated.
They can do it right out here with nobody to see, under the
sky, under the sun, in the dry hot air, with nothing on their
minds but the innocent gambol of it. (Forget their spouses for
a moment.) Are they caught? Are they found? Are they betrayed? Oh no, but they are on a steep slope of hill and, dam-
mit, they just can't get a grip to hold to one place long enough
to effect this unfamiliar conjunction—they *can't*. The gravel
and pebbles slip, they stumble, little landslides barrel down
the mountain each time they try some friendly contemporary
stunt. They can't even manage a traditional stunt.

When they return to their families, they are neither sadder
nor wiser, but rather, they are happier and more ignorant.
They are happy because the adventure has left them with cuts,
bruises, scrapes and aching muscles, and yet no guilt. They did
their best. They couldn't manage. The holy terrain saved
them. And they are innocent of evil, still horny, hornier in
fact, and so it's a hot time in the old home foyer this night.
Both their partners feel that the day in the sun ("I wanted to
walk, dear"; "I took a little hike, honey") really stimulated
them, turned them on. There's nothing like nature except unnatural acts.

Perhaps a nice epilogue in the hippie coffeehouse of Salt Lake City. They go out for a candlelit evening. The couples salute each other. As they stare, show the puzzled looks: one wife has scratches and cuts, so does one husband. Fadeout.

There's nothing wrong with sexual comedy. I like writing it. In fantasy I laugh at fantasy, my own and others'. But is the world suffering for lack of this story? Is it unique? Well, it's never been done to the Wasatch Mountains, so far as I know, and that gives it an exotic aura. Make them fallen Mormons, perhaps—Jack Mormons, as they're called. But do I really need to tear the lid off the Wasatch Mountains and the Mormons? I have pleasant memories of Salt Lake City, except for the time the police chief hassled me in the coffeehouse. He came in with his light meter to test the level of the illumination for immorality. It got to be a peculiar scene with the cops, so I took my date to see a movie, *Teen-Agers from Outer Space*. The Martian adolescents landed on earth with their dissolve guns, climbed out of their spaceships, and I noticed they were wearing Booster Keds. Perhaps that's the story— movie night in Salt Lake City. No exposé of sex and laughter, but a dead little sketch about bored vistors going to a double feature in the dirtless, sanitized, geometric capital where Brigham Young said, "This Must Be the Place!" (honored by the This Must Be the Place monument of Brigham Young) and the sea gulls ate the grasshoppers to save the crops, and God made them throw up and eat more grasshoppers, and eat more and more, and it was a miracle. But now its pretty quiet out there in Salt Lake City. Where have all the regurgitating sea gulls gone? Another possibility for a story here.

Well, I know other exotic places. Let's see.

4

HAITI. I lived there, and I've written more than enough stories from Haiti to make a book of Haitian Tales. An editor who has published many of my stories used to say to me, "Come on, how much will it cost us to get you out of Haiti?" He took to refusing to read anything that mentioned Creole, Port-au-Prince, voodoo, Choucoune. But it's a part of my nightmare life and someday I must do a book about this lovely, desperate, sad, and beautiful land. A story I haven't written yet: My friend the dentist visited me in Port-au-Prince. What to show him after the usual tourist pleasures (voodoo, Choucoune, Creole beauties)? Well, how about a mass arrest? I knew of some revolutionists, I knew the police knew about them, many of the revolutionists wanted to be martyrs, there was to be a meeting and the police would be arresting everybody. Fine: a Latin farce. We dressed for spectator sport. Here come the Booster Keds again—young adults from outer space. My friend draped two cameras around his neck. The custom was for the arrest to be made, the traitors kept in jail briefly, and then family pressures would get them released. Police and revolutionaries, ins and outs, were generally related, anyway.

We watched the little secretive band of conspirators enter the house in the Canapé-Vert district of Port-au-Prince. We stood on the flowered street, smelling bougainvillaea. Then suddenly a screech of sirens and a mass of police Buicks and Army jeeps converged on the house, and what seemed like a small army burst out, with submachine guns and light mortars. Oh Lord, this wasn't going to be just another playful arrest, this was to be a massacre. But the commanding officer caught sight of us, the American writer and the American tourist. The command was given not to blow up the house. The CIA, they decided, was watching. They got into their cars and roared away. An American dentist had inadvertently saved the lives of a group of Haitian élite. Someplace a report went down that the U.S. of A. was "interested" in the matter.

Now we have another problem. The story is true, but too amazing to be easily believed unless I simply tell it as fact, as personal history, and not as story. But as soon as it's told that way, it becomes part of my memoirs and loses the magic of created fiction. Personality is diminished through being presented as mere personality. I dislike the current fashion of putting the writer forward as his chief character. Mostly this self-dramatization depends for its glamour on the background material, media and TV and literary fan puffing of writers, and there will be the reaction to them that there was to, say, the Goncourt brothers' journals. Who cares now, other than perhaps a few scholars and literary historians? (Goncourt, Edmond [Huot] de, 1822–1896, and Jules [Huot] de, 1830–1870.) Of course, through the personal voice of an Orwell or a Proust, in their different ways, the real story emerges and the person is only the setting for a subtle and complex refraction of light.

Something ordinary and true—the death of a friend, war experience, falling in love—can be made extraordinary by the gift of telling. The general is made particular, and blazes. My adventures in Haiti may make a curious history, but turning the search for adventure into thinly disguised fiction is like the late Hemingway's courting of attention. "I, I, I," howls the operatic star, and the truth of that blessed lying which is fiction recedes before the tender self-concern of a dramatic actor.

The great events of my times in Haiti should be written as reportage or history. The small horrors and blessings of Haiti —the children, the hope, the misery, the love-making and death-fearing—can be ripened through time and feeling into stories.

5

THERE's this young psychiatrist who feels uneasy with his career. His mother wanted him to become a doctor, so he became a doctor. His mother wanted him to become a psychiatrist, so he got himself that diploma, too. Then he went into analysis and worked himself up and around to be a psychoanalyst. Now are you happy, Mother? But she just wants to know why he doesn't tell her his problems any more. She has a point there. He's gotten secretive. And with all her experience in human nature, having one herself—a human nature—who better should help a young doctor diagnose the human mind (with the troubles she's had, raising her own children) than his very own mother? So she sits in the other room, and while the patient talks, she listens, just like on the telephone, and later on she tells him what to do. A bit of admonition here, a nice girl there. Why is that patient so whiny? Why doesn't he stand up straight?

Surprisingly enough, his patients do very well under this regimen. He writes learned papers on a new variation of the idea of group analysis—one patient, but a balanced group of therapists, such as one doctor and a lay person. One day, however, when he happens to have a cold, his mother insists on minding the store alone and he can stay home and the patients are clearly going to do even better without him . . .

But as soon as I say "black humor" to myself, the impulse dies. To tell a story must involve a personal and individual propulsion that has nothing to do with categories, schools, or principles, and if possible it should avoid the 1959 Mike and Elaine routines which tend to be Peter Sellers movies in 1969.

Some of the unwritten stories that come to fret my mind have tricky endings. Life often has tricky endings, plus middles, too, and even the beginning of life is sometimes a peculiar trick. But a story shouldn't seem odd and quirky and made-up in that way. So I turn against these stories regretfully because they seem like neat tricks. Still, a nice trick needn't be forgotten without some memorial pleasure in its niceness. Kindness and generosity and all the grand feelings may be extended to cunning and cleverness, too, in a truly forgiving world.

If the day is cold and gray, and the air is foggy over North Beach and the bay, and the coffee is strong and my fingers itch, almost anything can seem justified as I wiggle the straw between my fingers or punch at the typewriter. Writing is a physical pleasure, like swimming, love-making, or sculpting. There's an agreeable floating in the mind and an agitated expense of muscle and blood. The pencil is an awl, the typewriter is a riveting machine or an acetylene torch; the body wields these tools like weapons against unyielding paper and teasing imagination. Men and women heave into view, ideas shove them about and are moved by them; I am exhausted at the end of a confrontation between what might have been and what should be.

Not every good story that a writer conceives can be written. Certain kinds of virtue are imaginable in the abstract, but not in the concretely moving and personal fashion that enables a particular storyteller to work the mystery of his own personality around the mystery of the characters he hopes to bring into life. A film producer once said to me, "How do you block out a story?" and I stared at him with blocks in my eyes and a block on my tongue. You don't block out a story. You let it grow. You nourish it, encourage it, even push it a bit with sweat and ferocity, but you go where it goes. You try to travel on with it. It surprises you. Any tentative outline or scenario is made to be destroyed. You are the victim of its will. Therefore, a "good story" may turn out to be impossible, and sometimes, for mysterious reasons, a trivial (James Joyce: "No, quadrivial") story may have meanings beyond meanings which engage you in the parental task of watching over its development. A blocked-out story is like a blocked-out child: "Congratulations, we've given birth to a nice Jewish doctor." Or like an overplanned evening: "From eight to nine, discussion of current events. From nine to ten, drunken banter. From ten to eleven, sexual overtures. Twelve o'clock: lights out." That's not how children or parties or stories get to be vibrant and healthy. Planning kills. Damn plans. But bless proposals . . .

And so the writer stares out the window, looking within. He gives up childish things to take up the responsibility of infantile pleasures. He seeks to master what he knows and, more important, what he doesn't know. He looks to illuminate blood, terror, spirit, catastrophe, energy, the complex of hope and desire, fear and death—the commonest truths and, in short, what we will never understand, no matter how much we learn. He looks into the dark secret chambers of the soul, where there is knowledge beyond knowledge and moralities beyond the prescription of morality. He uses the rhythm method to make the invisible visible and the visible invisible. He abandons the hope of utter closeness in favor of a sense of intimacy with men in their lonely rooms, crowds on their lonely streets everywhere. He knows that there is nothing more boring than someone else's dream, and yet he is sure that his waking fantasy can tell everyone what life means.

Ah, now I've got the action for a great full-length novel. It sums up our condition. There is the murder of a father—I see it so clearly—and a crazy half-brother. And one brother is a dark rationalist, tormented by doubt and disappointed faith, and one is a saint with turbulent human feelings, and one is a passionate gambler and lover, enraged and tender, and they all care for one another—show how deeply they care—and the world and their world and the world of all of us closes down upon them, and I'll call them Ivan, Alyosha, and Dmitri Karamazov . . .

ABOUT THE AUTHOR

HERBERT GOLD's novels include *The Great American Jackpot, Fathers, Salt,* and *The Man Who Was Not With It.* He has also published a volume of short stories, *Love and Like,* and one of essays, *The Age of Happy Problems.* He has taught at the University of California at Berkeley, at Stanford, Cornell, and Harvard. He has received numerous literary awards, published essays and stories in many magazines, and his books have been widely translated abroad. He lives in San Francisco and is working on a new book.